A Symphony of Glass

PAPERWEIGHTS FROM THE ELLIS COLLECTION

FIA Flint Institute of Arts
MUSEUM + ART SCHOOL

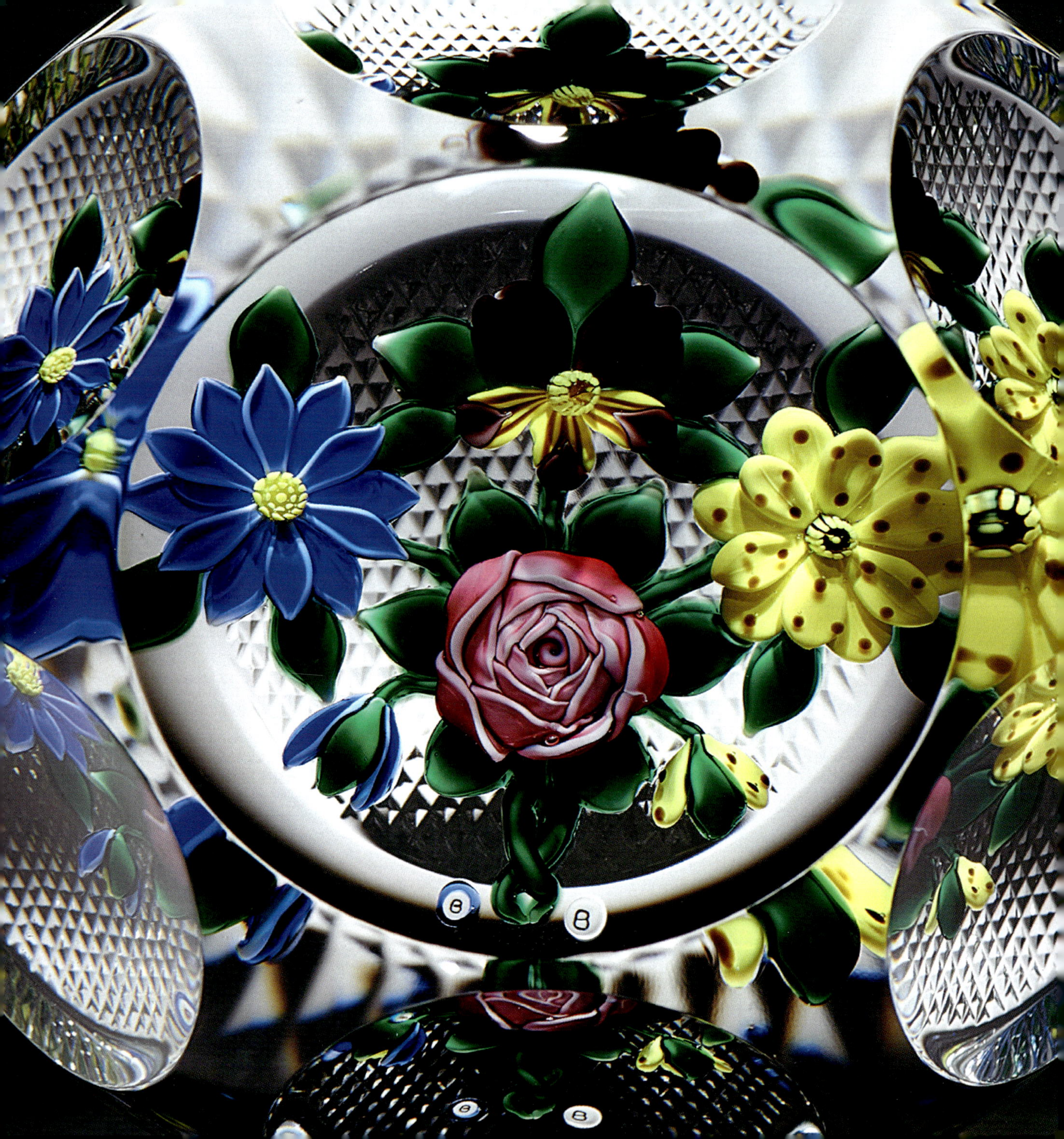

CONTENTS

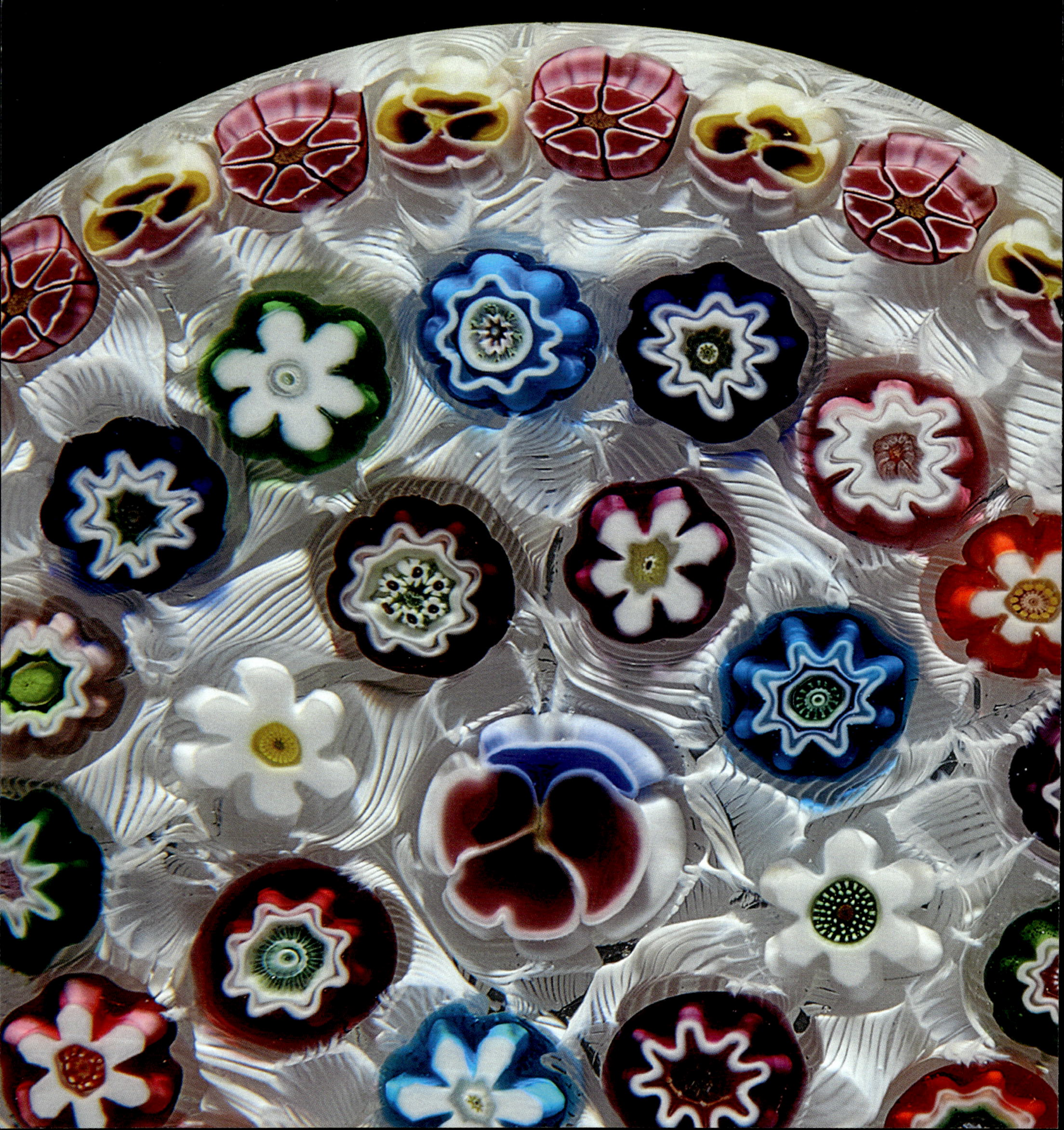

Foreword

Tracee J. Glab

Executive Director

Flint Institute of Arts Museum + Art School

Through knowledge its rooms are filled with rare and beautiful treasures.
—Proverbs 24:4

This proverb from one of the wisdom books of the Hebrew Bible aptly describes how Eileen Ellis amassed a wonderful collection of more than 400 paperweights, from the classic period of the nineteenth century to contemporary works of present day. What began as a token of love from her husband blossomed into a passionate pursuit guided by Eileen's deep knowledge of paperweights. Once Eileen started to collect paperweights, she decided to educate herself by reading scholarly articles and attending conventions. The result of her study is indeed a room full of rare and beautiful treasures as seen in the exhibition *A Symphony of Glass: Paperweights from the Ellis Collection* at the Flint Institute of Arts Museum + Art School (FIA).

LEFT: Detail of Cat. 173

This catalogue provides an overview of not only the most important aspects of paperweights in the Ellis Collection but also offers insight into the mind of a collector. Director of Donor Relations and Special Initiatives Kathryn Sharbaugh curated the exhibition and wrote the text that follows. Sharbaugh has an extensive knowledge about paperweights having curated three exhibitions at the FIA about this subject, including the 2019–2020 exhibition *Postscript,* which featured 68 weights from the Ellis Collection.

The FIA has a long history with paperweights, starting with the large gift of weights from the Viola E. Bray Collection in 1969 from her son-in-law and daughter Mr. and Mrs. William Richards. In fact, as detailed in Sharbaugh's essay, Ellis has memories of visiting the FIA and seeing these weights on view. In 2011, an area in the galleries was created to have a permanent display of 60 weights along with nearby visual storage drawers that open to reveal the rest of collection. In 2018, the FIA renewed its commitment to glass by creating a contemporary craft wing, a state-of-the-art Hot Shop, and a flameworking studio. Since then, many contemporary paperweights have been exhibited and several paperweight artists have worked or taught in our Art School.

I would like to thank Eileen Ellis for sharing her collection with our audience and for her support of the FIA in various projects connected with our historical and contemporary glass collections. I am grateful to Kathryn Sharbaugh for her thoughtful and interesting work on the exhibition and catalogue. I would like to acknowledge Doug Schaible's work on photographing the collection and Paul

Dunlop's work on editing. I would like to thank the Curatorial Department's Director and Curator of Collections and Exhibitions Sarah Kohn and Associate Curator Rachael Holstege for overseeing catalogue production, and Curatorial Assistant Emily Legleitner for her graphic design work.

Since 1928, when the FIA was founded as an art school, we have had at our core the idea that arts and education are a vital part of life. This exhibition and catalogue of the Ellis Collection supports this value and is in line with the FIA's mission to *connect diverse communities through fun, creative, and inspiring visual arts experiences.*

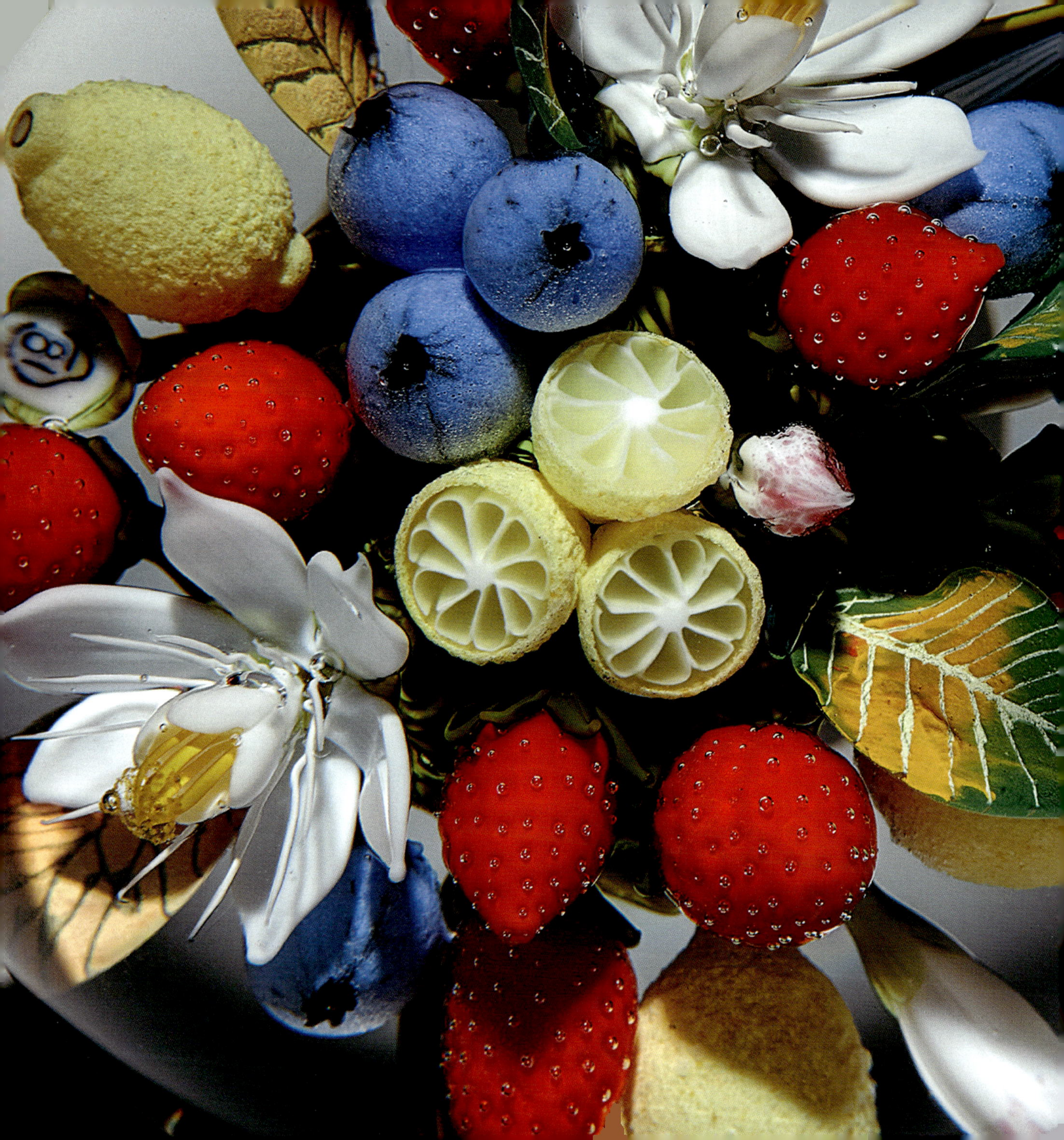

About the Collector: Eileen Ellis

Kathryn Sharbaugh
Director of Donor Relations & Special Initiatives
Flint Institute of Arts Museum + Art School

Eileen Ellis has immersed herself in the pursuit of collecting, learning about, and enjoying paperweights for several decades. After receiving her first gift of a weight in the early 1990s, she became increasingly committed to focusing on specific makers and styles within the genre. What is revealed as one studies her collection is a microcosm of paperweight production from classical to contemporary. Her collection exemplifies the distinctive nuances within the nineteenth-century classical production through to the virtuosity of today's makers. Her collection is not restricted to one technique (lampwork or millefiori), country of origin (France or Great Britain), or one era—antique Classic (1845–1870), Classic Revival (1950–1960), or Contemporary (1960–present). What one notices throughout the Ellis Collection is that it celebrates and encompasses subtle and unexpected surprises (sometimes within a single weight) or an avant-garde rarity of style. Her collection requires the viewer to take notice.

LEFT: Detail of Cat. 217

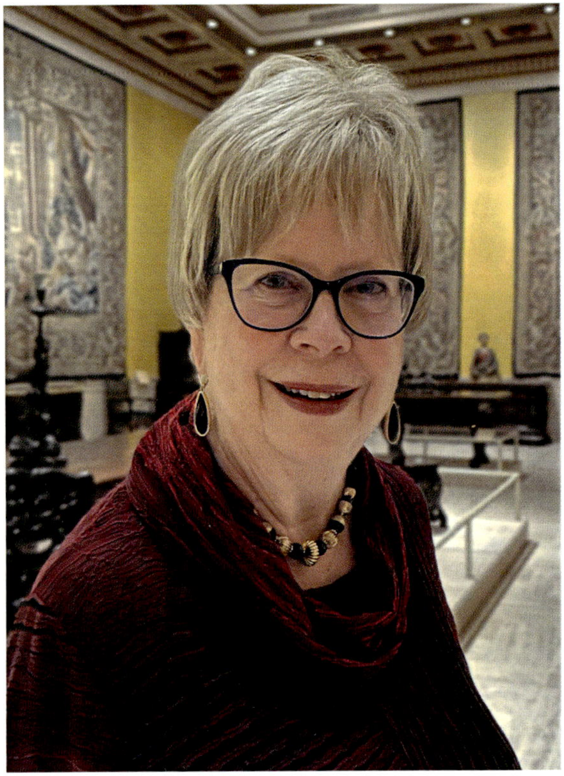

Eileen Ellis in the Bray Gallery

One cannot help but wonder what motivated Eileen Ellis to build this collection. The best way to understand why and how it came to be is to first learn about her. What we find when we look at her formative years are a group of specific building blocks that later support Eileen Ellis as a collector.

Music

Eileen grew up in Lansing, Michigan. Her introduction to collecting began as a child through a membership, along with her sister, in the Columbia Record Club. The first LP in their fledgling collection was Beethoven's Seventh Symphony. The allure of a record collection also speaks to her desire to study different instruments including piano, organ, and, most recently, hand bells.

Understanding the structure of classical music seems to directly correlate with her fine-tuned response to paperweights. Classical music, when read, displays elements that are specific. A sheet of music defines, through the use of symbols, how one is to produce each sound with their instrument, individually or as a whole with a small group or orchestra. A score presents a code that defines the beat, tempo, note values, rhythm, measures, and pauses. The language is fundamental to playing an instrument and understanding the composer and his or her intent. The fluency of the musician's acuity is critical for the listener's enjoyment. Similarly when viewing artwork, there are visual elements that are transposed within the brain into a language or score that prompts the viewer to use insight and knowledge of rhythm, pauses, and visual acoustics, in order to enjoy a work of art. Certainly this harmony is illustrated within the format of classical paperweights. The score is clearly present, encased forever in glass.

Eileen's early interest in music also led her to present a high school term paper on the history of Russian music. Her subsequent awareness of history and her study of an artist's country of origin serve to form another block in her foundation of becoming a collector. A work of art can reveal cultural influences, resources, and techniques, often rooted in indigenous folklore. This understanding can identify the time period of the work, the maker's ethnicity, as well as other information. Nuances, within periods, frequently show departures from tradition caused by external influences including cultural trends, revolutions, class, leadership, inventions, and immigration. Classical music is one of the foundations of Eileen's later pursuit of being a serious collector of paperweights.

Mathematics

After graduating from high school, Eileen left Spartan country to earn degrees in mathematics at the University of Michigan in Ann Arbor. She returned to Lansing to pursue her career in the financial aspects of health care. Her career was dedicated to facilitating funding and affordable medical plans for hundreds of thousands of low-income residents of Michigan.

The nature of mathematicians tends to be investigative, inquisitive, and curious. Mathematicians also tend to be detail-oriented, organized, and structured. They take risks willingly rather than impulsively. As with a musician, timing, pattern, and memory are basic cognitive skills exhibited by mathematicians. In building a collection, Eileen has exercised her mathematical acumen by understanding the structure and discipline of music that is instrumental in stimulating mathematical comprehension.

Visual Arts

Interest in the visual arts enters Eileen's life through her relationship with her husband Jim. Before they were married, they visited Chicago, passing time strolling through the galleries of the Art Institute of Chicago. They frequently paused to spend time with the Impressionists, in particular, looking at a favorite work by Renoir or Monet. In July of 1970, Jim proposed marriage in the gardens of the Art Institute of Chicago. Chicago became their honeymoon destination with the idea of spending time in the museum too. During a later

Chicago visit, Eileen was at the Art Institute and decided to visit the collection of miniature Thorne Rooms located in the lower level. While there, she moved into an area with a new exhibition, which included selected weights from 1,200 pieces that were recently given to the museum by the real estate developer Arthur Rubloff (1902–1986). The Rubloff Collection of fine paperweights represented all periods, designs, and techniques with the majority fabricated during the Classic era. She recalls that they were not displayed very well, but she was amazed by their beauty and the complexity of designs. She can recall that was the day that she truly fell in love with the art form. From that day forward, Eileen was taken with paperweights.

Eileen remembers as she walked out of the museum thinking, "I enjoyed looking, but I wonder if ordinary people can collect them?" In 1991, on a visit to Rau's Country Store in Frankenmuth, she discovered many paperweights from several different Scottish companies including Selkirk Glass and Edinburgh Crystal (for more information see page 119). She purchased an Edinburgh millefiori weight and put it into the "gift" drawer at home for her husband Jim to give to her on the next special occasion.

Eileen first encountered paperweights at the Flint Institute of Arts (FIA) about the same time, when visiting the FIA during one of her frequent business trips to Flint. She remembers there were glass-topped tables displaying many Classic weights given to the museum by William and Bertha Bray Richards, son-in-law and daughter of collector Viola Bray (1873–1961). An avid art collector and patron of the FIA, Viola Bray collected more than 200 Classic paperweights, most of them on display since they were given in 1969. In subsequent visits, Eileen was concerned that the weights were not on view as before. To her delight, after a major renovation in 2011, the FIA expanded the collection galleries to include a permanent area dedicated to displaying the art form. The visual storage drawers in the Ann K. Walch-Chan Decorative Arts Gallery also offers access to the weights not currently on view.

Becoming a Collector

Collecting became intentional in 1994 when Eileen learned about a sale of contemporary weights from American artists from a classified ad in *The New Yorker* magazine. The sale was through an auction by L. H. Selman Gallery, located at the time in Santa Cruz, California. Coincidently, in September, her husband Jim had a business convention in San Francisco. Eileen went along, rented a car and drove to Santa Cruz. She discovered, to her chagrin, that all ten of the weights she most wanted had been sold, including a triple weight by Parabelle. However, she did make an important purchase of a weight by Rick Ayotte titled *Sweet Summer Bouquet* **(cat. 178)**. She recalls that when she first started buying paperweights, she never envisioned a large collection. She bought what she liked and what her budget would allow at the time, as she had other priorities, her daughter was in college, and her husband Jim had his own interests that also used some of their available funds.

Eileen started to build a library and joined the Paperweight Collectors Association (PCA). For the library, she acquired issues of the *Annual Bulletin of the PCA* going back to the first one published in 1954. This resource, exclusive for PCA members, contains scholarly and historic research as well as profiles and articles on contemporary works. The bulletins present information on paperweight making techniques and discussions of all aspects of collecting. The bulletins also contain detailed information by collectors, artists, art historians, and dealers from around the world. They have become an important educational resource for anyone interested in weights. Eileen also traveled to the PCA's biennial conventions. For a weight collector one cannot overestimate the value of these conventions. The convention's location changes to include cities that have museums and private collections to tour, as well as studios to visit, and artist demonstrations. Conventions also present a variety of lectures and panels that provide informative discussions on market trends. The convention venue hosts a "Dealer's Fair" and an "Artist's Fair." For a collector, it is important to meet artists and become more familiar with what they are making and to meet dealers that may help collectors acquire wanted pieces. This PCA affiliation makes a collector a part of a community.

Evolution & Focus of the Collection

As her collection grew, Eileen committed to collecting mid-nineteenth-century weights from four French factories: Baccarat, Clichy, Pantin, and Saint-Louis. She admits to a special emphasis on, and love for, Clichy weights. However, at the same time, through the PCA and their biennial conventions, she began to meet many contemporary artists and became supportive of their work. So while the goal was to collect antiques, she could not resist great pieces by many of the artists she met. Directly knowing artists has expanded Eileen's interest to include work by contemporary artists. These relationships have given her insight into their process, history, personality, achievements, and often their families, many of whom are creators too. Undeniably, the study of the history of weights has informed the makers of today, and Eileen's collection illustrates the relationship between the nineteenth-century makers and contemporary artists.

As a collector, Eileen has become the chief curator of the Ellis Collection. She has a cataloging system, spreadsheets of inventory, appraisal information, and receipts. She knows the market, checks auction houses, works with dealers and continues to share information with the paperweight community. She also has organized and changed the display of the collection in her home. She periodically rearranges her display to groupings of individual artists or makers. Occasionally, she exhibits the weights to feature a subset around a theme. Changing how she views her collection has encouraged her to study recurring themes within the collection including, to her surprise, the number of weights she has that include pansies (twelve weights to be exact): six Classic, three Classic Revival, and three Contemporary.

Currently, her intent is to buy only what she especially likes, it must "sing to her." She has become a well-educated collector. Space is never a consideration for her—she will make space. While she does not see herself as an impulsive buyer, she admits that she has sometimes adjusted her budget to make a purchase. Her main purpose of interest is to purchase important paperweights—ones that are rare, with remarkable artistry, and museum worthy. She cites that both the Pantin and Russian weights from the Dyat'kovo Imperial Glassworks, add a dimension of extreme rarity to her collection.

Thoughts on Starting a Collection

Eileen advises to first, have a plan. Know what you value before you go to antique fairs or bid during an auction. Do not spend your limited funds on "seconds" but hold out for the good weights. Join the PCA and find a local chapter if there is one in your part of the country. Visit museums and galleries and study weights. Over time you will develop preferences that will inform your collection. Eileen says, "Collecting is joyful." However, she warns, "Be prepared to adjust your budget if a very rare Pantin paperweight called *Bird in the Nest* becomes available!"

A Symphony of Glass

HIGHLIGHTS FROM THE ELLIS COLLECTION

Kathryn Sharbaugh
Director of Donor Relations & Special Initiatives
Flint Institute of Arts Museum + Art School

The Ellis Collection presents an extensive selection of glass paperweights and related glass objects made in Europe and the United States. Included in this collection is an extraordinary variety of techniques and styles, incorporated in an array of motifs, types, and shapes. Every weight in the Ellis Collection displays its own distinct properties to study and enjoy.

History of Fine Paperweights

The art form of paperweights, or weights, began in European glass factories in the mid-nineteenth century referred to as the Classic Period ca. 1845–1870. Within a few years paperweights were produced by workers in glass houses in France, Great Britain, Russia, and the United States. More than a hundred years later in 1950, a number of manufacturers revived the art form referred to as Classic Revival. In the late 1950s major advancements in technology allowed artists to work independently rather than in glass factories.

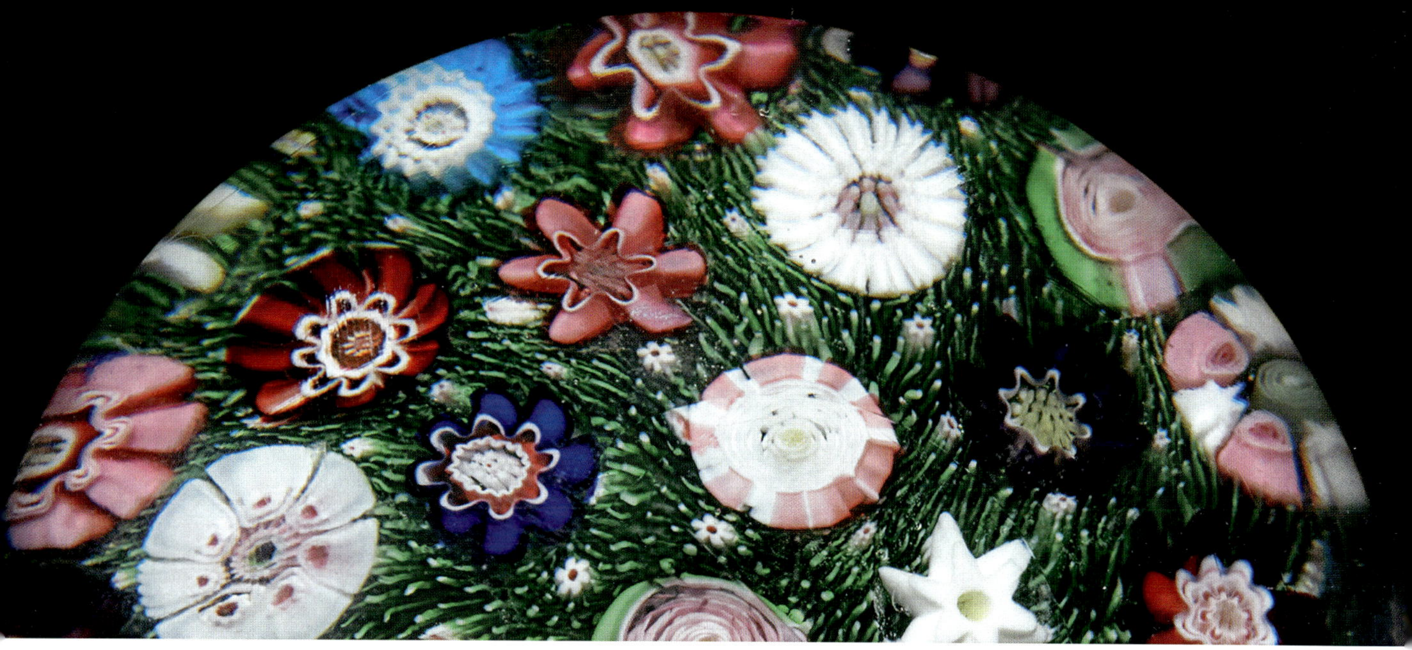

This period is referred to as Transitional. As a consequence, the ability to create without the constraints of a manufacturer's requirements, individual artists and independent studios took the art form in new directions; glass artists were known as being part of the Contemporary Studio Glass movement. Looking at the twenty-first century, we see new designs, techniques, and shapes, although artists are still working within the historical vernacular of glass paperweights.

This catalogue divides the Ellis Collection by chronological period. The Classic and Classic Revival periods are organized by country of origin. The Contemporary weights are alphabetical by maker.

ABOVE: Detail of Cat. 68

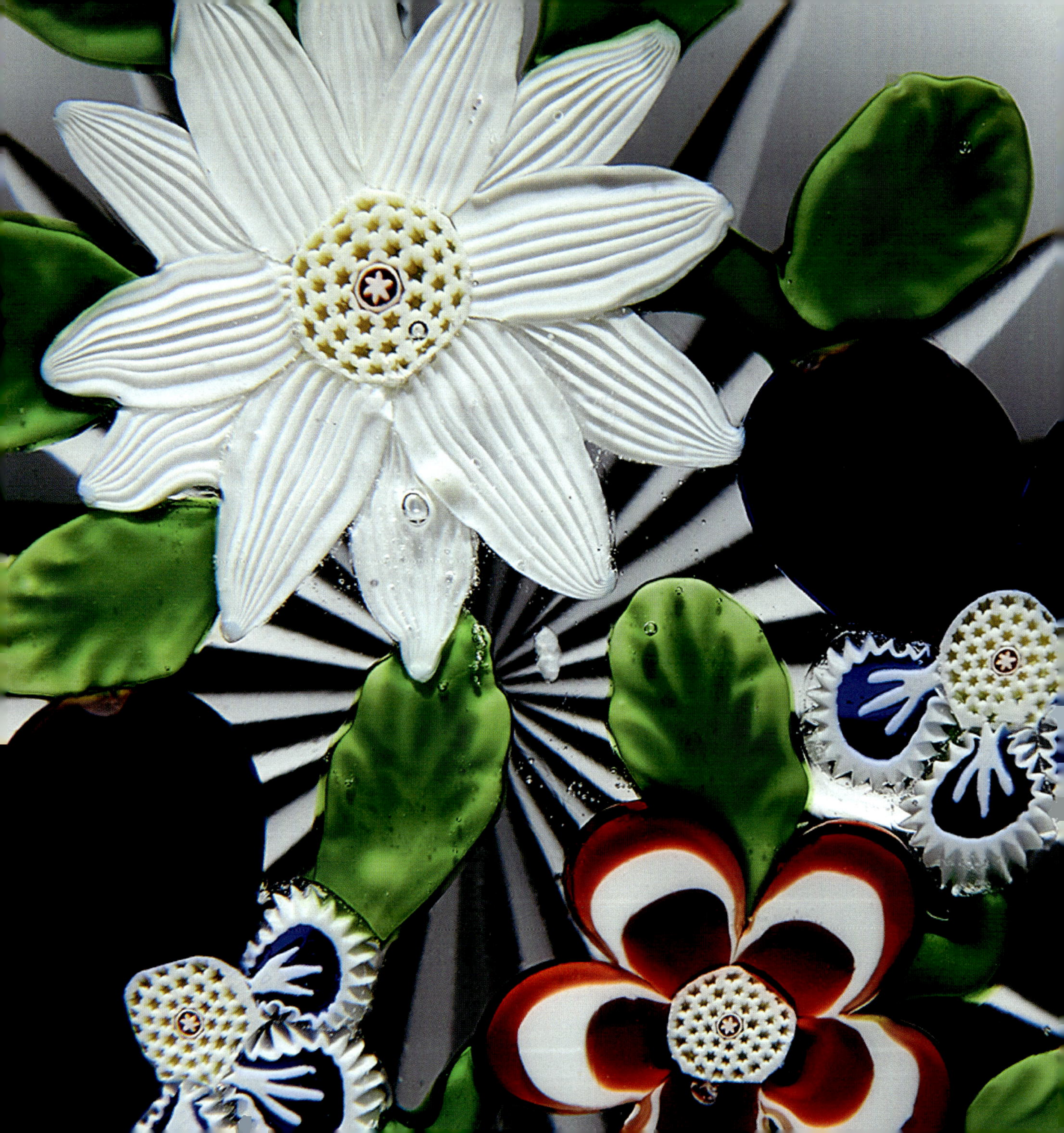

Classic & Post-Classic *circa 1845–1890*

Paperweights of the Classic Period were produced during an era when Europe and the United States experienced rapid and profound socio-economic changes. Between 1845 and 1870 urbanization was spawned by two Industrial Revolutions, which defined the period as the age of the machine. Major advancements in technology impacted every level of society, improving everyday life. Breakthroughs in transportation, especially railroads, sailing, and shipping, fueled communication and immigration across countries and continents. New ideas and artistic influences were able to spread quickly throughout Europe and the United States. Politically and geographically these regions were changing, which brought land acquisitions, new statehood, revolutions, civil war, and the breakdown of old empires and growth of new ones. Art—decorative or applied, as well as fine art, sculpture, and painting—during the nineteenth century was changing as well. The changes were dramatic, transitioning from the historic works of the Old Masters to the brink of unconventional works created during the eve of modernity.

LEFT: Detail of Cat. 1

The Classic Period's weights, at first glance, may appear to look similar but manufacturers used their own specific designs, palettes, cutting, and finishing techniques to make their work unique. Production was a coordinated effort of several glassworkers within each factory working collaboratively but making different parts of each design. The weights were primarily composed of *millefiori* (Italian for "thousands of flowers") canes and lampworked elements.

Large glass manufacturers employed workers that were highly specialized and able to produce a complex product line from large chandeliers to small vials and paperweights. Every object, including paperweights, had intricate parts requiring unique skills to fabricate and finish them. Some people worked alone using lamps to form the interior assemblages of flowers. Lamps were small oil-fueled torches that were fed oxygen with foot-operated bellows, to heat the glass to a malleable temperature. Others worked in teams at large furnaces gathering hot glass at the end of long pipes. The glass would be rolled on a marble table into thick cylindrical shapes. Once formed, a second worker would attach another pipe at the opposite end of the cylinder and then pull the glass into a long narrow rod as one would pull taffy. The rods would be cut into many long segments, usually the diameter of thick pencils. Many rods were produced. Workers would then form assemblages of glass rods in a variety of colors and predetermined alternating patterns to heat together to become a cane. Heated again, the cane was stretched to the diameter of a thin pencil. Once the elements were cooled they were then cut into fine, tiny, cylindrical segments, with many segments to be used in cross-section to reveal an image or millefiori.

Recurring design elements included garlands, crowns, silhouettes, and an infinite number of different configurations of canes. Flowers occur singularly or in a variety of arrangements and bouquets; some flat, some upright, and surrounded by garlands and torsades (Italian for twist/ribbon). Flowers are also constructed of bundled millefiori canes clustered tightly together resembling the shape of a mushroom. Once all of the parts are assembled, or set up, the design is encased in clear glass and annealed (slowly cooled) in an oven. Once cooled, the weights are then polished. Some weights are overlaid with colored glass completely covering the weight's exterior. These weights are cooled and then cut and ground with facets or windows to juxtapose and reveal the display that has been encased within the interior. The base of the weight, referred to as the ground, may be clear, transparent or opaque. Bases, when cold, might be etched and polished with precision cuts to refract light creating a prismatic effect. Many weights contain extraordinary base layers of canes that appear to look like lace, muslin, or a carpet. They also impersonate sand, grass, or coral. Weights also include lifelike elements that truly appear to be from nature rather than fabricated out of glass—magnified forever in an incredible, intimate micro world.

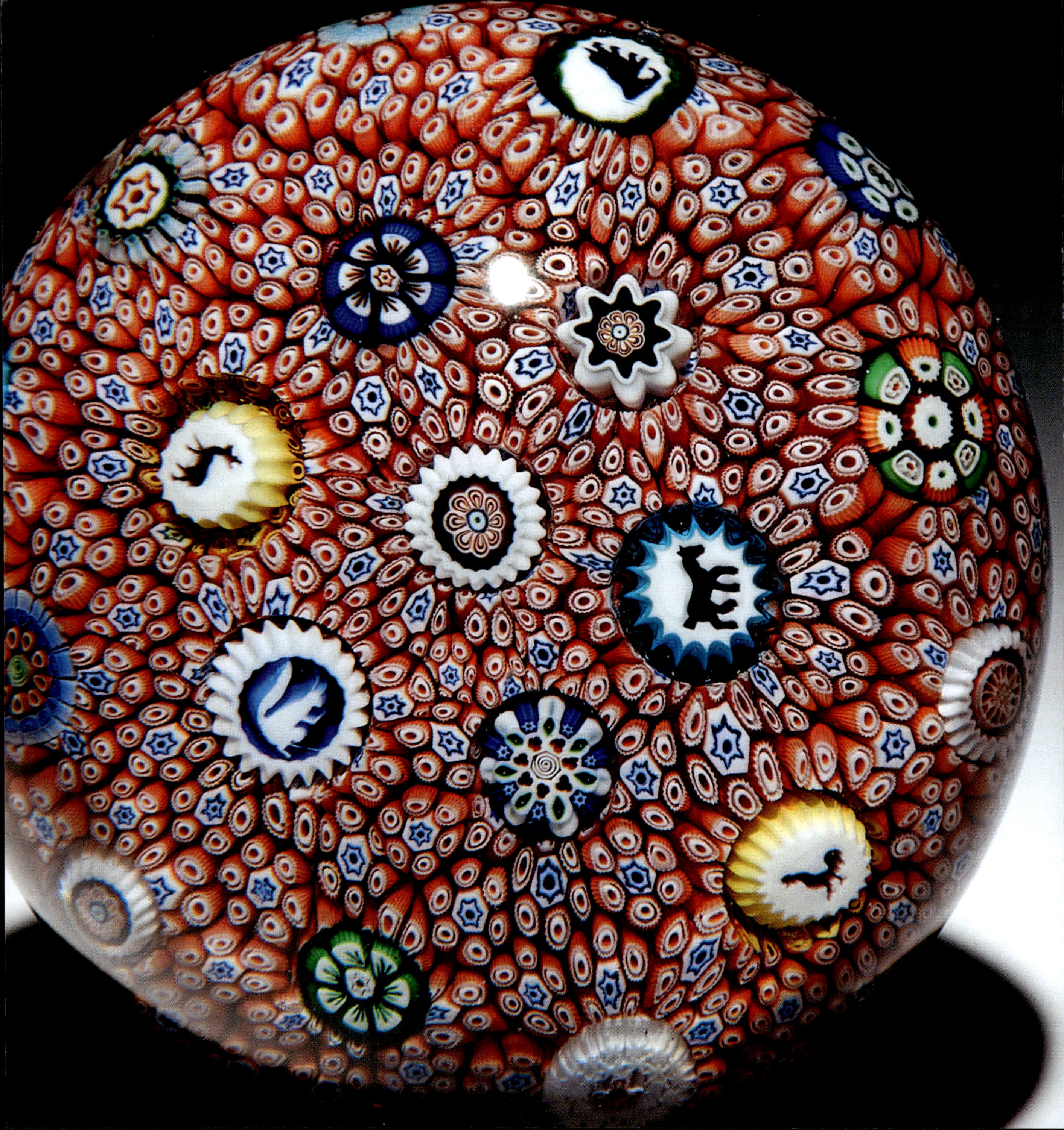

France *CLASSIC & POST-CLASSIC PERIOD*

Baccarat

Baccarat was founded in 1764 outside the town of Baccarat in the Alsace-Lorraine district of Northern France. Baccarat became the first company in France to manufacture leaded glass paperweights with dates appearing in the object in 1846. Leaded glass weights became a popular part of their product line for more than fifteen years. Nearly a century later, early in the 1950s, Baccarat once again put weights into production continuing until the turn of the twenty-first century.

The Ellis Collection includes many fine examples of Baccarat's weights in a variety of their distinctive styles. Among the most varied are weights containing lampworked pansies, the most common flower produced by Baccarat. Many other companies during the period also incorporated pansies into their product lines. The flower's popularity became part of the era's lexicon known as floriography, the language of flowers. Gifts of flowers and specific floral arrangements were used to send a coded message to the recipient, allowing the sender to express feelings that could not be spoken aloud. The name *pansy* is derived from the French word *pensée,* which means thought. It was a sentimental symbol encased in glass to say someone was thinking of you.

LEFT: Detail of Cat. 14

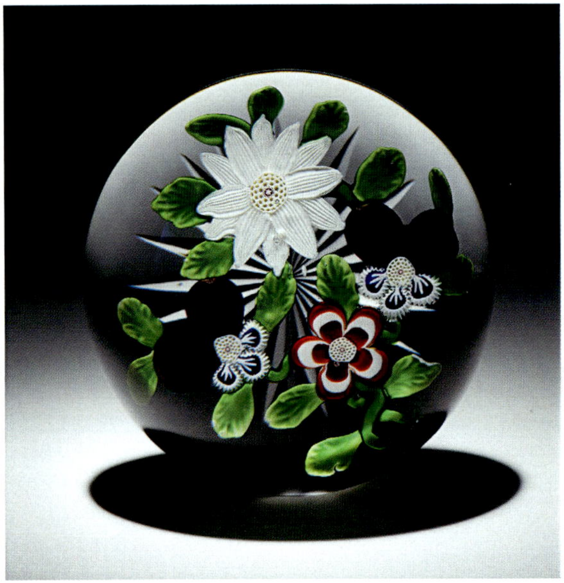

1. Baccarat, French, founded 1764
Bouquet with Type I Pansies, ca. 1850
Glass, D. 3 ⅜ inches

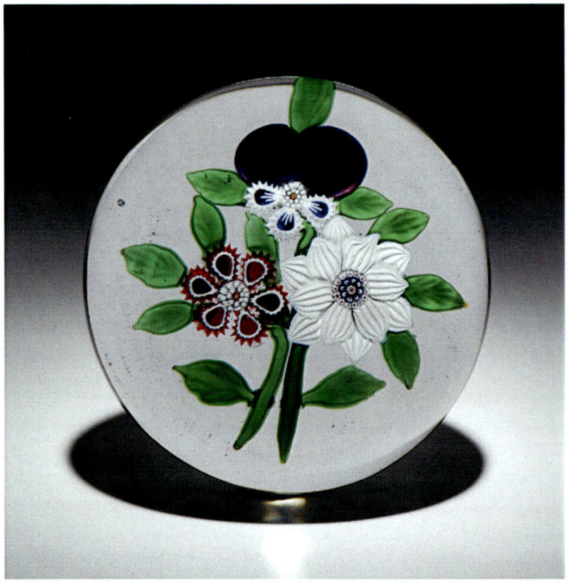

2. Baccarat, French, founded 1764
Three Flowers Type I Bouquet, ca. 1850
Glass, D. 3 ¹⁄₁₆ inches

Baccarat Pansies

Baccarat produced three distinctive types of pansy paperweights all of which are represented in the Ellis Collection. They all have two dark purple upper or posterior petals and millefiori cane centers. What changes in each type is a different approach to fabricating the two lateral and anterior petals.

In **Type I** the flower's lower petals are constructed with canes resembling a crow's foot known as arrowhead canes.

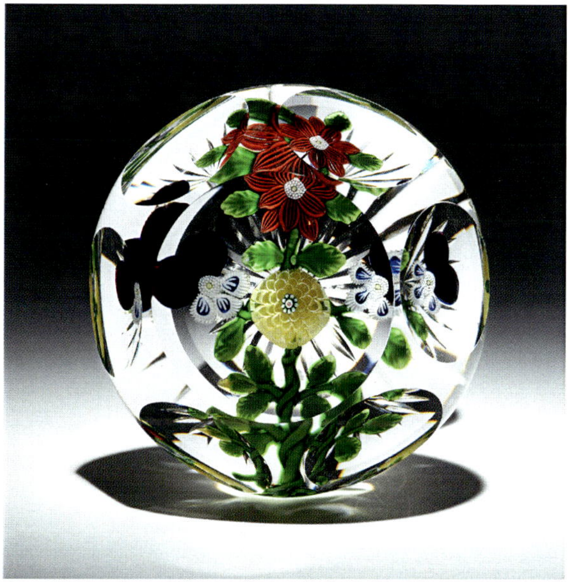

3. Baccarat, French, founded 1764
Faceted Bouquet with Type I Pansies, ca. 1850
Glass, D. 3 3⁄16 inches

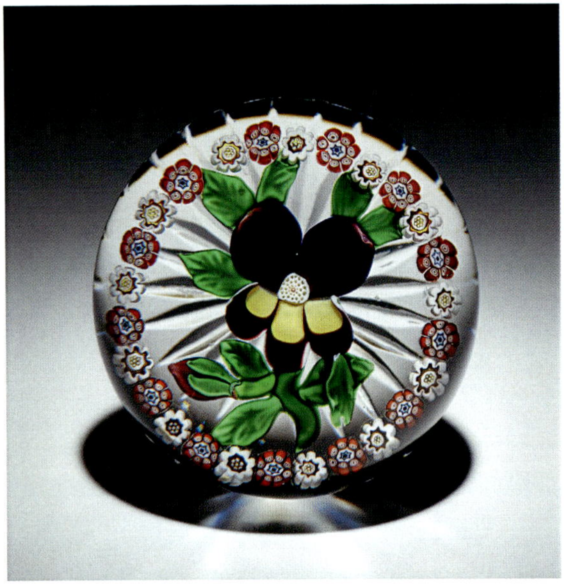

4. Baccarat, French, founded 1764
Type II Pansy with Garland, ca. 1850
Glass, D. 2 ⅞ inches

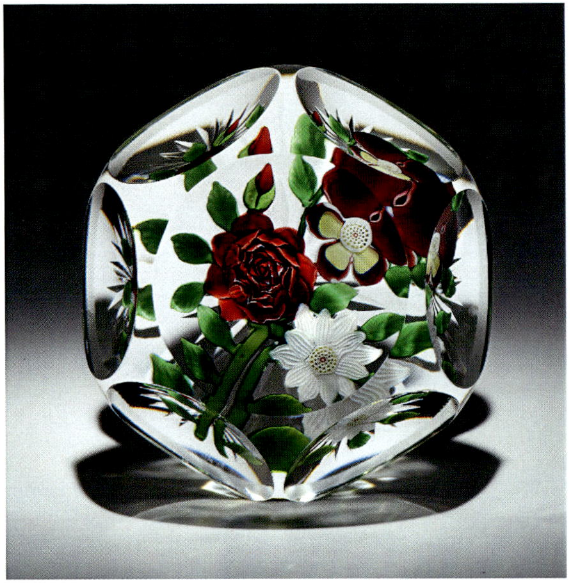

5. Baccarat, French, founded 1764
Type II Magnum Faceted Bouquet, ca. 1850
Glass, D. 3 $^{9}/_{16}$ inches

Type II weights have a solid dark purple "U" shape covering the tips of the yellow lateral and anterior petals.

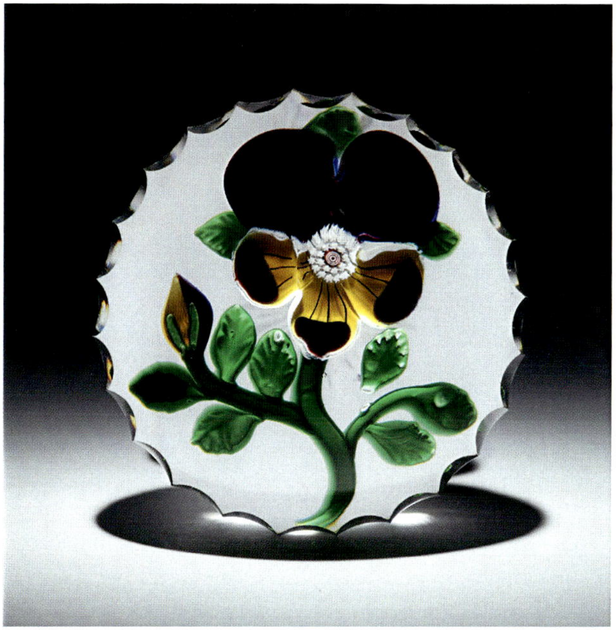

6. Baccarat, French, founded 1764
Type III Pansy, ca. 1850
Glass, D. 3 ⅛ inches

Type III includes lower petals that have dark purple half-circle shapes at their base.

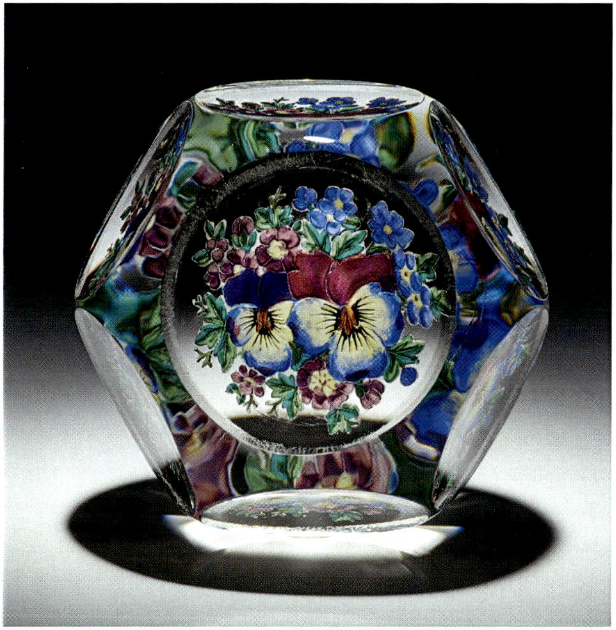

7. Baccarat, French, founded 1764
Faceted Enameled Bouquet, ca. 1850
Glass, D. 3 ⅛ inches

A departure from Baccarat's typical types of pansy weights is **cat. 7,** an enameled, faceted bouquet.

Baccarat Grounds and Millefiori

The Ellis Collection illustrates the diversity of Baccarat's innovative bottom backgrounds called carpet grounds. From stars to organic forms like a *choufleur* (French for "cauliflower"), these richly textured repetitive grounds serve as a uniform wall-to-wall habitat to feature figured canes nestled snugly within the ground known as spaced millefiori. All these weights also contain Baccarat's "Gridel" silhouette canes. These distinctive canes are based on eighteen original silhouette designs created in the 1840s by eight-year-old Emil Gridel. Gridel was the nephew of Baccarat's general manager, Jean-Baptiste Toussaint. His drawings inspired Baccarat's glass workers to create eighteen silhouette canes that depicted butterflies, a red devil, deer, dogs, elephants, goats, horses, love birds, a man with rifle, pelicans, pheasants, pigeons, roosters, storks, swans, squirrels, a black monkey, and a white monkey. Many of these weights are dated by including tiny complex white canes that contain the letter *B* placed above the dates of 1847 and 1848 in combinations of navy, red, and green.

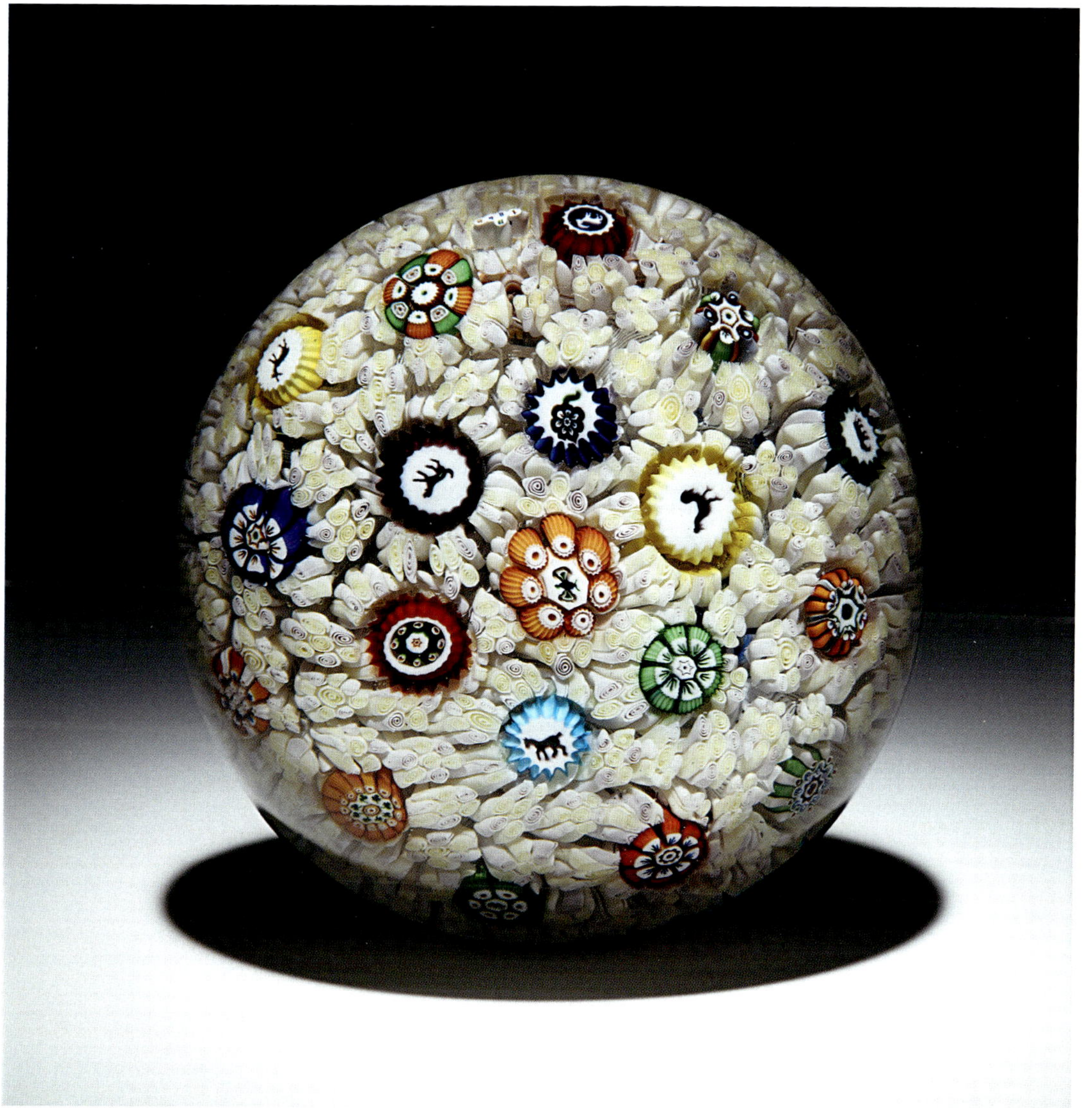

8. Baccarat, French, founded 1764
Millefiori and Silhouette Canes on Choufleur Ground, 1848. Glass, D. 3 3⁄16 inches

9

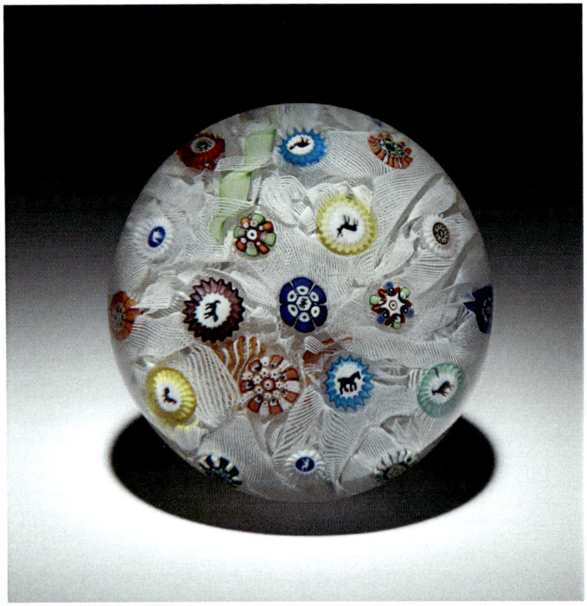

11

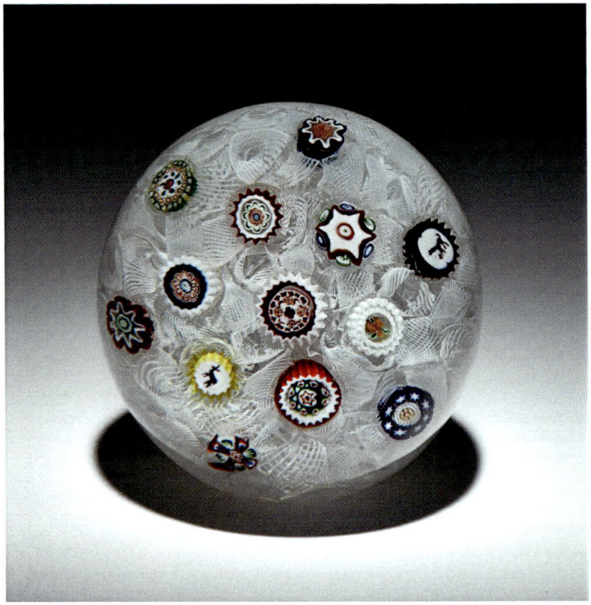

10

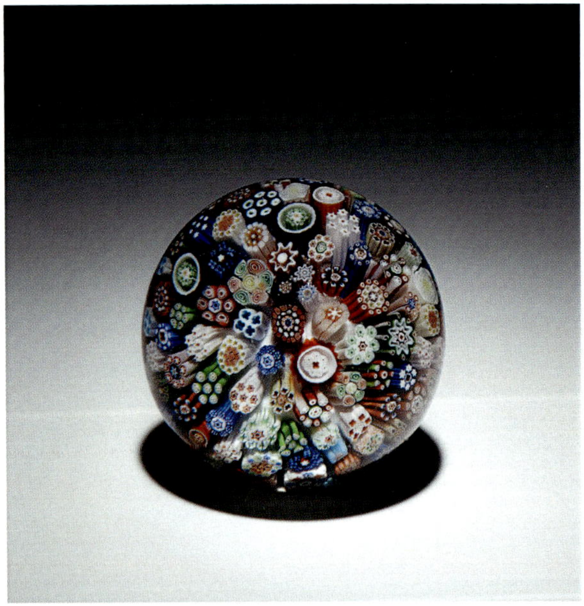

12

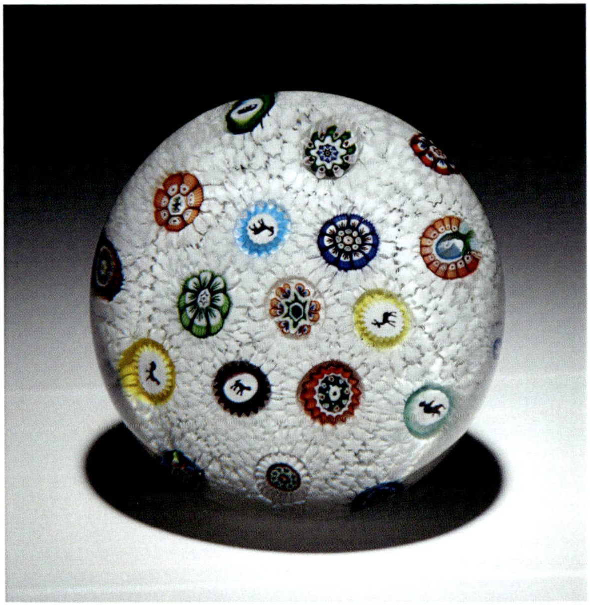

13

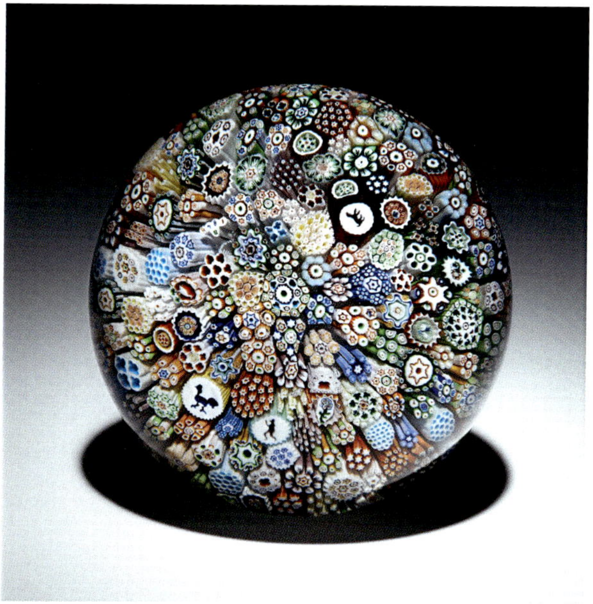

14

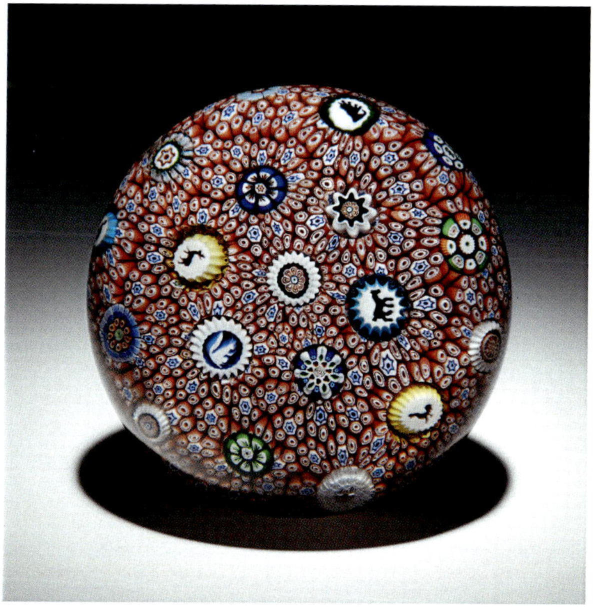

9. Baccarat, French, founded 1764
Spaced Millefiori on Upset Muslin, 1848
Glass, D. 2 5⁄16 inches

10. Baccarat, French, founded 1764
Miniature Close Pack Millefiori on Sodden Snow, ca. 1850
Glass, D. 1 3⁄4 inches

11. Baccarat, French, founded 1764
Spaced Millefiori on Muslin, ca. 1850
Glass, D. 2 3⁄16 inches

12. Baccarat, French, founded 1764
Millefiori and Silhouette Canes on White Stardust Carpet Ground, 1848
Glass, D. 2 3⁄4 inches

13. Baccarat, French, founded 1764
Close Pack Millefiori, 1848
Glass, D. 3 inches

14. Baccarat, French, founded 1764
Millefiori and Silhouette Canes on Red Carpet Ground, 1848
Glass, D. 3 inches

15

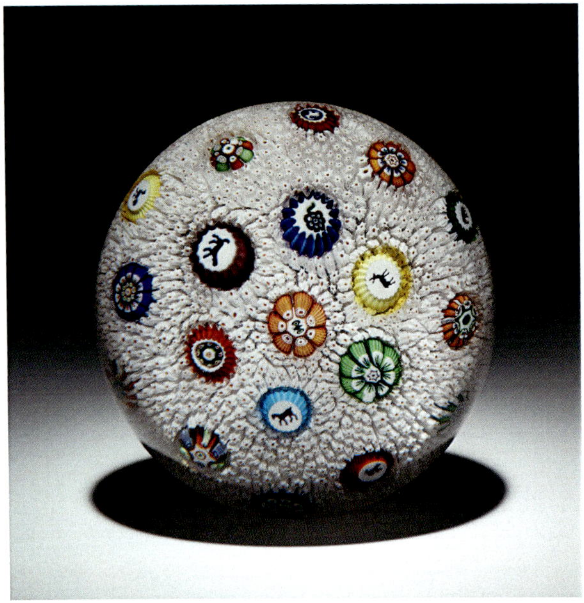

17

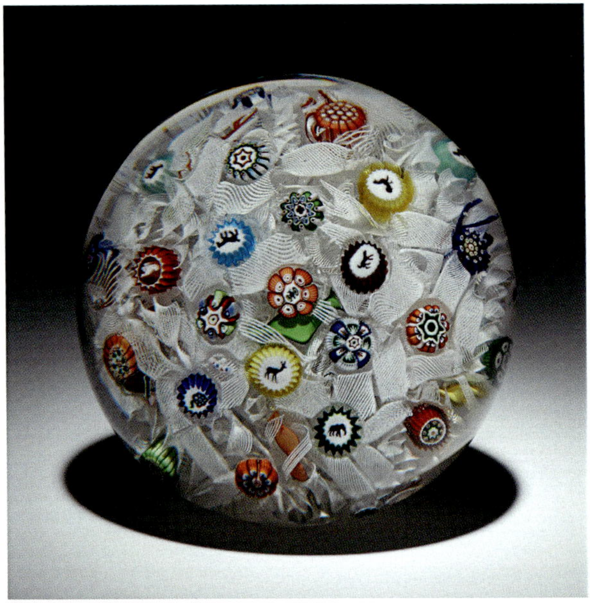

16

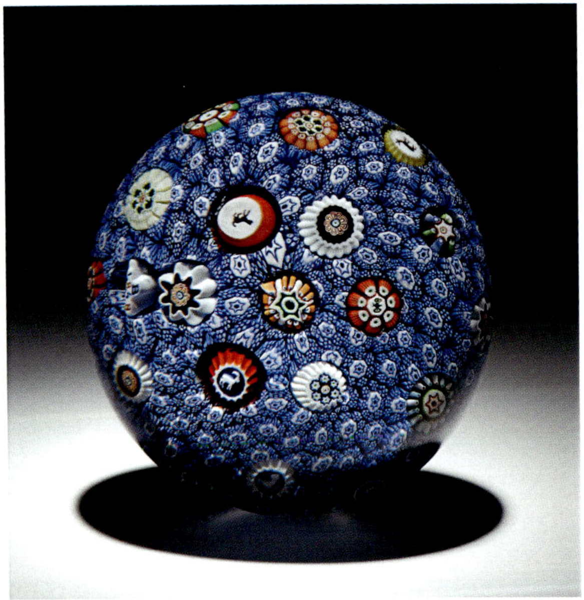

18

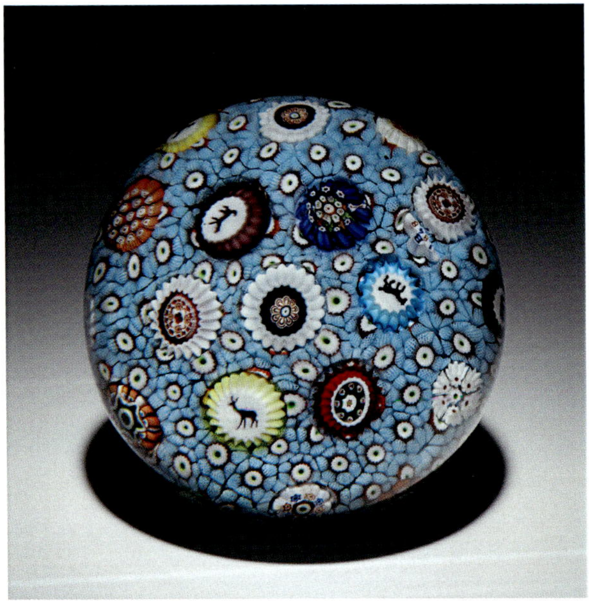

19

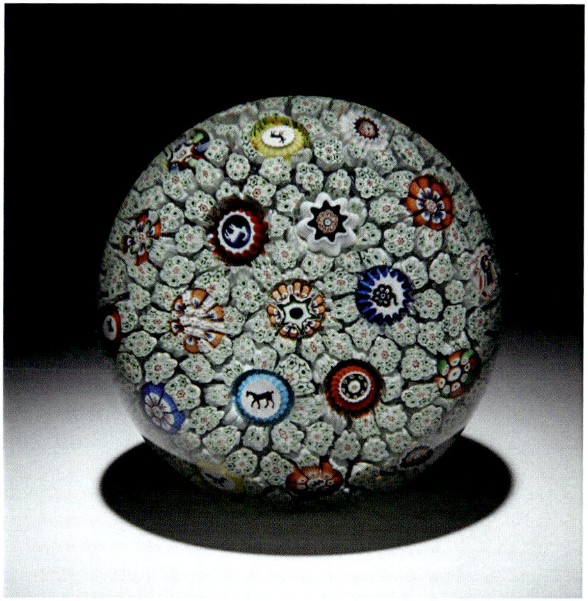

20

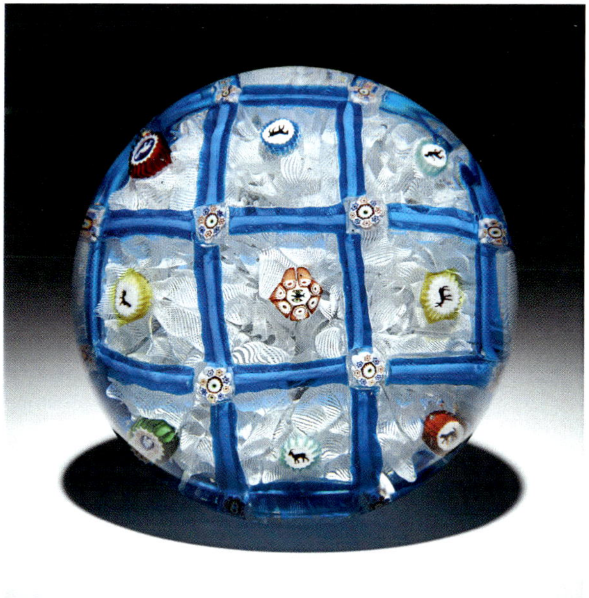

15. Baccarat, French, founded 1764
Millefiori and Silhouette Canes on Stardust Ground, ca. 1850
Glass, D. 3 3⁄16 inches

16. Baccarat, French, founded 1764
Scattered Millefiori and Silhouette Canes on Blue and White Carpet Ground, 1848
Glass, D. 3 1⁄8 inches

17. Baccarat, French, founded 1764
Magnum Spaced Millefiori on Upset Muslin, 1848
Glass, D. 3 3⁄4 inches

18. Baccarat, French, founded 1764
Spaced Millefiori and Silhouette Canes on Aquamarine Honeycomb Carpet Ground, 1848
Glass, D. 3 inches

19. Baccarat, French, founded 1764
Complex and Silhouette Canes on Green Carpet Ground, 1848
Glass, D. 3 1⁄16 inches

20. Baccarat, French, founded 1764
Magnum Quadrille, 1848
Glass, D. 3 11⁄16 inches

21

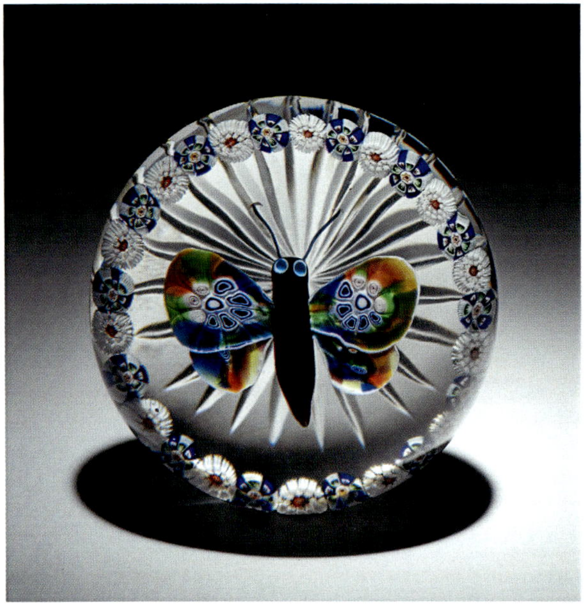

23

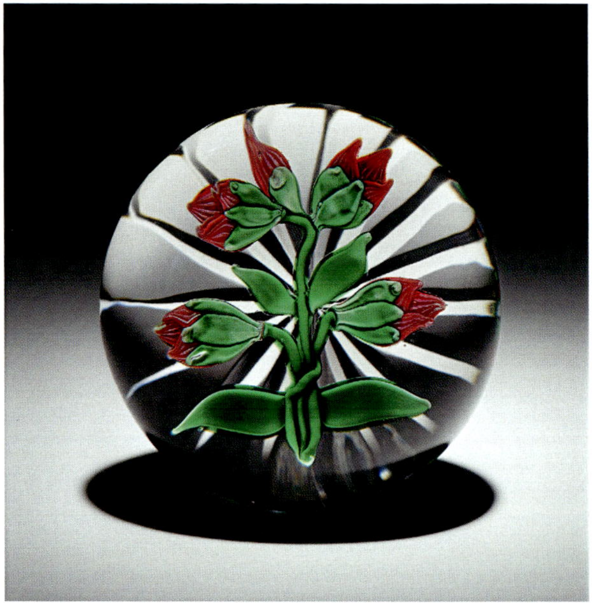

22

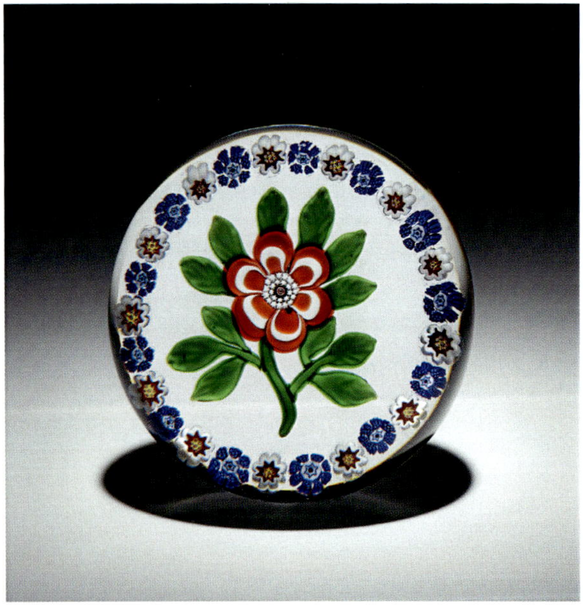

24

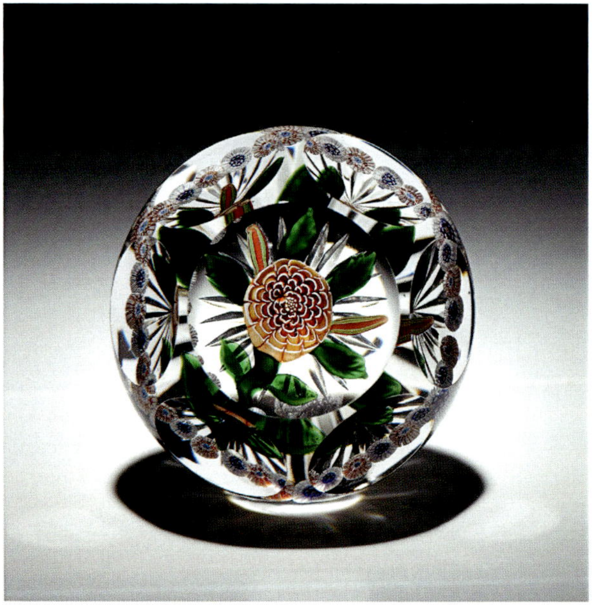

25

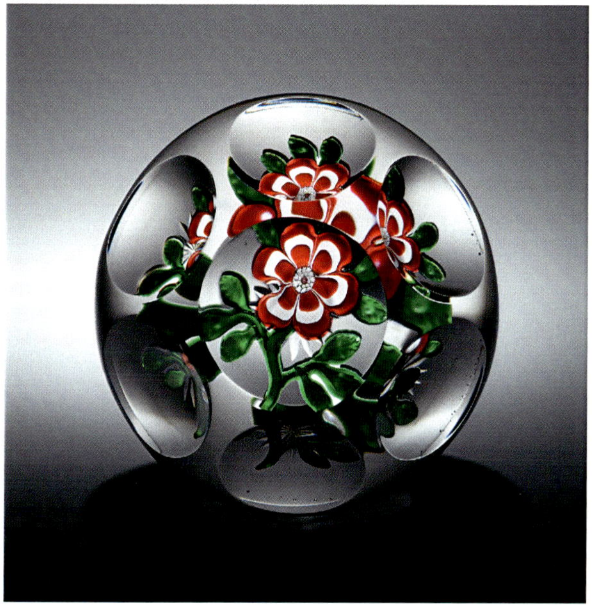

26

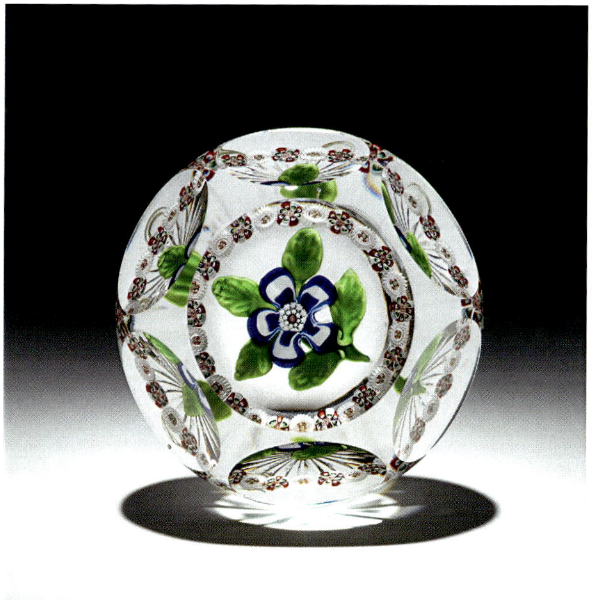

Baccarat Lampwork

Lampwork, also known as flamework, is a technique where colored glass is manipulated with small torches to create representational subjects.

21. Baccarat, French, founded 1764
Butterfly with Garland, ca. 1850
Glass, D. 3 inches

22. Baccarat, French, founded 1764
Primrose with Garland, ca. 1850
Glass, D. 2 ½ inches

23. Baccarat, French, founded 1764
Clematis Buds, ca 1850
Glass, D. 2 15⁄16 inches

24. Baccarat, French, founded 1764
Faceted Copper Chamomile with Garland, ca. 1850
Glass, D. 2 3⁄16 inches

25. Baccarat, French, founded 1764
Faceted Primrose, ca. 1850
Glass, D. 3 1⁄16 inches

26. Baccarat, French, founded 1764
Faceted Blue Primrose with Garland, ca. 1850
Glass, D. 2 5⁄16 inches

27

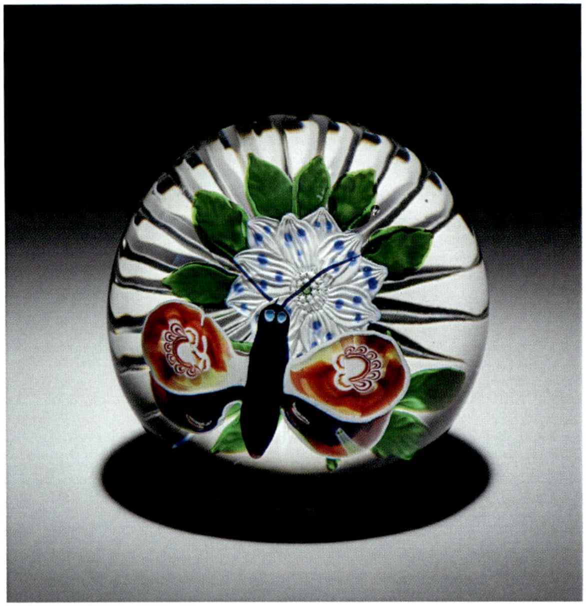

29

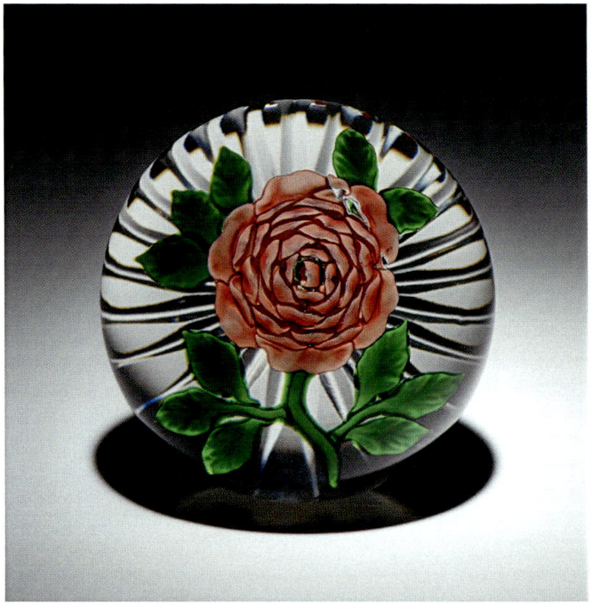

28

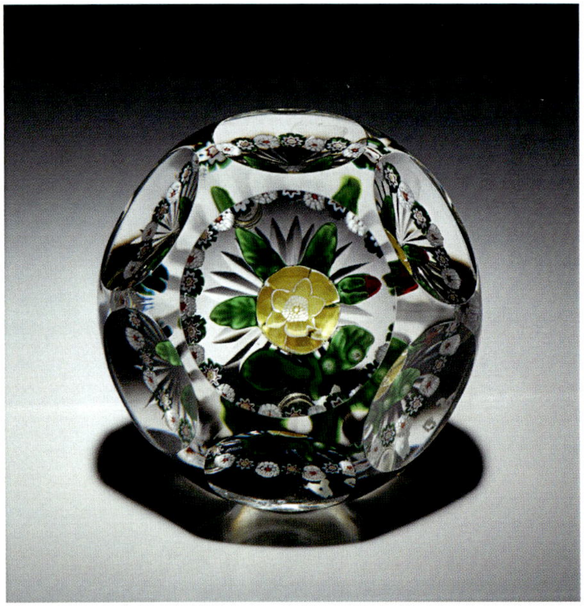

30

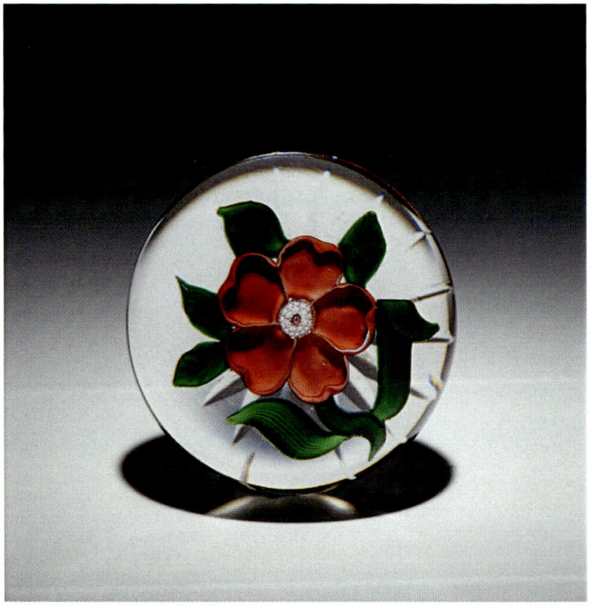

31

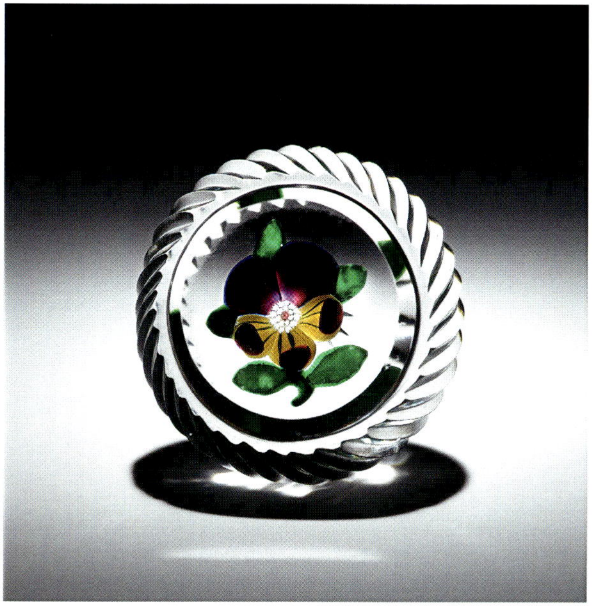

32

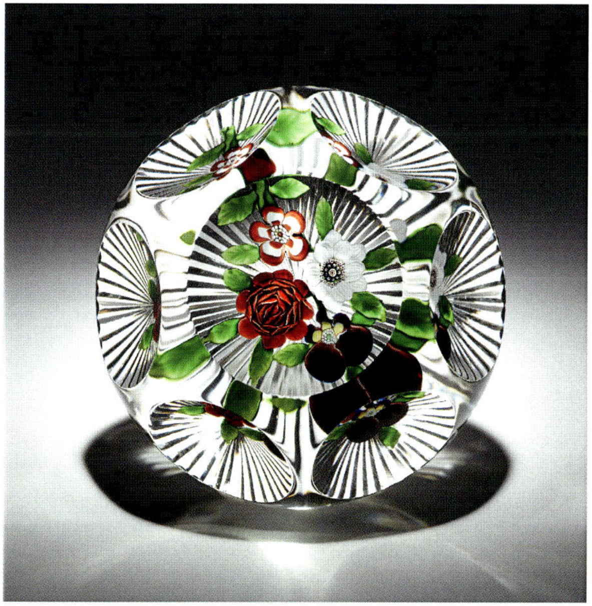

27. Baccarat, French, founded 1764
Butterfly Over Wheat Flower, ca. 1850
Glass, D. 2 7/8 inches

28. Baccarat, French, founded 1764
Yellow Buttercup with Garland, ca. 1850
Glass, D. 2 9/16 inches

29. Baccarat, French, founded 1764
Cabbage Rose, ca 1850
Glass, D. 2 7/8 inches

30. Baccarat, French, founded 1764
Miniature Red Dog Rose, ca. 1850
Glass, D. 2 inches

31. Baccarat, French, founded 1764
Miniature Type III Pansy, ca. 1850
Glass, D. 2 1/16 inches

32. Baccarat, French, founded 1764
Magnum Faceted Flat Bouquet, ca. 1850
Glass, D. 3 5/8 inches

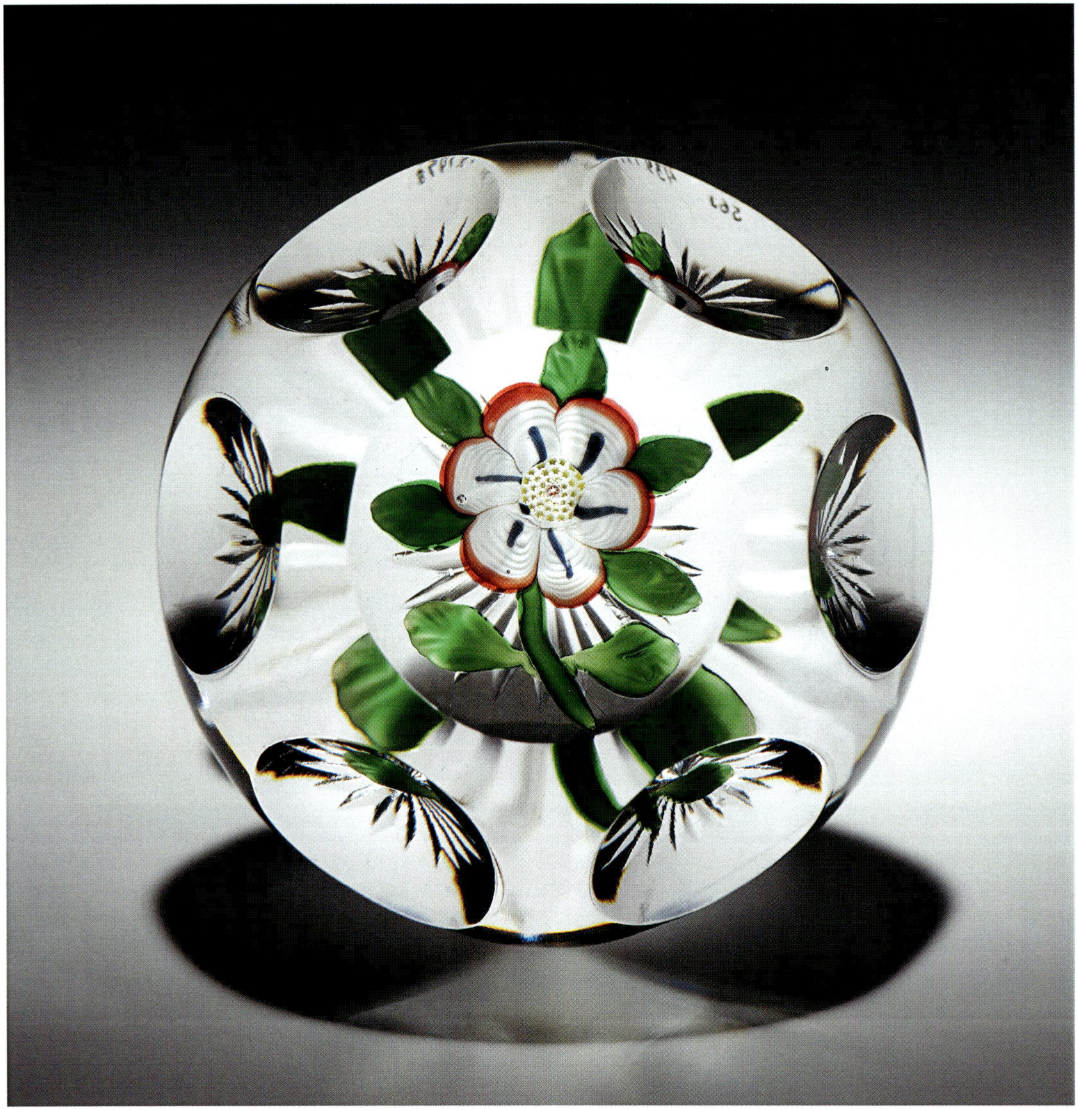

33. Baccarat, French, founded 1764
Faceted Periwinkle, ca. 1850. Glass, D. 2 ½ inches

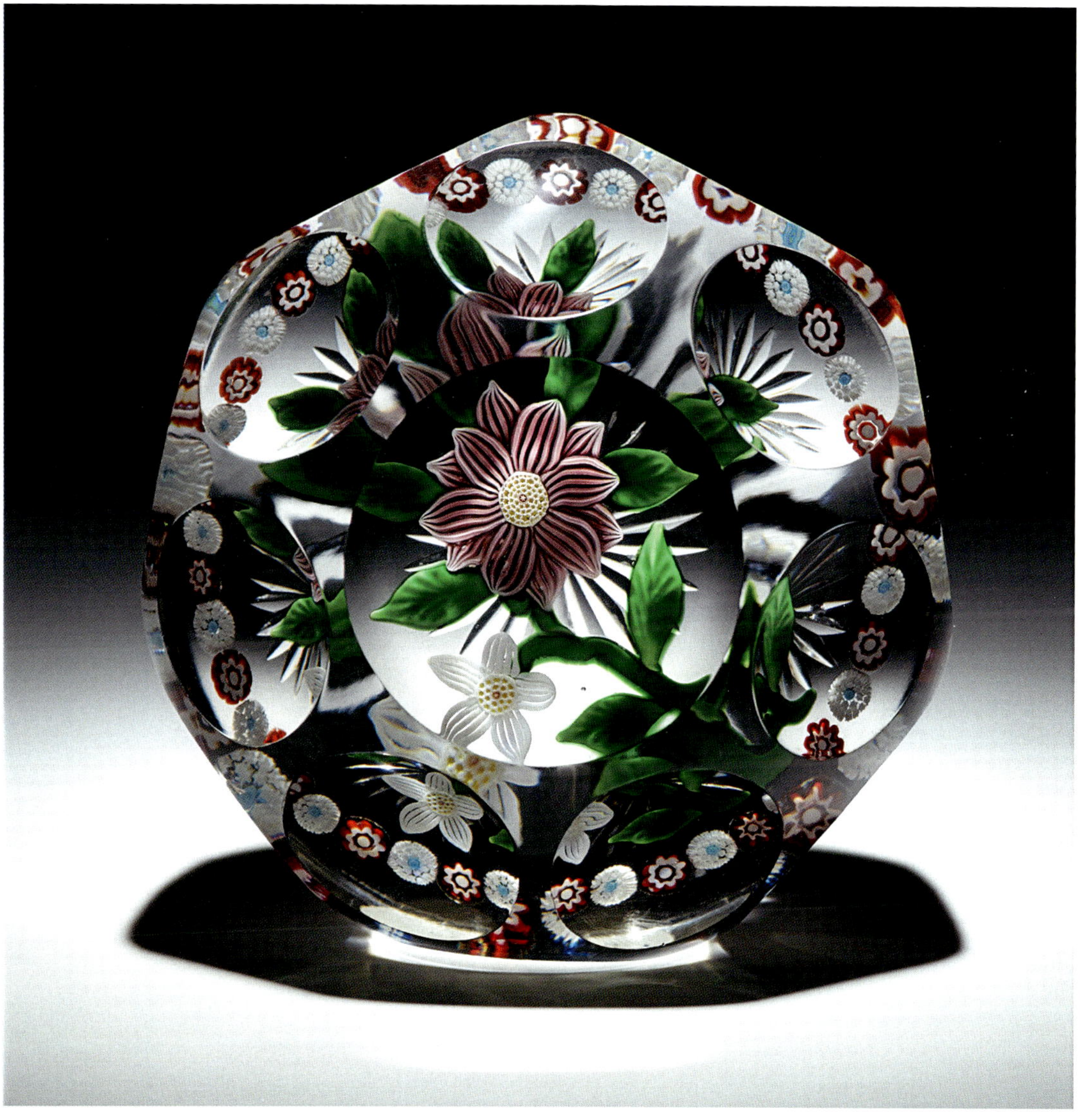

34. Baccarat, French, founded 1764
Faceted Bouquet with Garland, ca. 1850. Glass, D. 3 inches

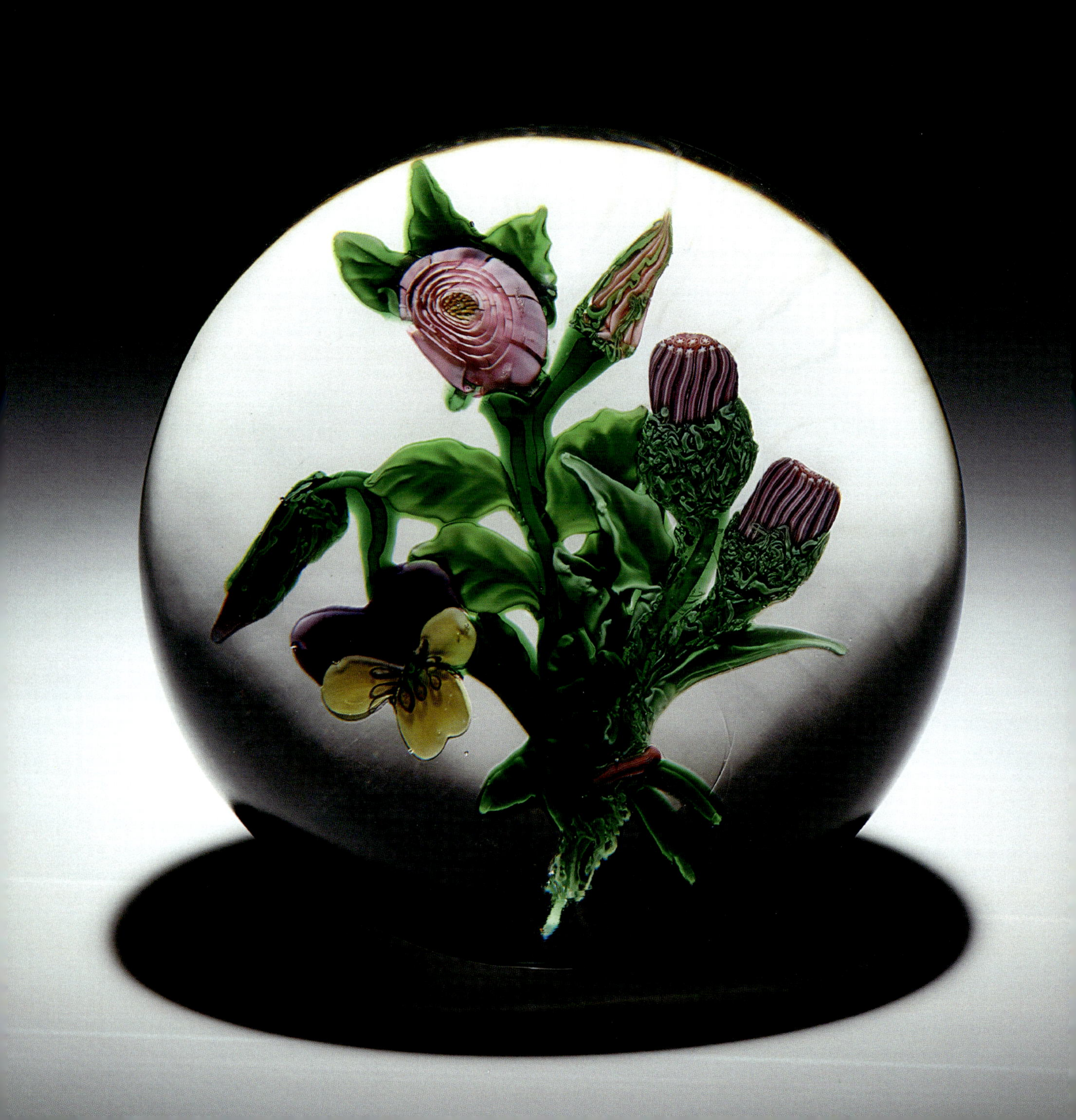

Clichy

Clichy was in operation from 1837 to 1885 at Clichy-la-Garenne, near Paris. The company merged with Cristaillerie de Sèvre in 1885 and ceased production by the late 1890s.

The canes and colors used were generally light and bright. Many Clichy weights display a trademark Clichy rose-shaped cane. It consists of a close overlapping arrangement of flattened hollow canes around a center millefiori cane. Pink, white, and yellow are the colors most found in Clichy roses. Sometimes the roses have green sepals around them. They are found individually and combined in clusters with canes of other designs. The variety of arrangements of the company's diminutive "signature" rose in the Ellis Collection is particularly notable.

35. Clichy, French, 1837–85
Rose, Pansy, and Thistle Bouquet, ca. 1850
Glass, D. 3 1/4 inches

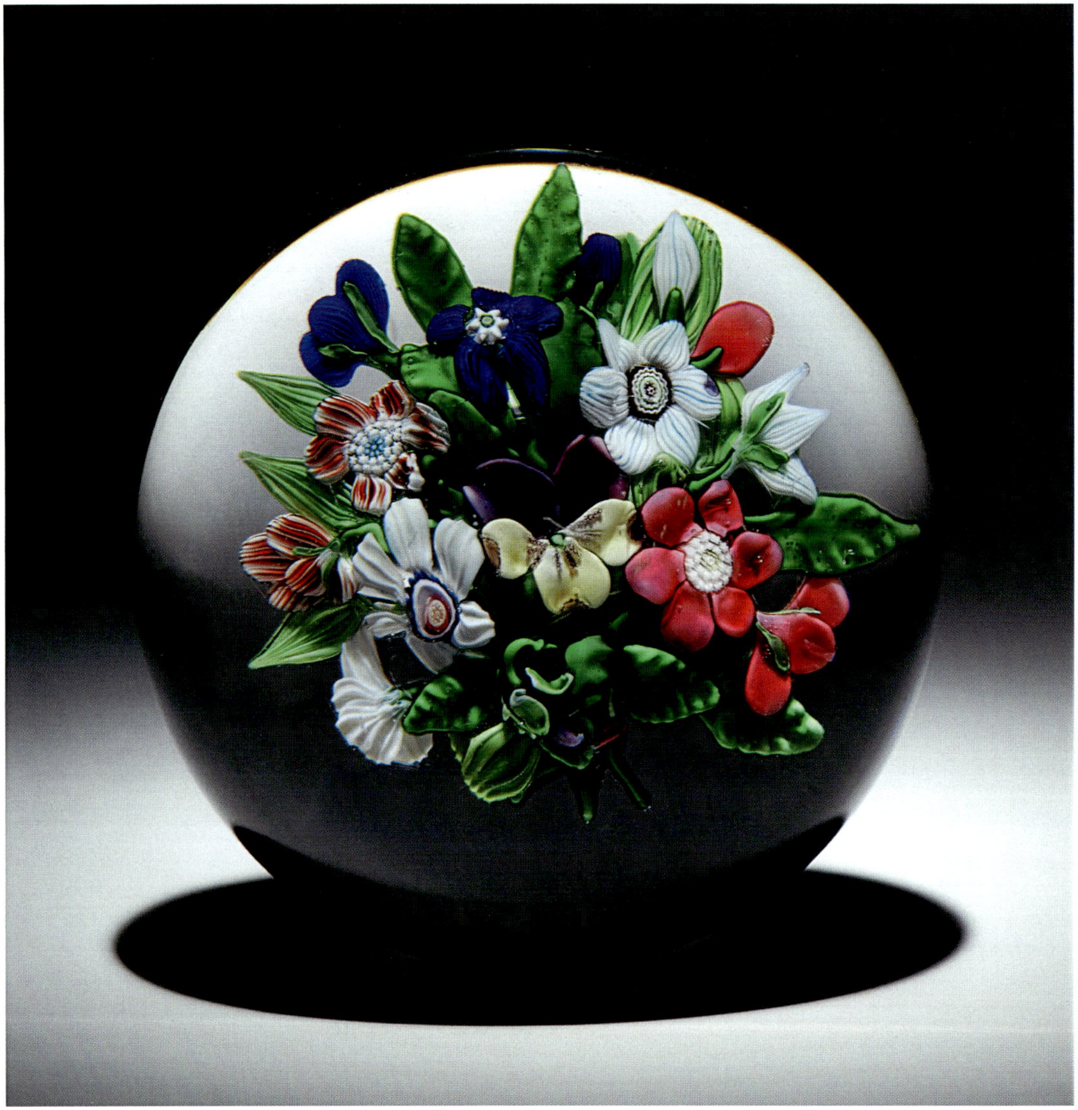

36. Clichy, French, 1837–85
Large Bouquet, ca. 1850. Glass, D. 3 5⁄16 inches

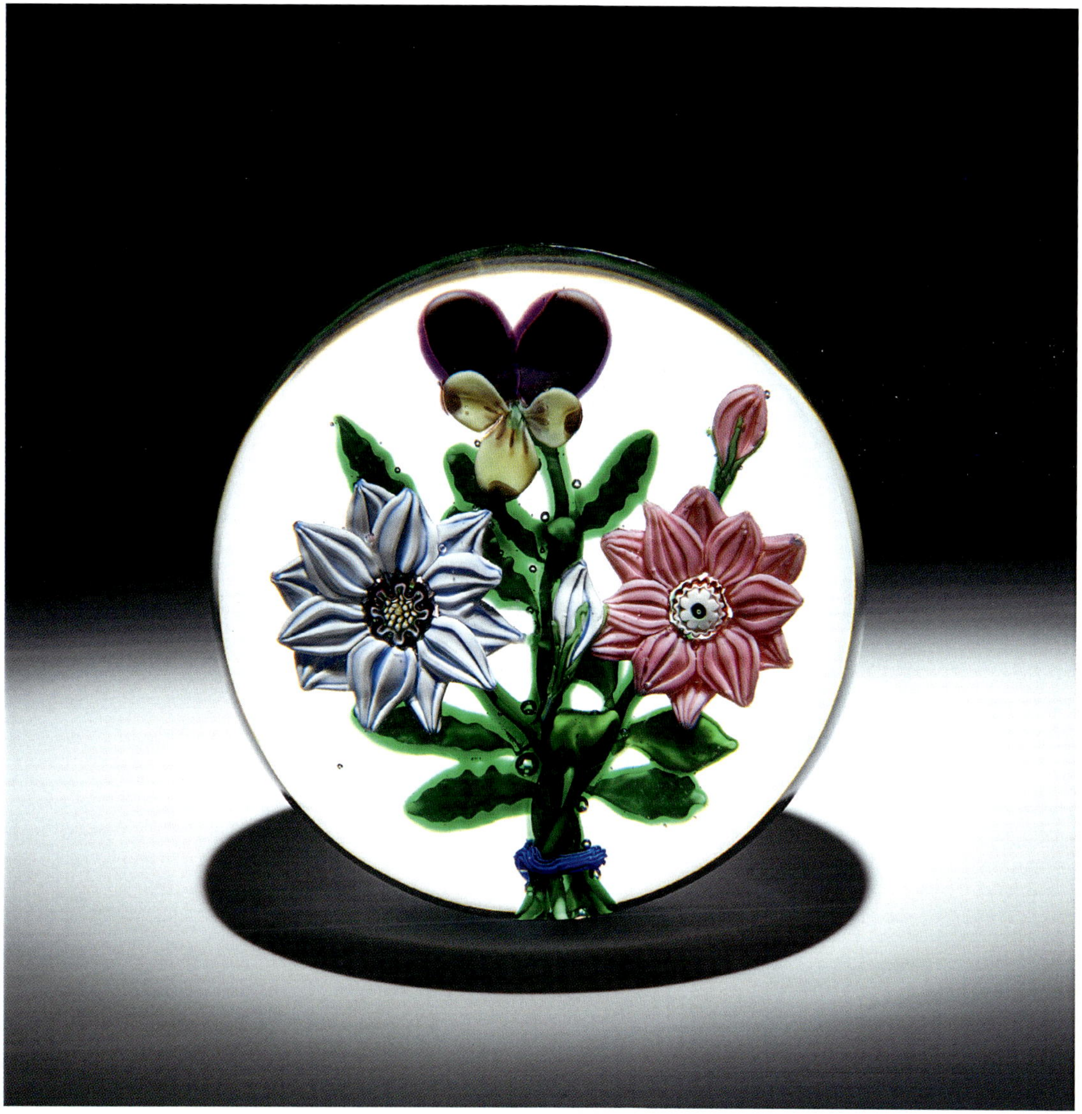

37. Clichy, French, 1837–85
Three-Flowered Bouquet, ca. 1850. Glass, D. 2 3⁄16 inches

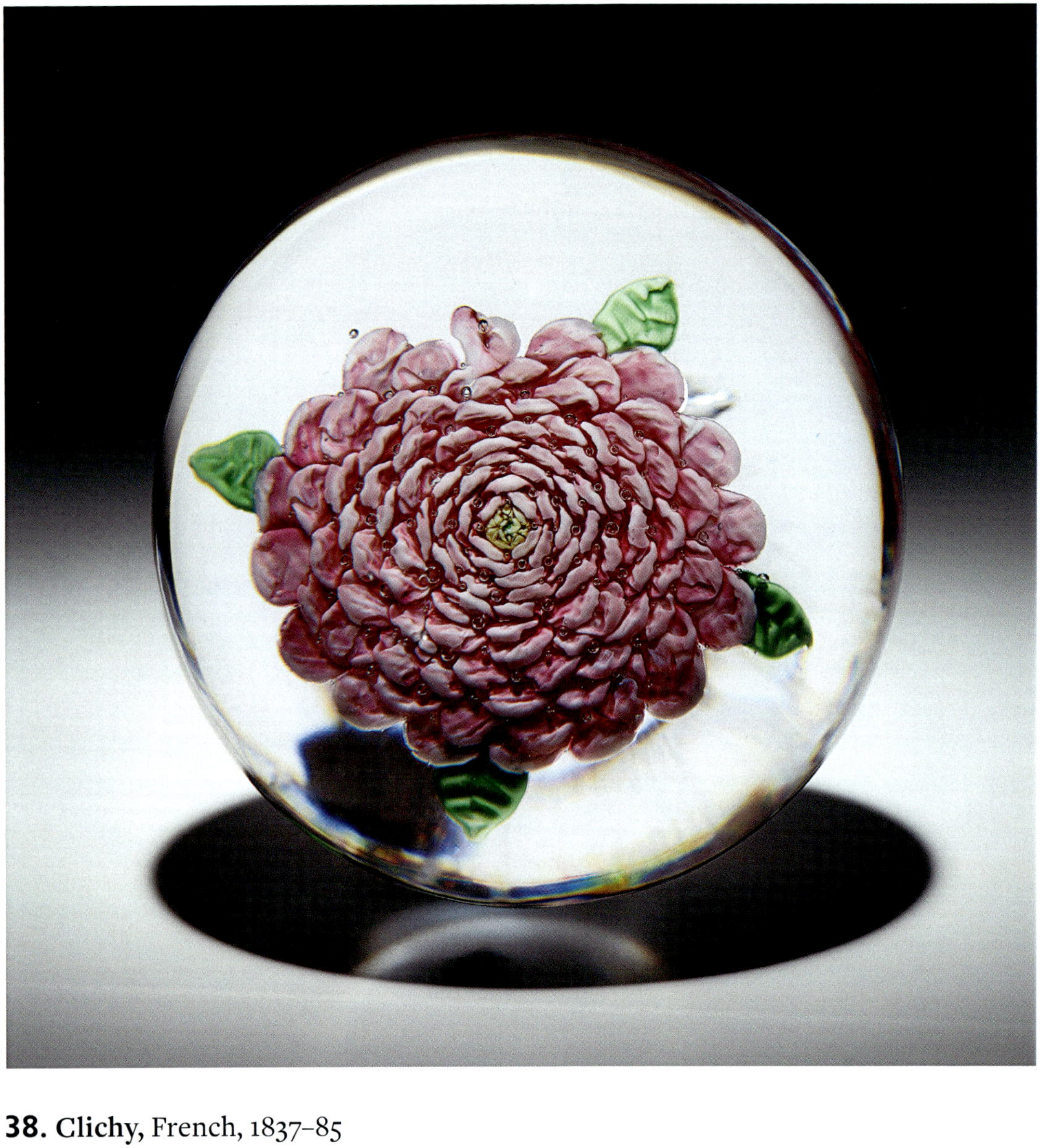

38. Clichy, French, 1837–85
Pink Camelia, ca. 1850. Glass, D. 3 $\frac{1}{16}$ inches

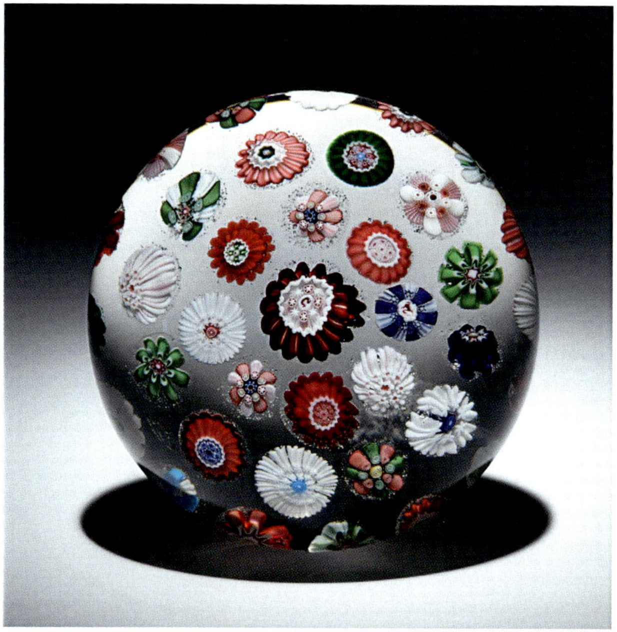

39. Clichy, French, 1837–85
Spaced Concentric Millefiori, ca. 1850
Glass, D. 3 ¹⁄₁₆ inches

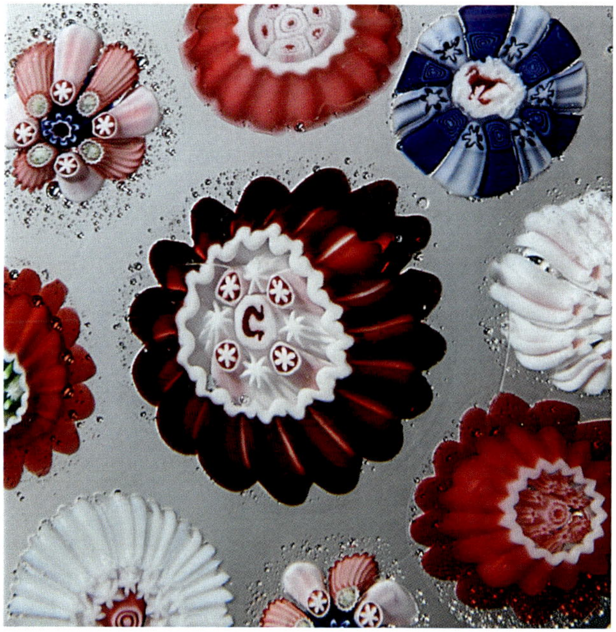

Detail of Cat. 39
Clichy paperweights were sometimes signed with a cane containing the letter "C." The letter in the cane usually appears in black, green, or red placed in the center of a white cane.

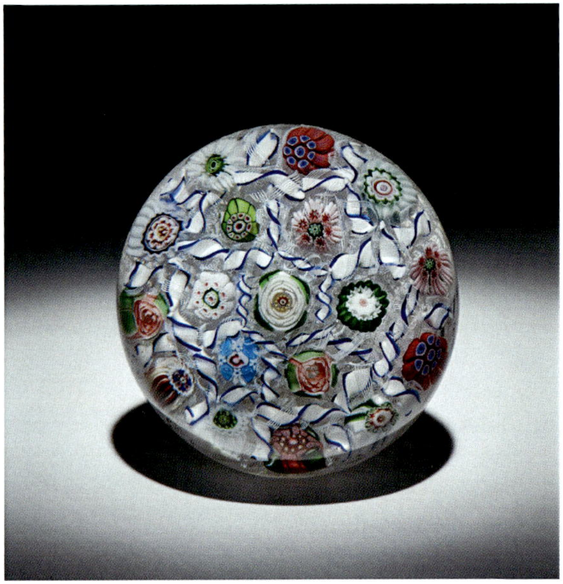

40. Clichy, French, 1837–85
Barber Pole Chequer on Upset Muslin, ca. 1850
Glass, D. 2 ½ inches

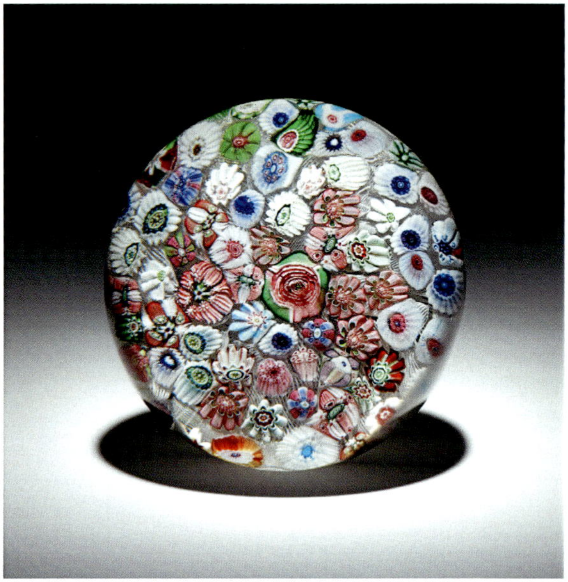

41. Clichy, French, 1837–85
Close Pack Millefiori, ca. 1850
Glass, D. 2 $^{11}/_{16}$ inches

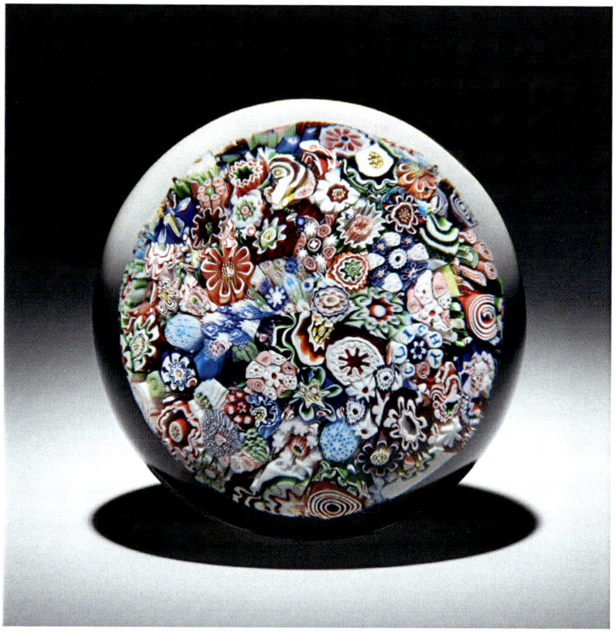

42. Clichy, French, 1837–85
Scrambled Millefiori, ca. 1850
Glass, D. 3 $\frac{3}{16}$ inches

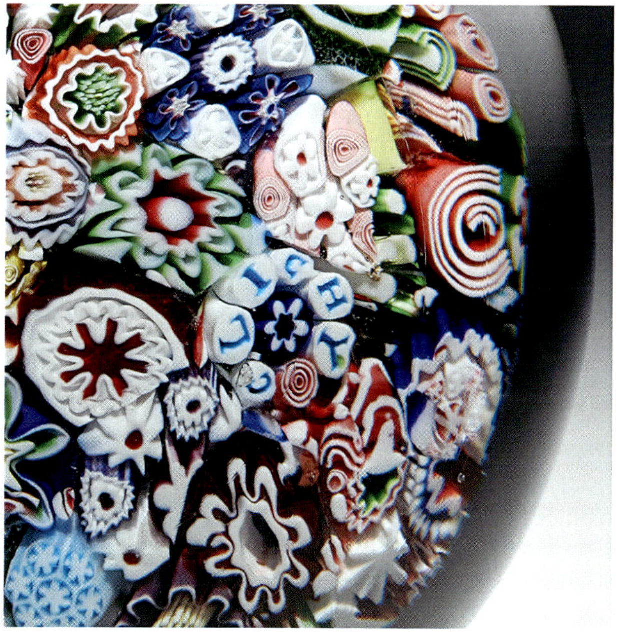

Detail of Cat. 42

Cats. 41 and **42** contain a fully signed "C.L.I.C.H.Y" signature composed of six individual letter canes placed together to spell the company's name.

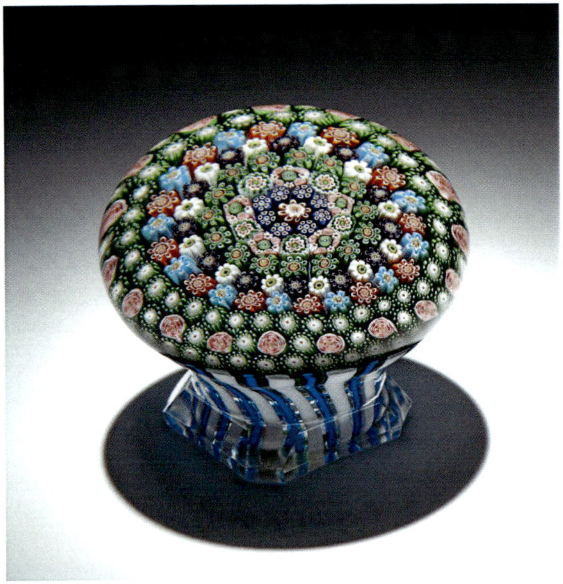

43. Clichy, French, 1837–85
Close Pack Concentric Millefiori Piedouche, ca. 1850
Glass, D. 2 15⁄16, H. 2 7⁄16 inches

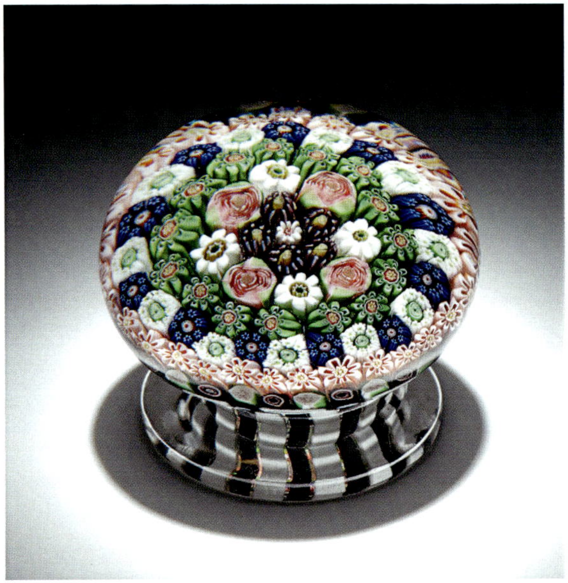

44. Clichy, French, 1837–85
Concentric Millefiori Piedouche
ca. 1850
Glass, D. 2 15⁄16, H. 2 inches

Cats. 43 and 44 are described as close concentric millefiori *piedouche* (French for "pedestal"). The pedestals of various heights are composed of alternating stripes of opaque white and colored staves, or rods drawn down to a clear base. Each contains meticulous arrangements of tight circular rows containing alternating colored flowers and Clichy roses and ends with a composed perimeter.

45

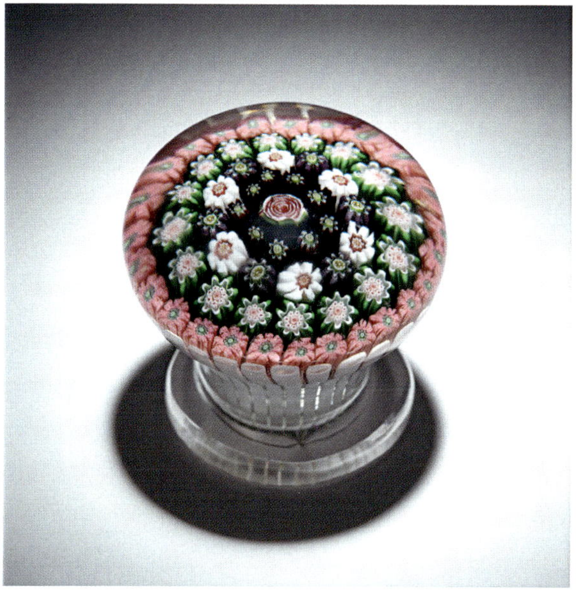

47

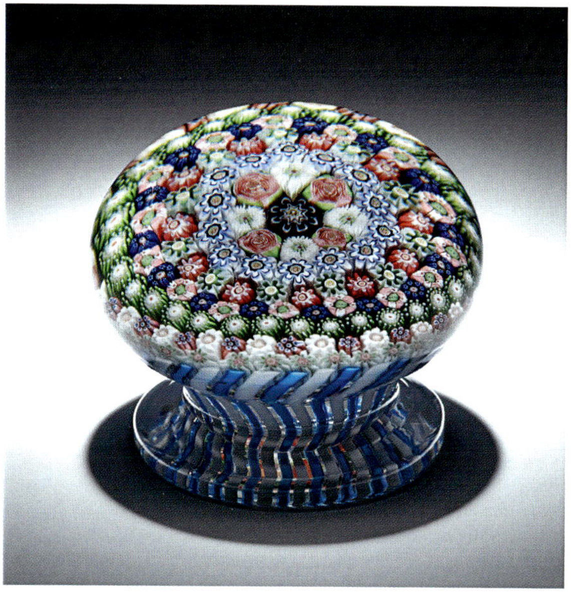

46

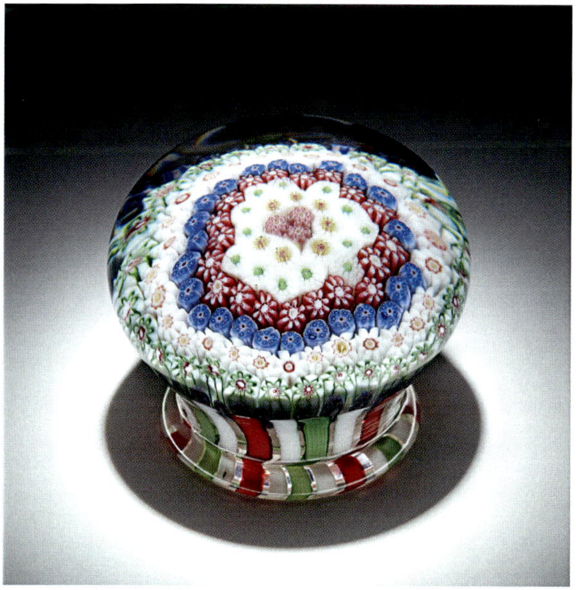

45. Clichy, French, 1837–85
Miniature Piedouche with Central Rose, ca. 1850
Glass, D. 1 3⁄16, H. 1 3⁄16 inches

46. Clichy, French, 1837–85
Piedouche with Tri-Color Stave Basket, ca. 1850
Glass, D. 2 ¾, H. 2 ¼ inches

47. Clichy, French, 1837–85
Concentric Millefiori Piedouche, ca. 1850
Glass, D. 3, H. 2 ½ inches

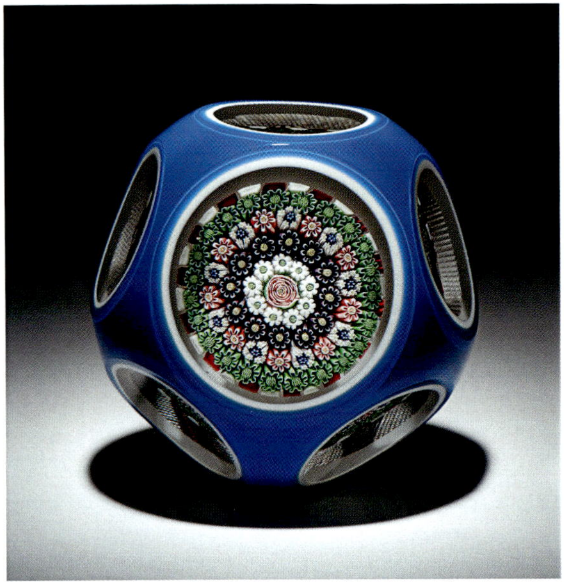

48. Clichy, French, 1837–85
Double Overlay Concentric Mushroom, ca. 1850
Glass, D. 2 ¾ inches

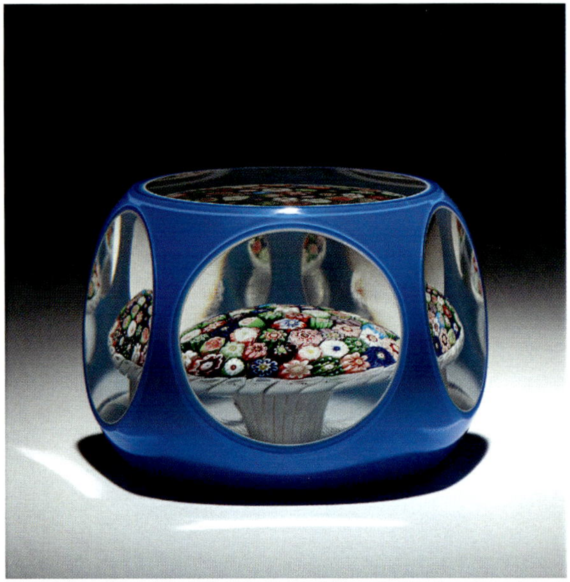

49. Clichy, French, 1837–85
Double Overlay Close Pack Mushroom, ca. 1850
Glass, D. 2 ¾ inches

Cat. 48 is a variation of a close-packed concentric arrangement with Clichy roses with a faceted concentric mushroom double overlay. This weight is overlaid with a layer of white then a layer of blue opaque glass. To achieve this effect once the glass is cold, the colored layers are cut through creating a large flat circular window. The weight's five faceted sides are treated with concave cuts, or printies, allowing for a view of the interior. The central motif rises vertically through the weight and opens to form a central bouquet.

50

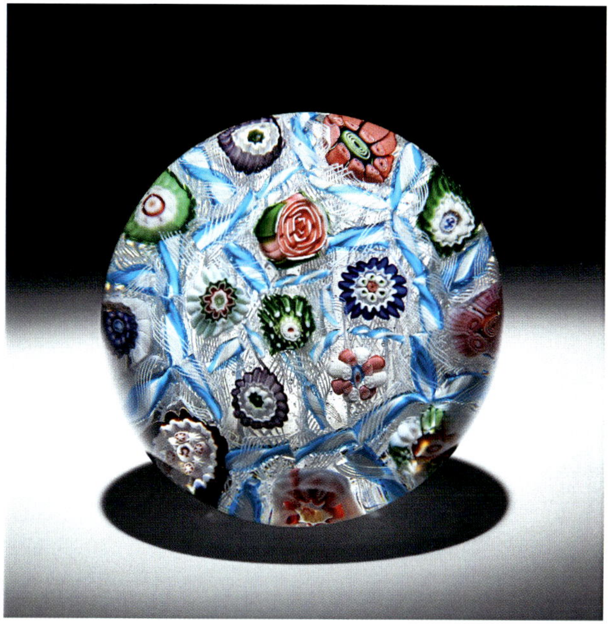

51

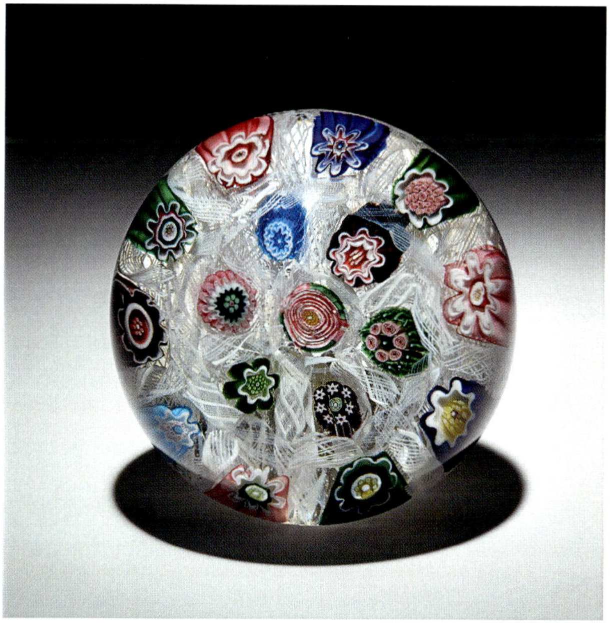

The Ellis Collection contains a playful array of Clichy weights that have a segmented or grid pattern made of canes. This style, known as a *chequer,* is fashioned to include spaced concentric millefiori separated by colored filigree pieces. **Cats. 50** and **67** resemble barber poles while creating a grid pattern. White, clear filigree canes resembling the fabric muslin add a soft, less active tone to **cat. 51** chequer.

50. Clichy, French, 1837–85
Barber Pole Chequer, ca. 1850
Glass, D. 2 7/16 inches

51. Clichy, French, 1837–85
Chequer Spaced Millefiori on Muslin Ground, ca. 1850
Glass, D. 2 5/8 inches

52

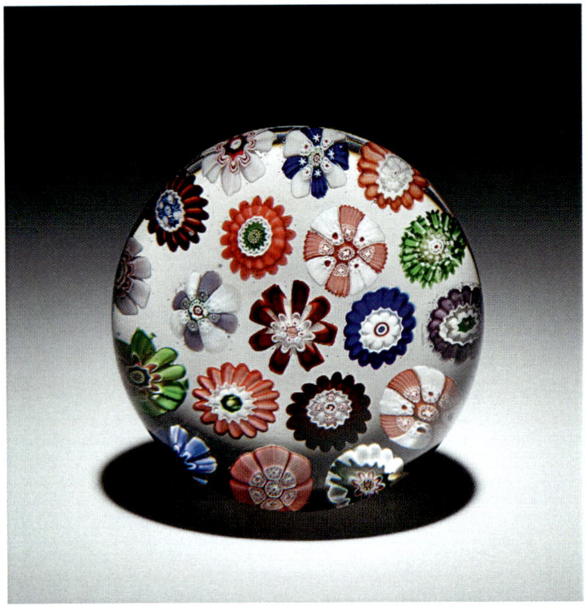

54

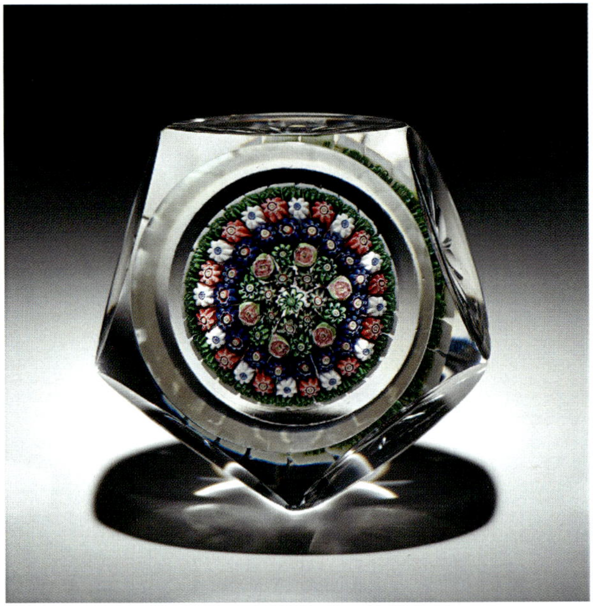

53

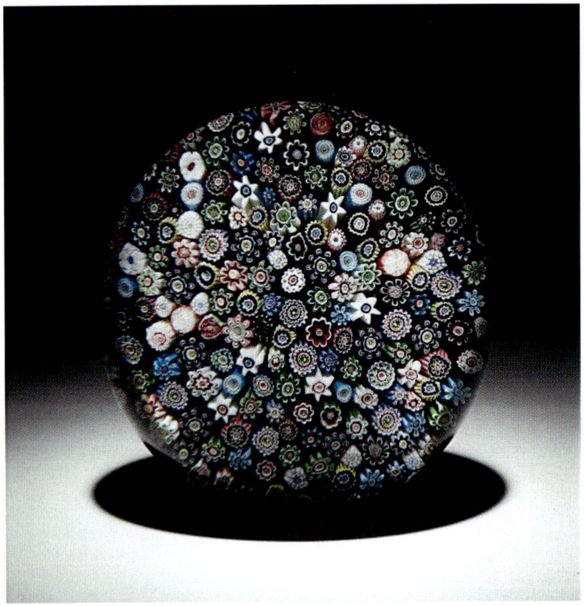

55

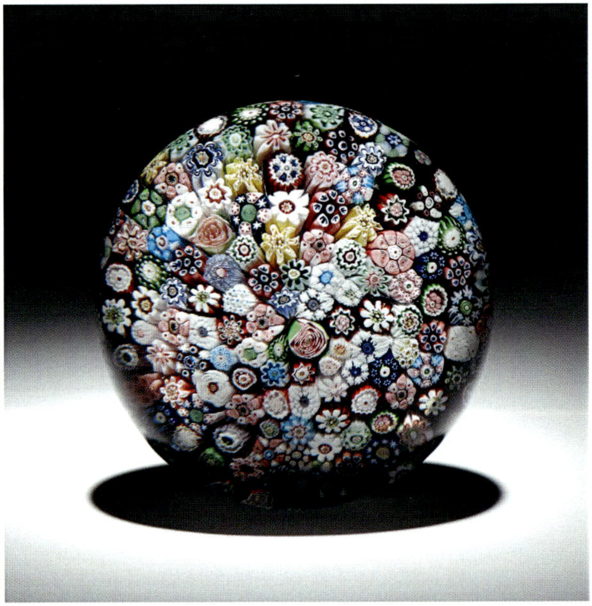

56

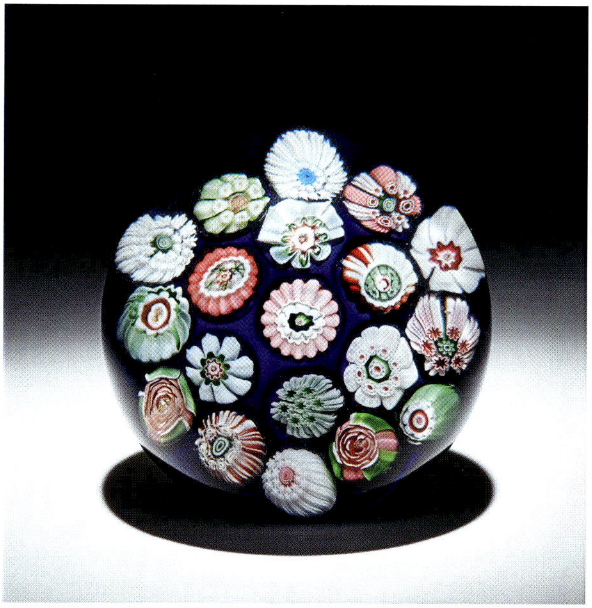

57

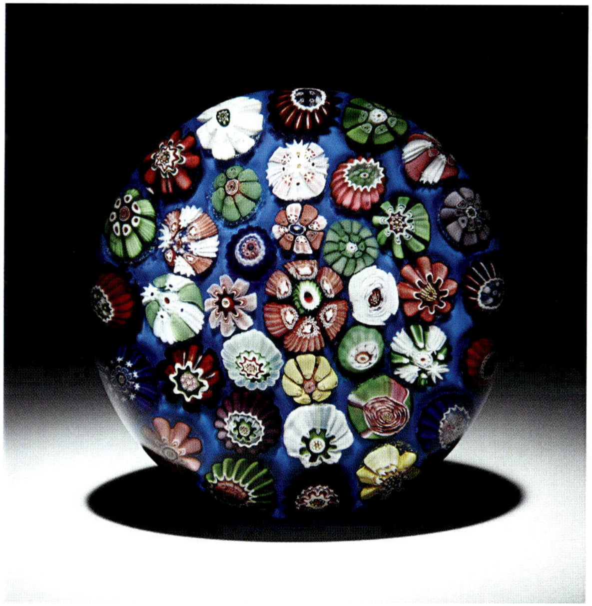

52. Clichy, French, 1837–85
Spaced Millefiori, ca. 1850
Glass, D. 2 ½ inches

53. Clichy, French, 1837–85
Close Pack Millefiori with Pink and White Stave Basket, ca. 1850
Glass, D. 3 ¼ inches

54. Clichy, French, 1837–85
Faceted Concentric Millefiori Mushroom, ca. 1850
Glass, D. 2 11⁄16 inches

55. Clichy, French, 1837–85
Close Pack Millefiori, ca. 1850
Glass, D. 3 ⅛ inches

56. Clichy, French, 1837–85
Spaced Millefiori on Indigo Ground, ca. 1850
Glass, D. 2 ½ inches

57. Clichy, French, 1837–85
Concentric Millefiori on Turquoise Ground, ca. 1850
Glass, D. 3 ¼ inches

58

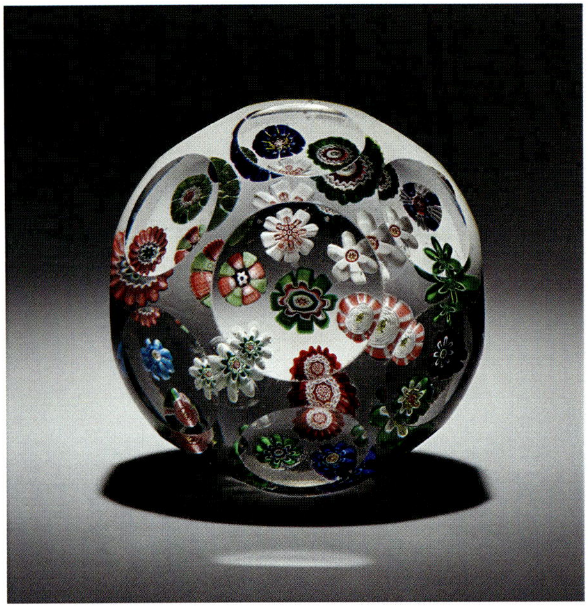

60

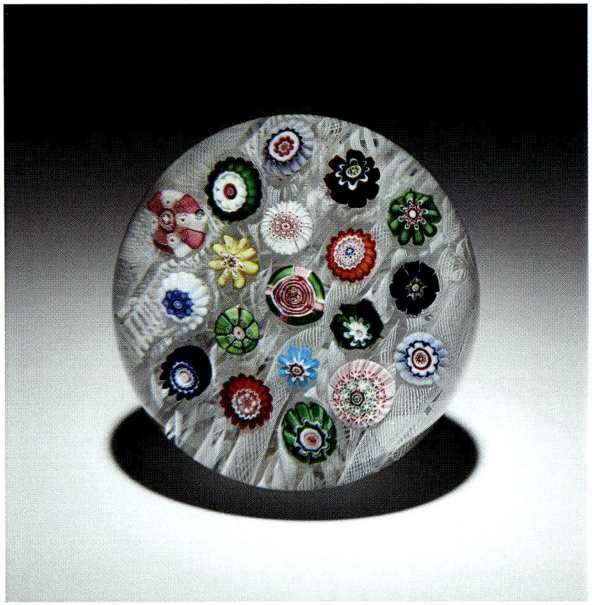

59

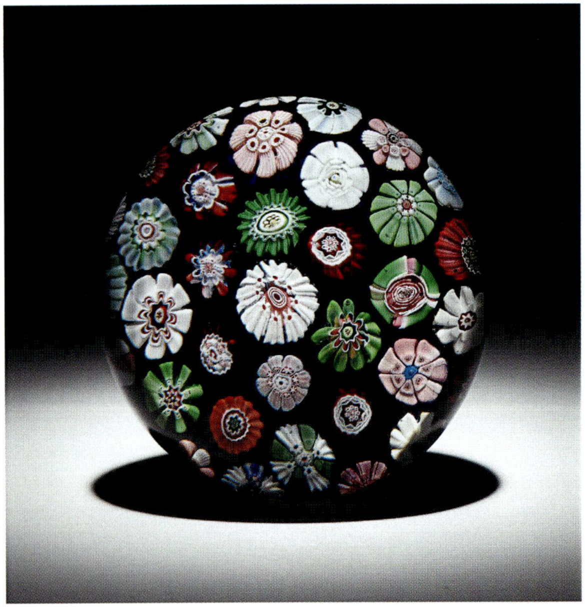

61

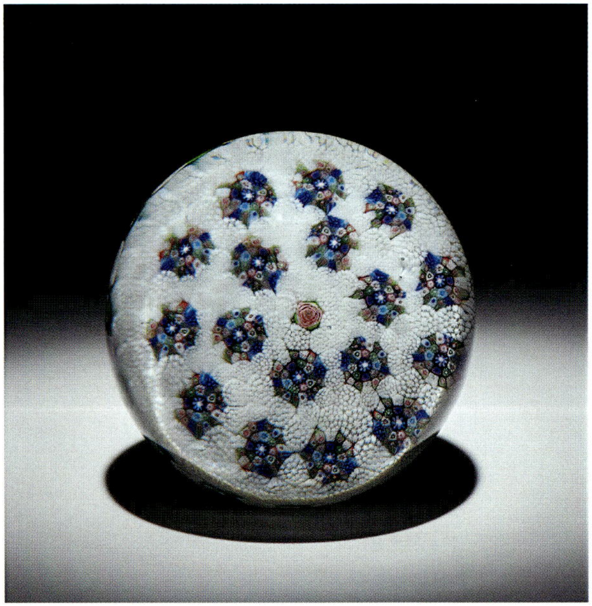

62

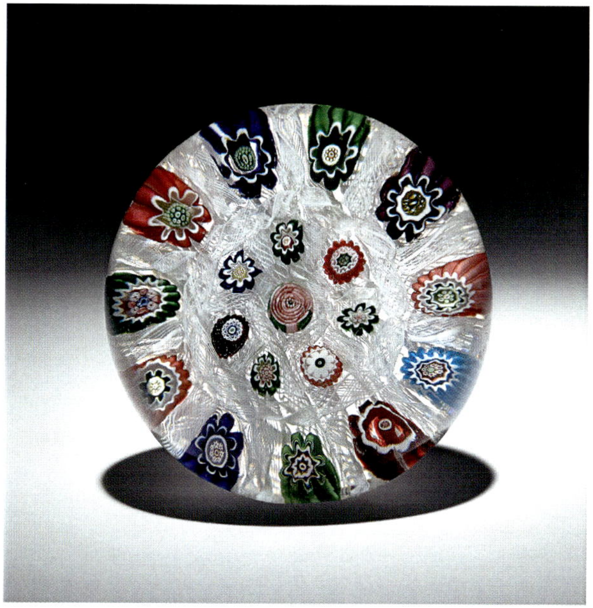

63

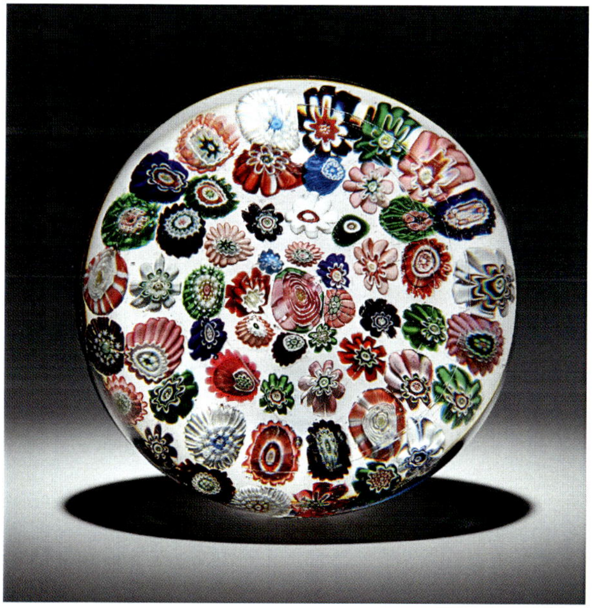

58. Clichy, French, 1837–85
Faceted Spaced Millefiori, ca. 1850
Glass, D. 2 ¾ inches

59. Clichy, French, 1837–85
Spaced Millefiori on Cobalt Ground, ca. 1850
Glass, D. 3 ¼ inches

60. Clichy, French, 1837–85
Spaced Millefiori on Parallel Filigree Ground, ca. 1850
Glass, D. 2 ⅜ inches

61. Clichy, French, 1837–85
Spaced Concentric Millefiori on Stardust Carpet Ground, ca. 1850
Glass, D. 2 ½ inches

62. Clichy, French, 1837–85
Millefiori Chequer, ca. 1850
Glass, D. 2 ⅞ inches

63. Clichy, French, 1837–85
Magnum Spaced Concentric Millefiori, ca. 1850
Glass, D. 4 ¾ inches

64

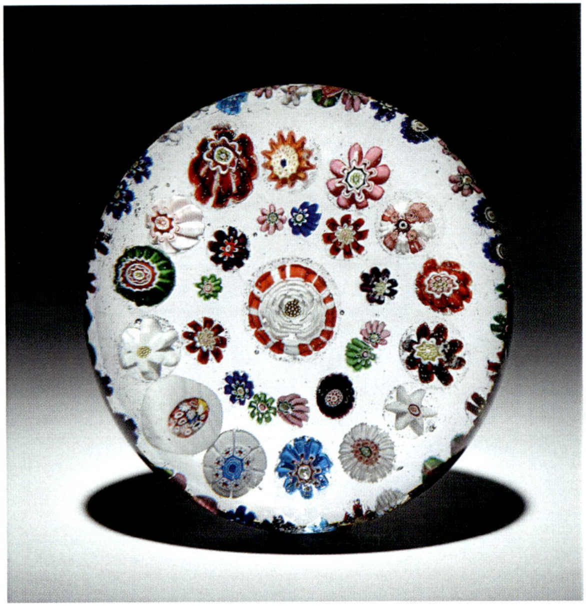

65

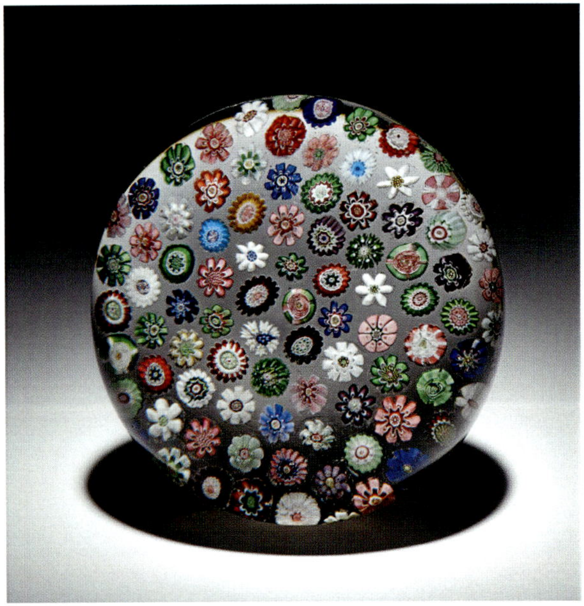

66

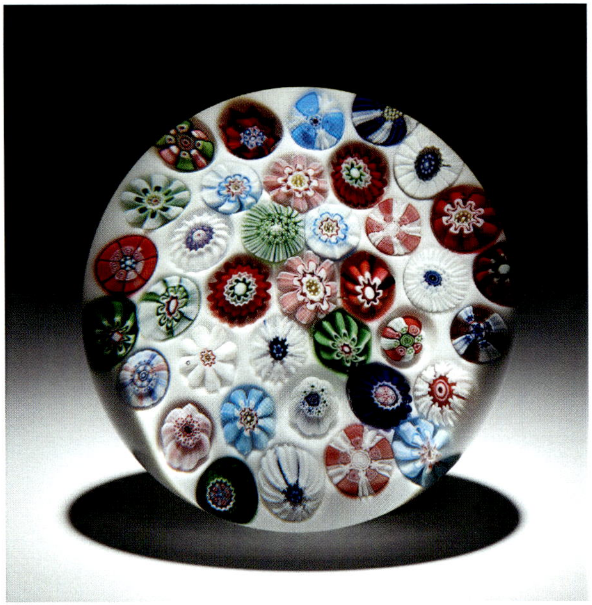

67

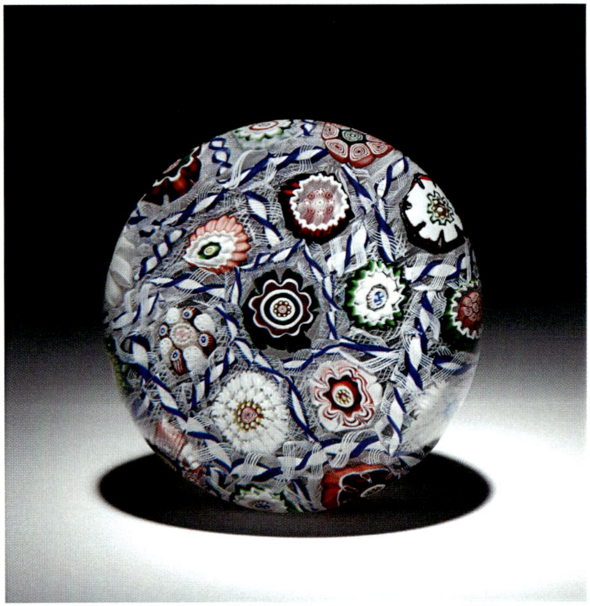

68

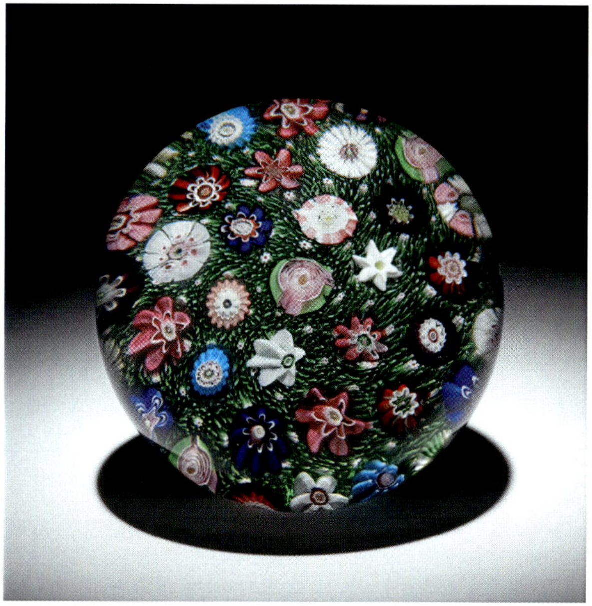

69

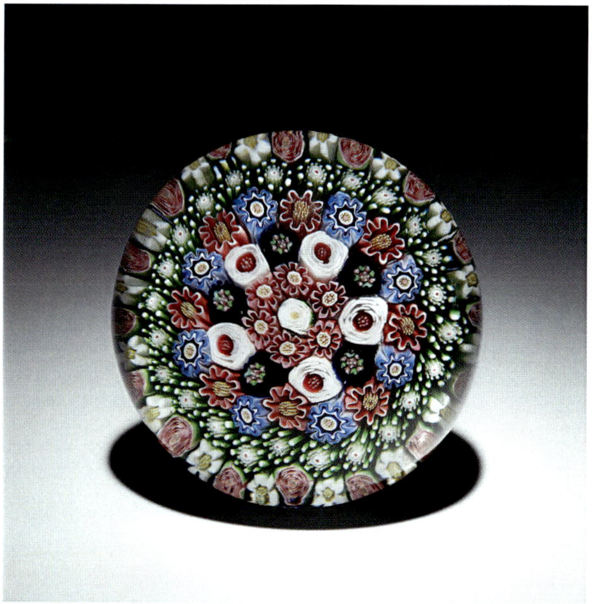

64. Clichy, French, 1837–85
Open Concentric Millefiori, ca. 1850
Glass, D. 3 ⅜ inches

65. Clichy, French, 1837–85
Spaced Millefiori, ca. 1850
Glass, D. 3 ¼ inches

66. Clichy, French, 1837–85
Millefiori on Sodden Snow, ca. 1850
Glass, D. 3 ⅛ inches

67. Clichy, French, 1837–85
Barber Pole Chequer, ca. 1850
Glass, D. 2 $^{15}/_{16}$ inches

68. Clichy, French, 1837–85
Millefiori on Moss Ground, ca. 1850
Glass, D. 3 inches

69. Clichy, French, 1837–85
Close Concentric Millefiori, ca. 1850
Glass, D. 2 ½ inches

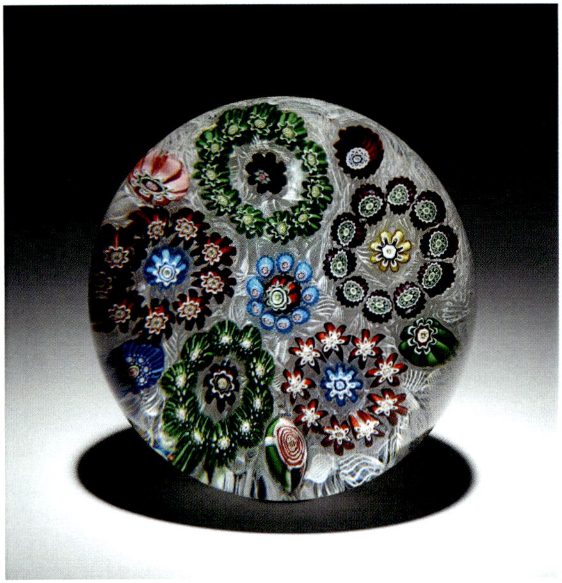

70. Clichy, French, 1837–85
Circlets on Upset Muslin, ca. 1850
Glass, D. 3 inches

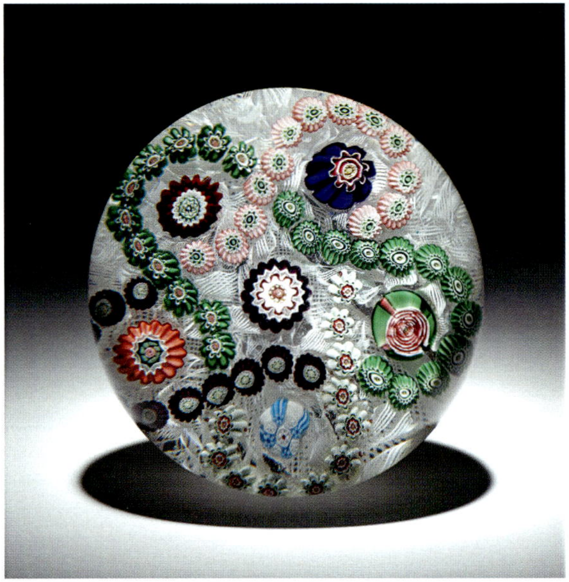

71. Clichy, French, 1837–85
Interlacing Garland on Muslin, ca. 1850
Glass, D. 3 $^3/_{16}$ inches

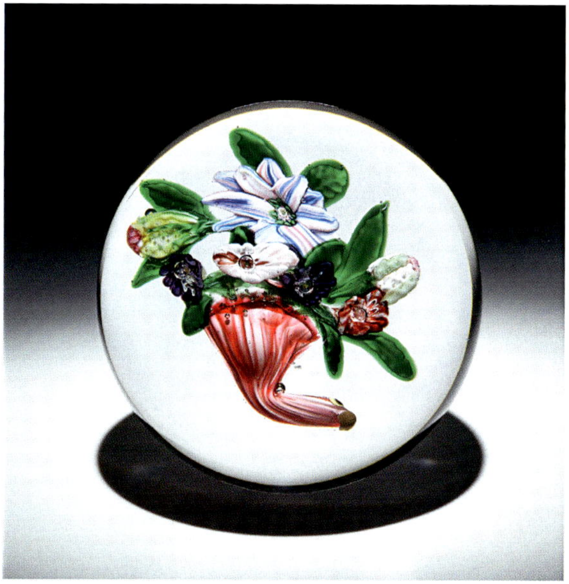

72. Clichy, French, 1837–85
Cornucopia Bouquet Facing Right, ca. 1850
Glass, D. 2 ⅞ inches

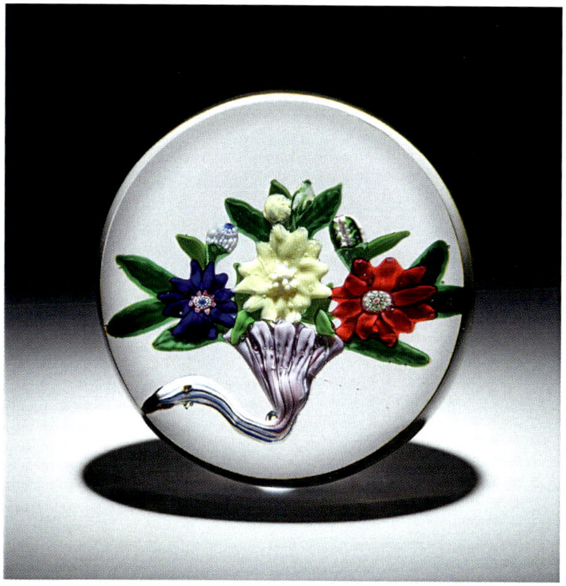

73. Clichy, French, 1837–85
Cornucopia Bouquet Facing Left, ca. 1850
Glass, D. 3 inches

Clichy Lampwork

The Ellis Collection also includes several Clichy weights containing motifs that were created by lampwork. Here are two rare cornucopia flat bouquet weights derived from the meaning of a "horn of plenty."

74

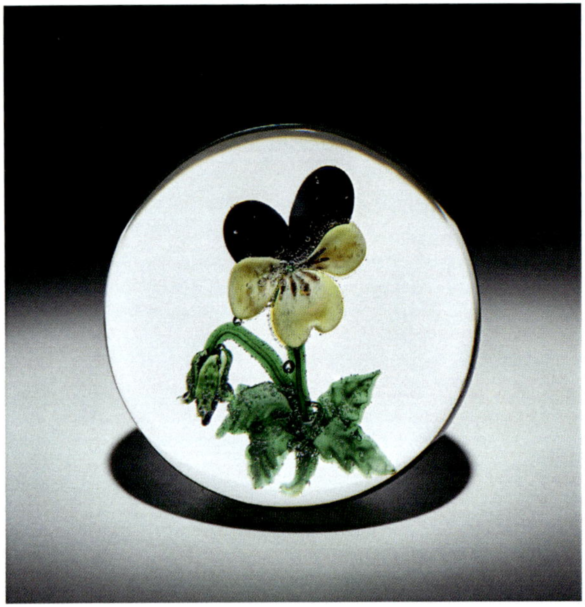

76

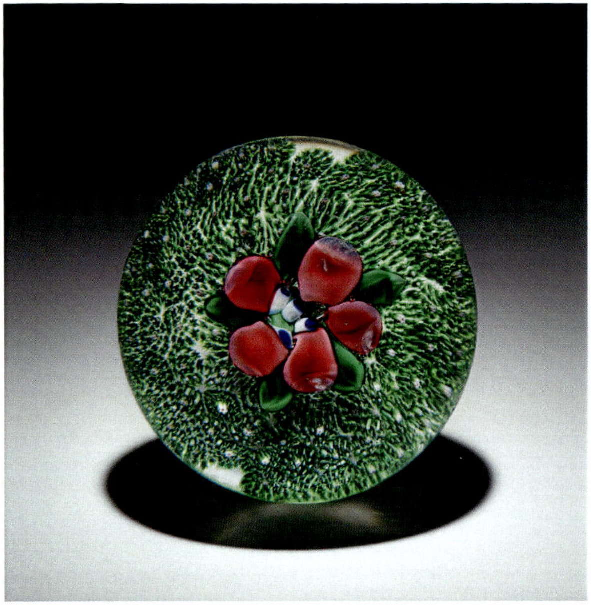

75

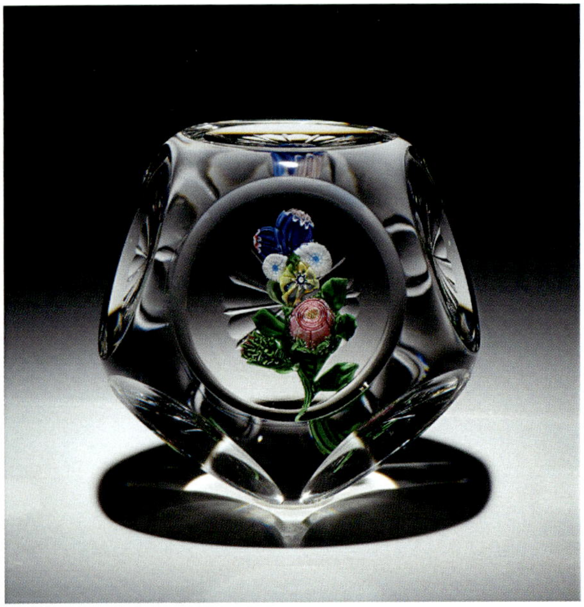

77

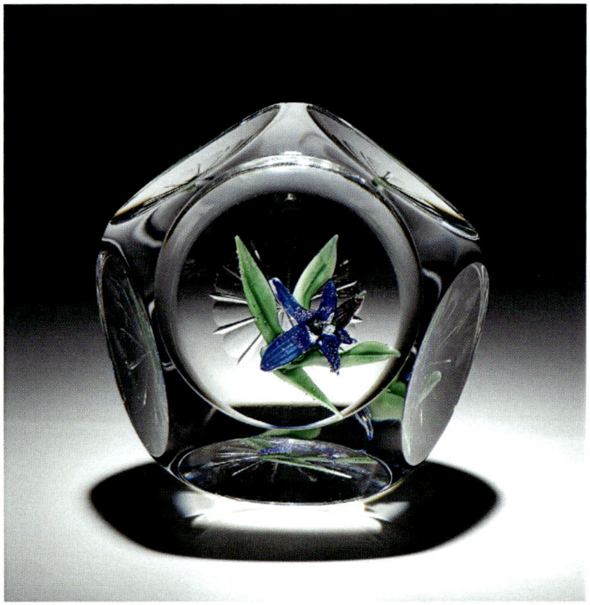

78

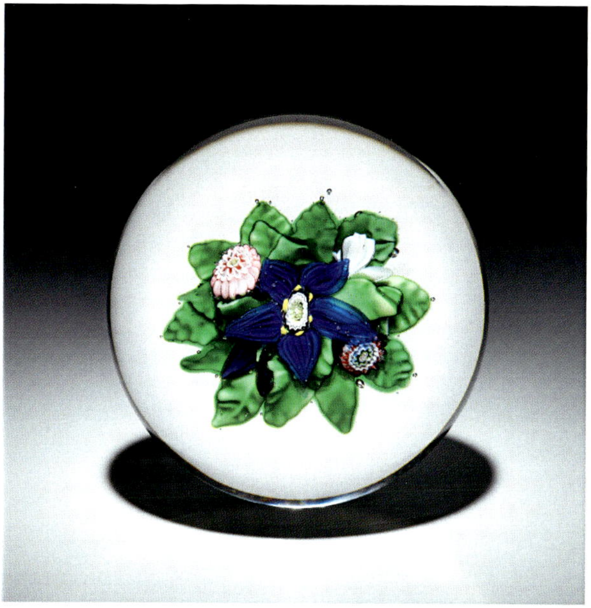

79

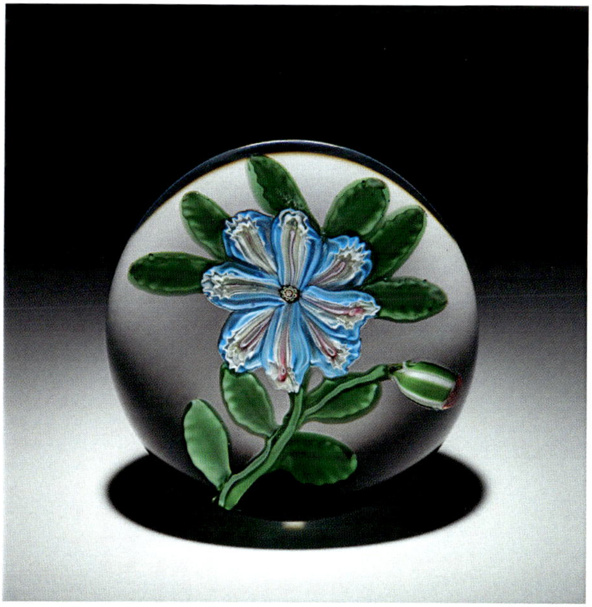

74. Clichy, French, 1837–85
Pansy, *ca.* 1850
Glass, D. 2 9/16 inches

75. Clichy, French, 1837–85
Two Flower Bouquet, ca. 1850
Glass, D. 3 1/8 inches

76. Clichy, French, 1837–85
Fantasy Flower on Moss Ground, ca. 1850
Glass, D. 2 3/16 inches

77. Clichy, French, 1837–85
Blue Orchid Blossom, ca. 1850
Glass, D. 2 3/4 inches

78. Clichy, French, 1837–85
Upright Bouquet, ca. 1850
Glass, D. 2 9/16 inches

79. Clichy, French, 1837–85
Fantasy Flower, ca. 1850
Glass, D. 2 1/2 inches

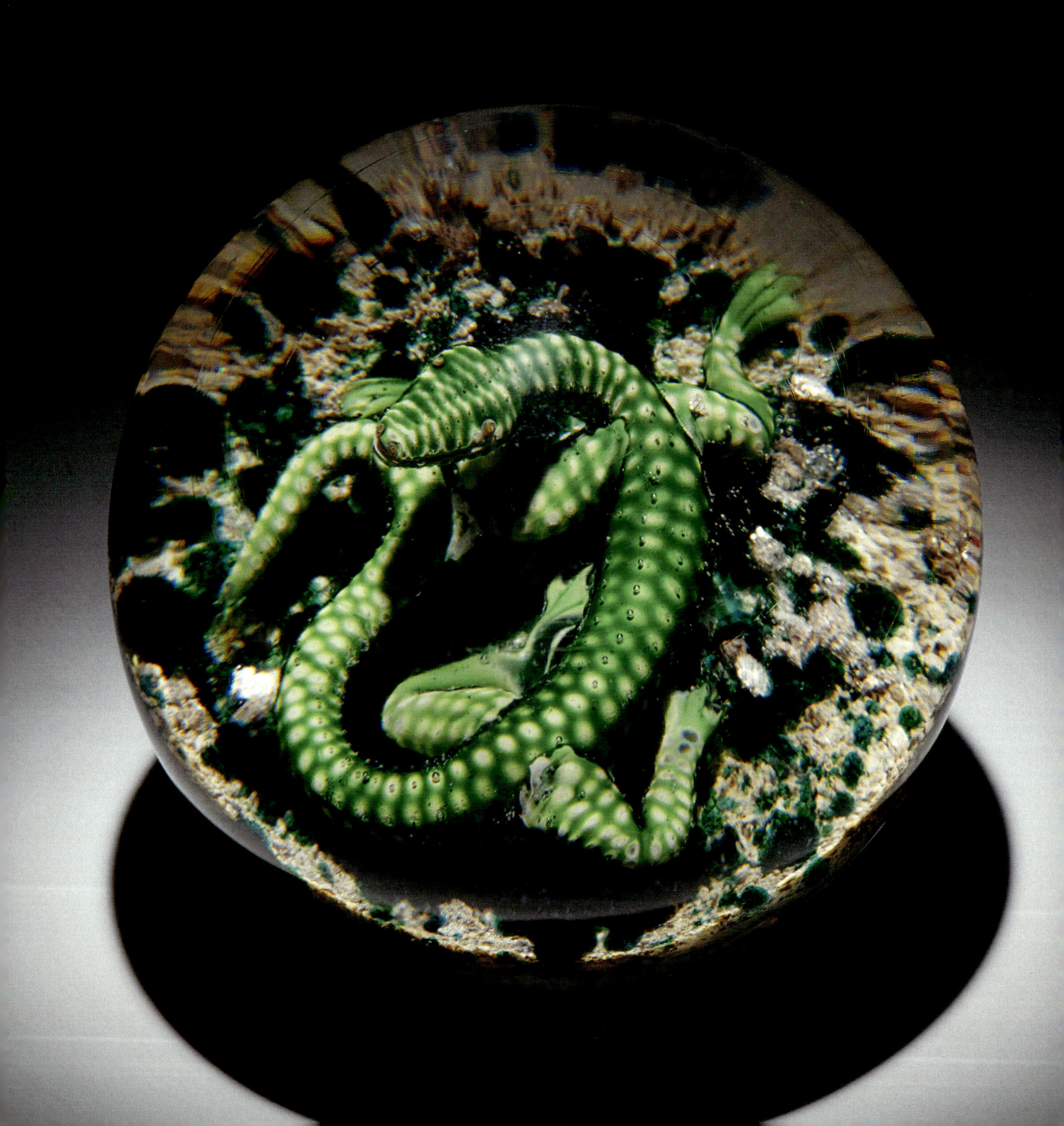

Pantin

Pantin (Monot, Père et Fils, et Stumpf, Cristallerie de Pantin) was in operation near Paris from 1850 to 1890, in the Post-Classic period. The earliest paperweights attributed to the company appeared in 1878 and were displayed that year in the Paris Universal Exposition. This was several years after the other French companies (Baccarat, Clichy, and Saint-Louis) all but ceased to include weights in their product line. Pantin created some of the most realistic, animated, and three-dimensional lampworked weights of the period, but only for a few years making them extremely rare. Only a few hundred are known to exist.

Noted by art historians to be among the most important and impressive weights ever produced is the Pantin magnum weight (**cat. 80**) that features a large dome incorporating a life-like animal. Referred to as a magnum, because of its extra-large size, it encases a lampworked glass coiled creature. The body was fabricated first with clear glass and covered with a layer of cream-colored glass. It was then overlaid with a thin layer of green glass. After cooling it was cut with an abrasive wheel to expose cream-colored scales. It was then heated again and encased in clear glass. The artist who produced this weight was highly skilled and was able to overcome the risks involved in encasing such a large, complex, fragile animal in molten crystal as it could have been broken easily.

80. Pantin, French, 1850–1915
Magnum Salamander on Sand and Moss Ground, ca. 1878
Glass, D. 4 3⁄16 inches
FIA collection; Gift of Eileen Ellis

The Ellis Collection also includes other rare Pantin weights.

Cat. 81 is a magnum weight that includes three-dimensional blooming flora and fauna serving as natural camouflage for the dark speckled Gila Monster placed on a realistic sandy ground.

Cat. 82, the *Bird and Rose* weight, is unique and unknown until recently. This special weight features a standing yellow bird with a deep purple beak and pink eyes and feet. The bird is placed opposite a dimensional pink rose with a green stem and leaves.

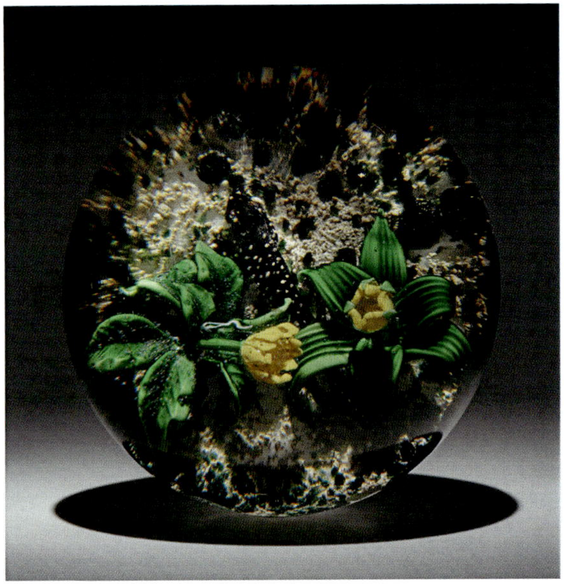

81. Pantin, French, 1850–1915
Magnum Gila Monster on Sand and Moss Ground, ca. 1878
Glass, D. 4 1⁄16 inches

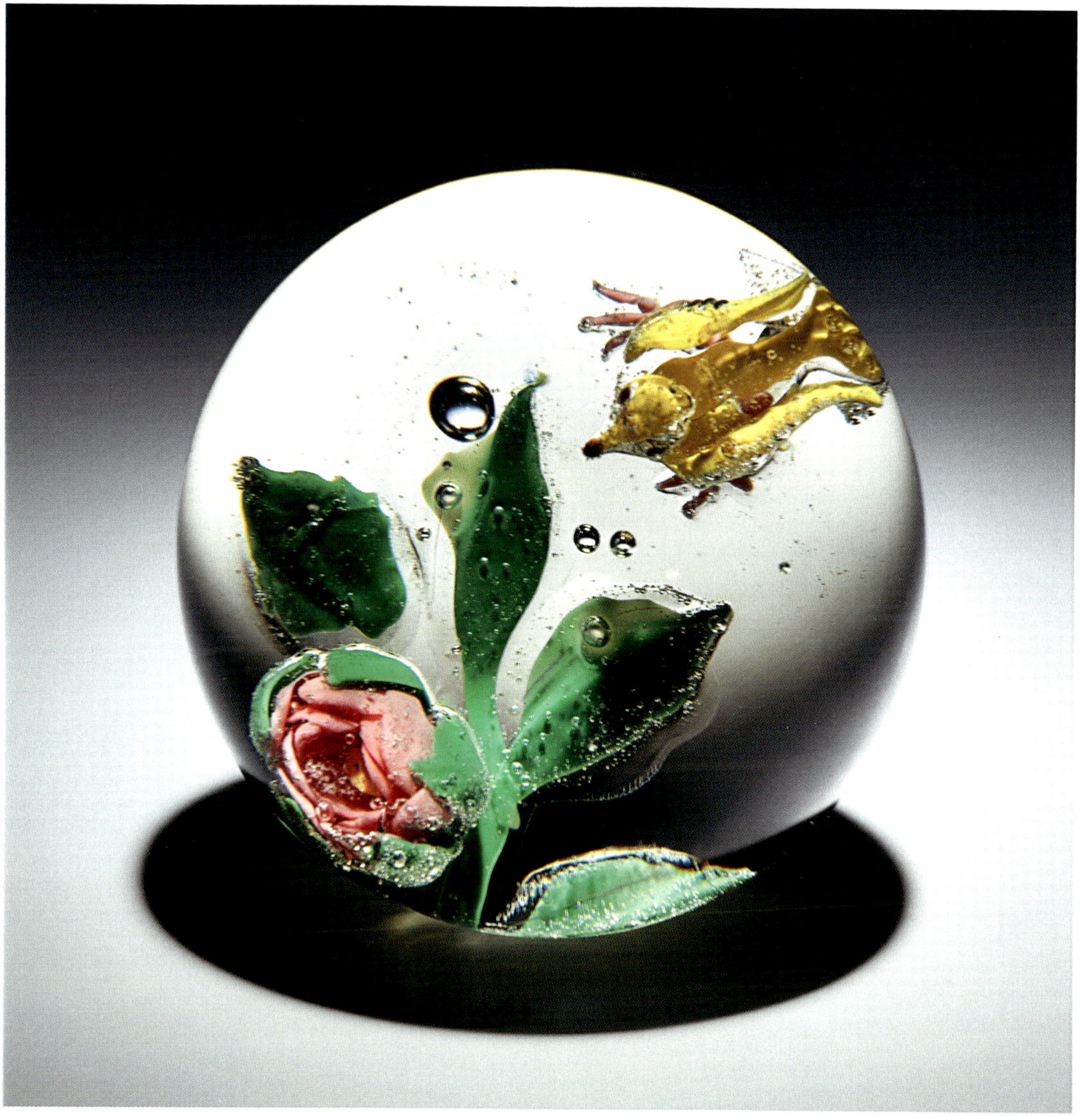

82. **Pantin,** French, 1850–1915
Bird and Rose, ca. 1878. Glass, D. 2 ⅞ inches

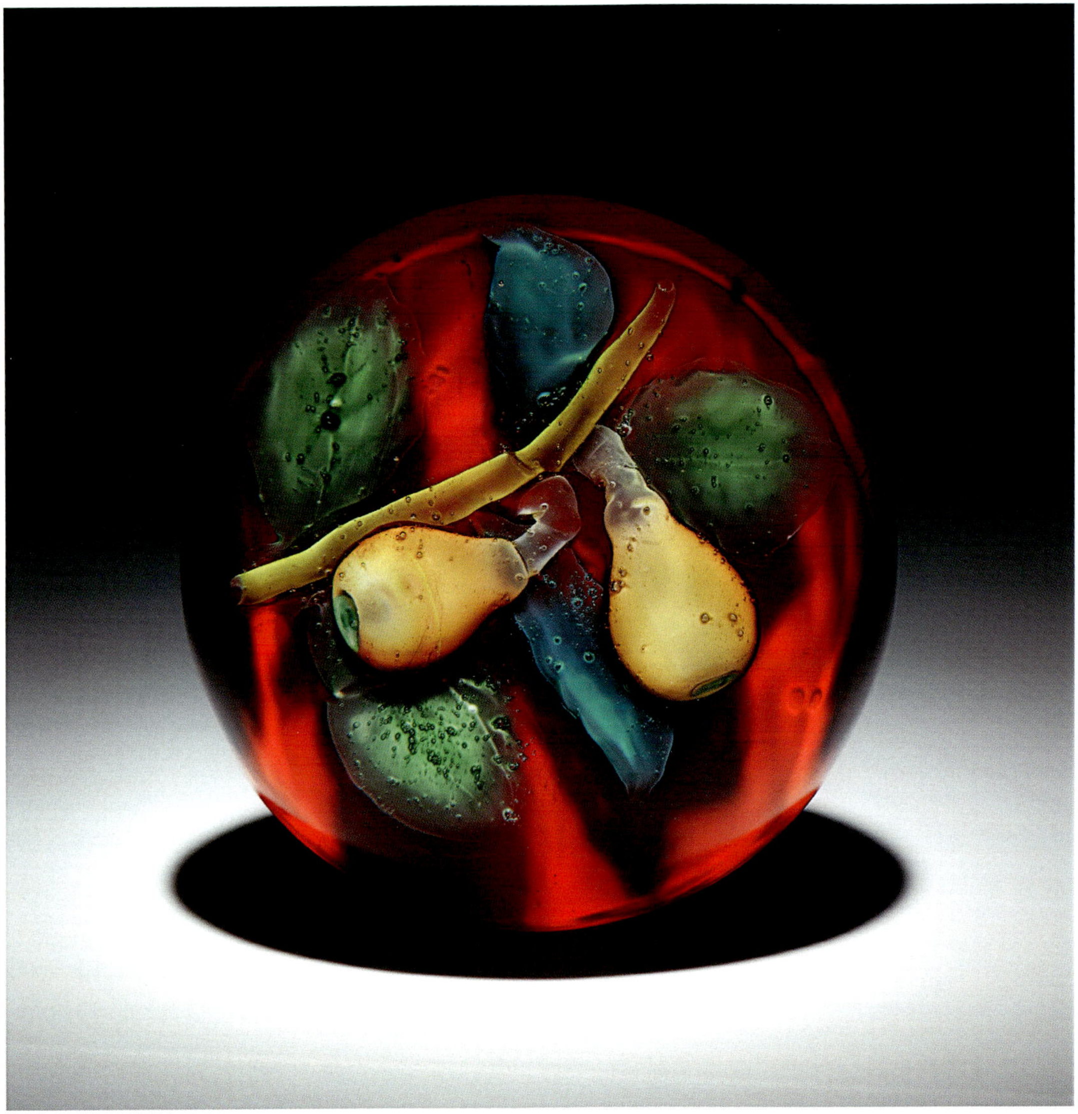

83. Pantin, French, 1850–1915
Pears on Red Ground, ca. 1878. Glass, D. 3 inches
FIA collection; Gift of Eileen Ellis

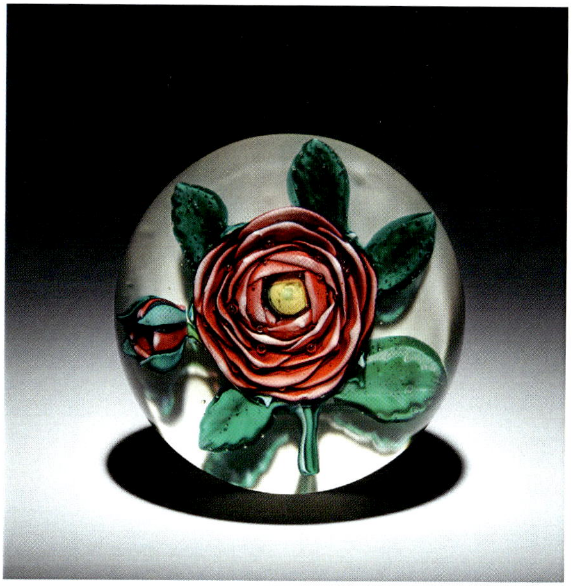

84. Pantin, French, 1850–1915
Large Rose with Bud on White Ground, ca. 1878
Glass, D. 2 3⁄16 inches

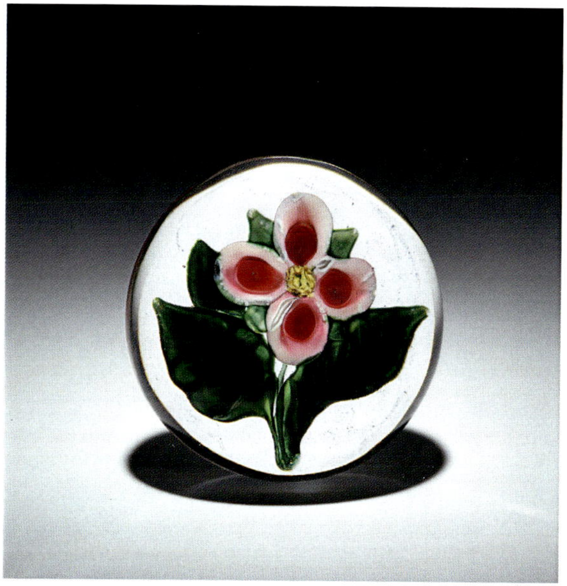

85. Pantin, French, 1850–1915
Miniature Red and White Flower, ca. 1878
Glass, D. 1 15⁄16 inches

86

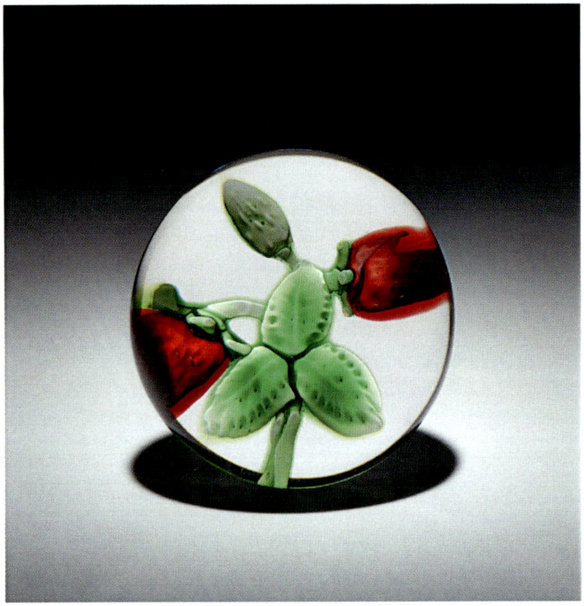

87

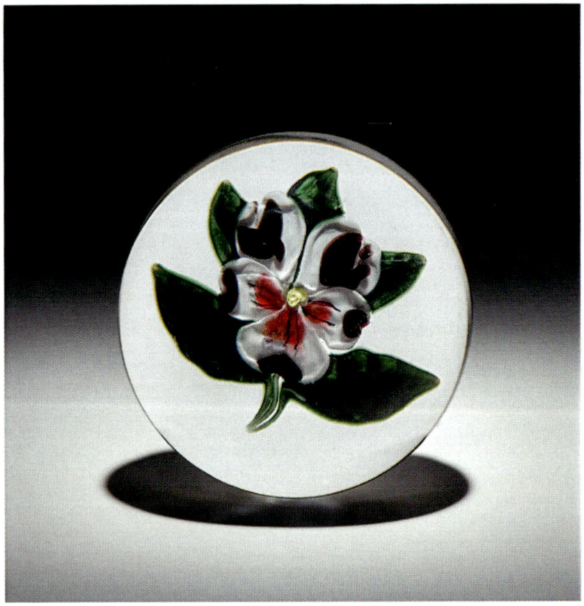

88

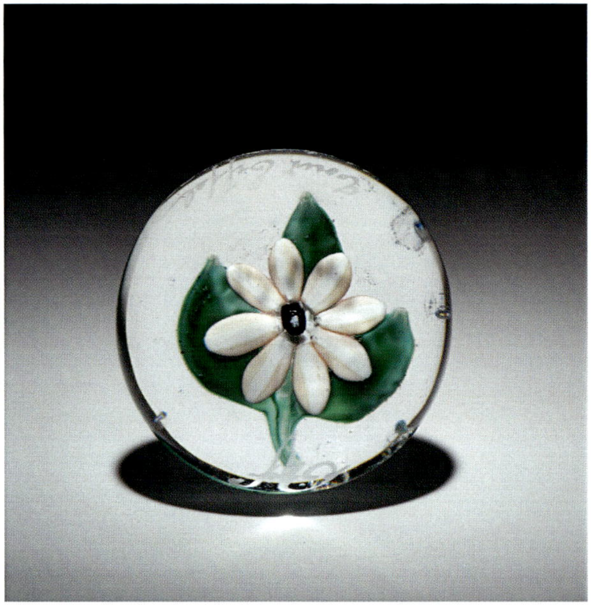

89

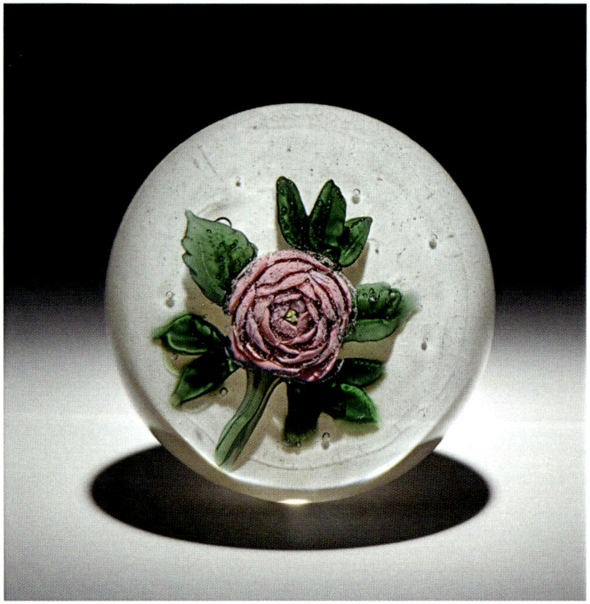

90
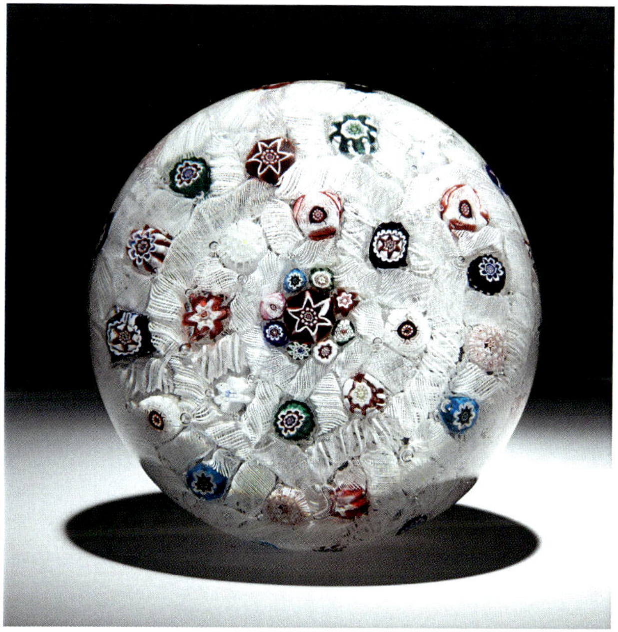

86. Pantin, French, 1850–1915
Miniature Strawberry with Bud, ca. 1878
Glass, D. 1 ⅞ inches

87. Pantin, French, 1850–1915
Pansy, ca. 1878
Glass, D. 2 13/16 inches

88. Pantin, French, 1850–1915
Miniature Flower on Clear Ground, ca. 1878
Glass, D. 1 15/16 inches

89. Pantin, French, 1850–1915
Rose on White Ground, ca. 1878
Glass, D. 2 ¾ inches

90. Pantin, French, 1850–1915
Magnum Chequer Finial, ca. 1878
Glass, D. 3 ⅞ inches

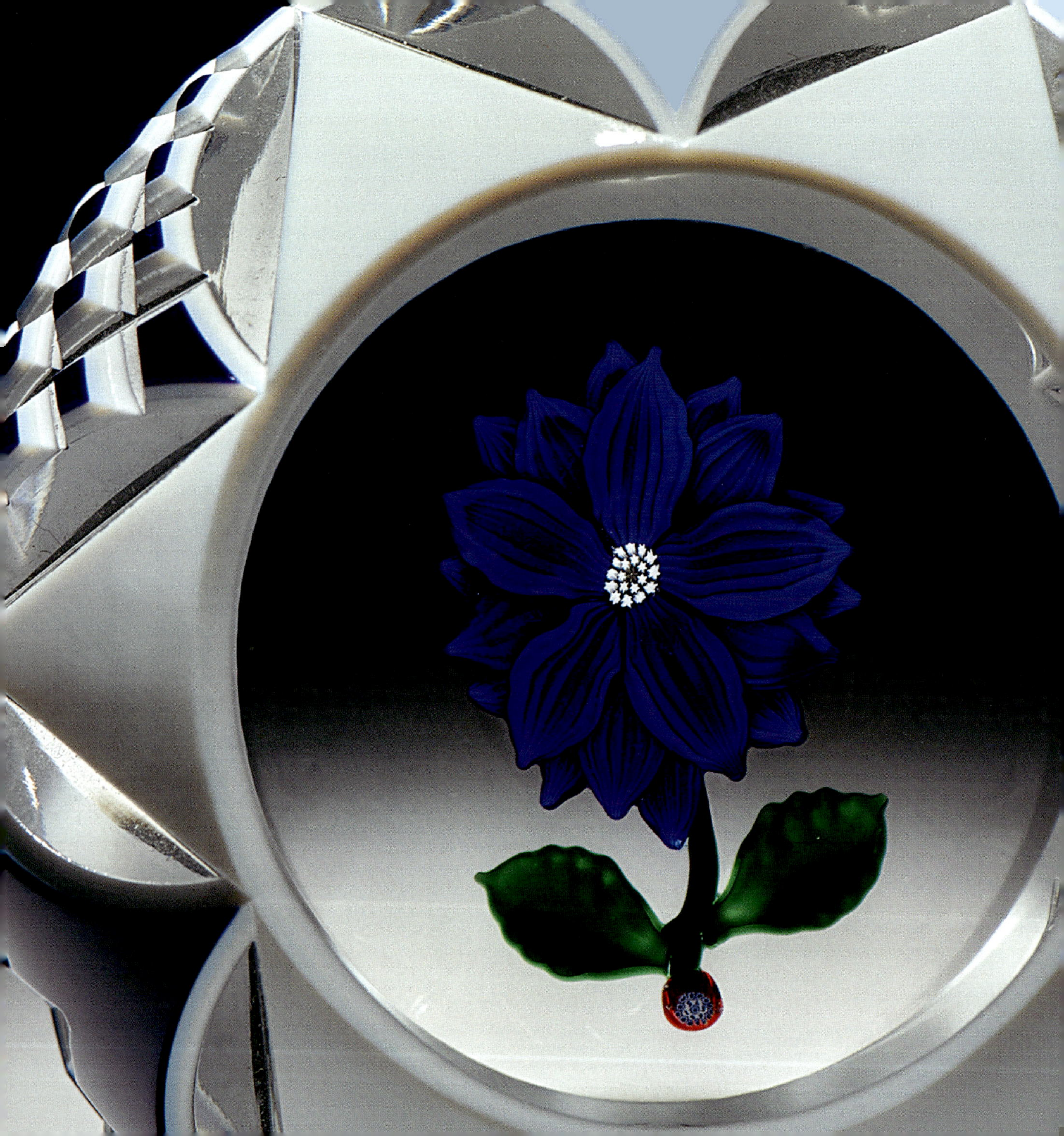

Saint-Louis

Saint-Louis was founded in 1767, in the province of Lorraine. Paperweight production began in the early 1840s with the first date to appear in Saint-Louis weights in 1845. Their production ended in the 1860s. In 1952 Saint-Louis resumed making weights again in their historic style for several decades and occasionally continues to include weights in limited editions as part of their product line today.

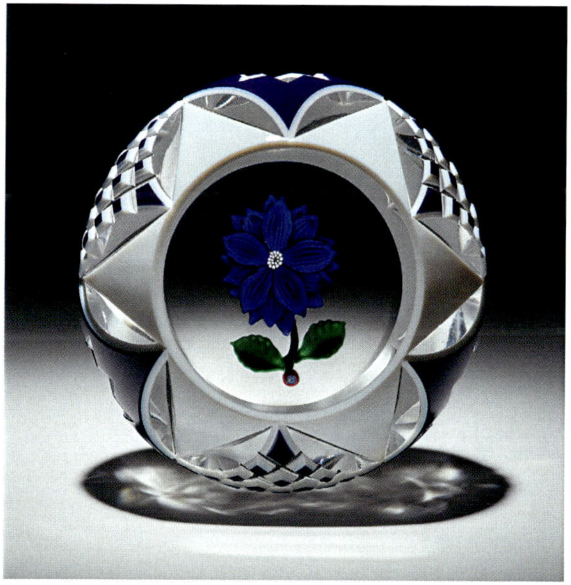

91. Saint-Louis, French, founded 1767
***Alaska* (*Blue Flower with Overlay*)**, 1993
Glass, D. 3 inches

This Classic Revival weight is an example of the precise coldwork that Saint-Louis mastered. Coldworking refers to many techniques, like grinding, cutting, and engraving, used to manipulate or decorate glass after the cooling process is complete. The weight has a double-cased overlay with sharp bevel cuts and a large open top window revealing a single blue upright flower.

LEFT: Detail of Cat. 91

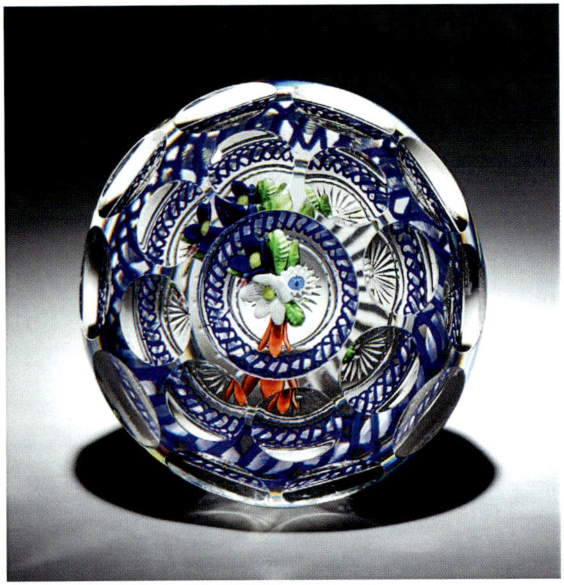

92. Saint-Louis, French, founded 1767
Faceted Upright Bouquet with Blue Torsade, ca. 1850
Glass, D. 3 ¼ inches

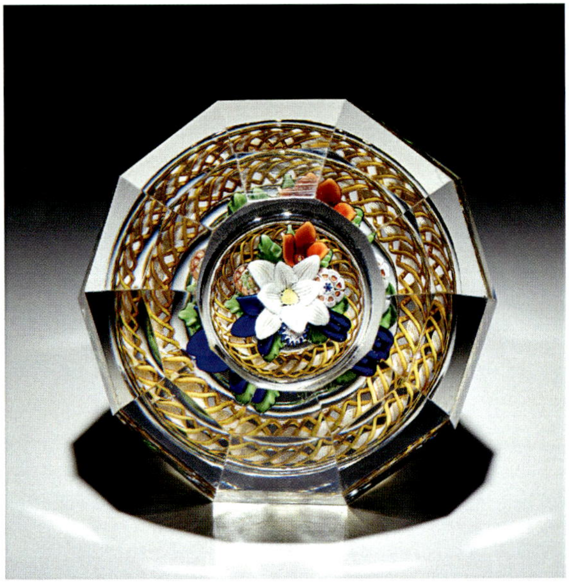

93. Saint-Louis, French, founded 1767
Faceted Upright Bouquet with Amber Torsade ca. 1850
Glass, D. 2 15⁄16 inches

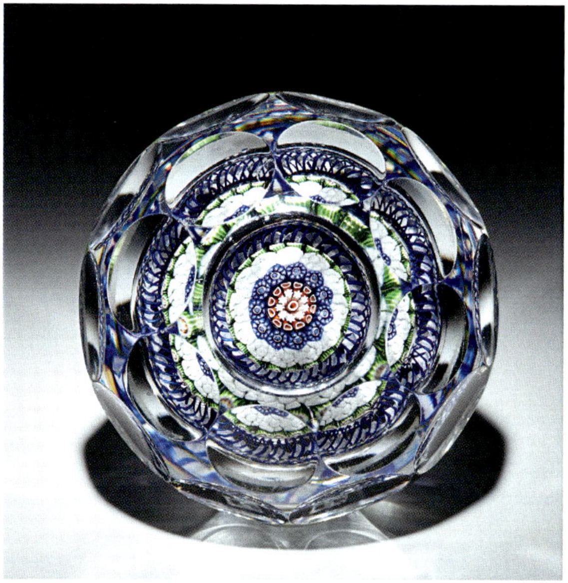

94. Saint-Louis, French, founded 1767
Concentric Mushroom, ca. 1850
Glass, D. 3 3/16 inches

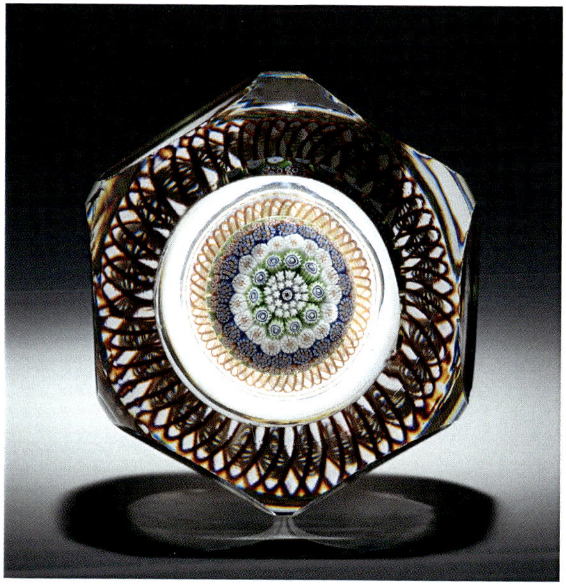

95. Saint-Louis, French, founded 1767
Magnum Faceted Concentric Mushroom with Torsade, ca. 1850
Glass, D. 3 5/8 inches

Saint-Louis perfected the optical play within a weight that is created by facets paired with colorful twisted ribbons called torsades. Many Saint-Louis weights have a marvelous array of coldworked cuts that create crystal lenses that enlarge or minimize the internal motif while allowing light to refract within the form.

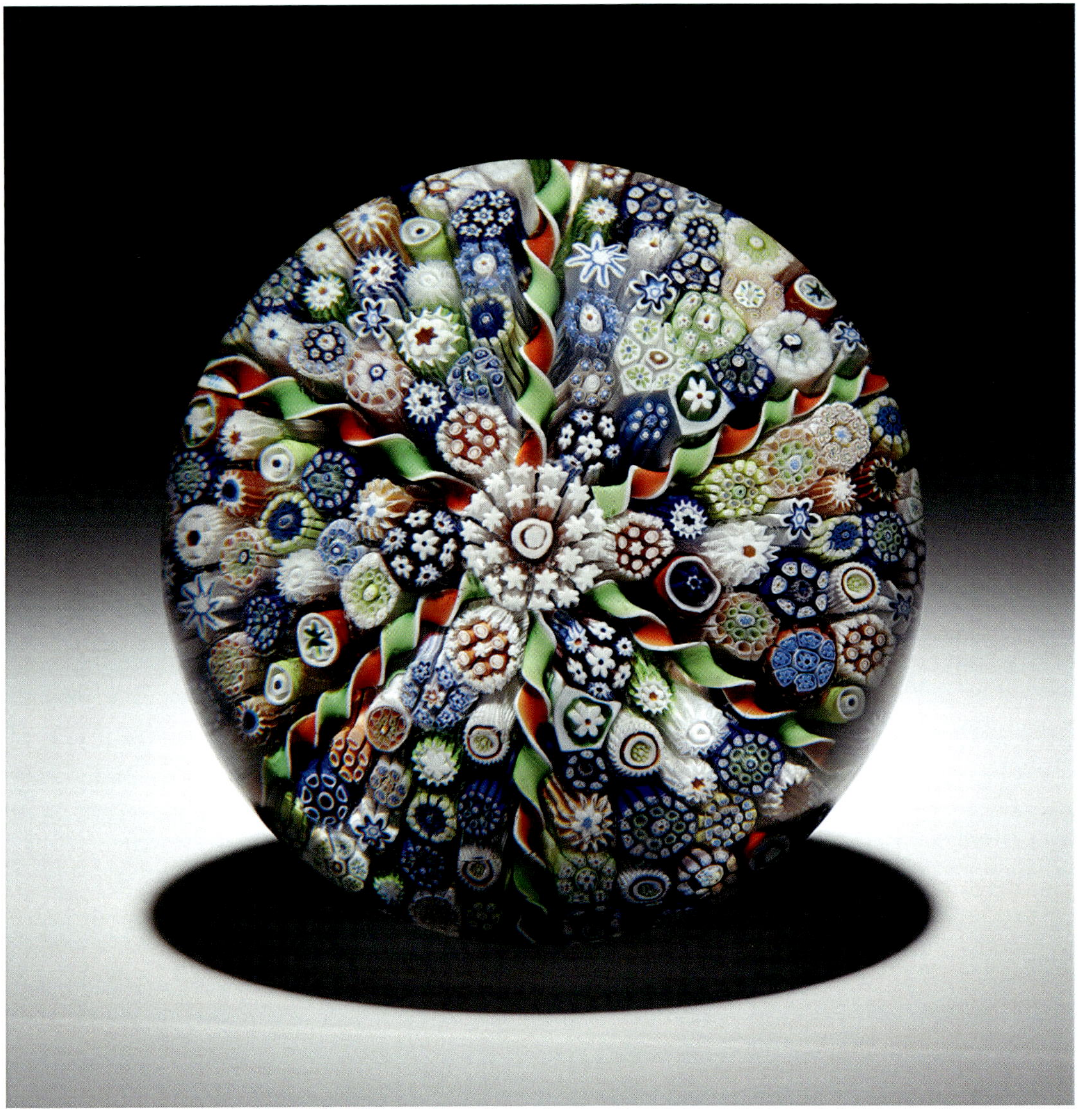

96. Saint-Louis, French, founded 1767
Paneled Close Pack Millefiori, ca. 1850. Glass, D. 2 ⅞ inches

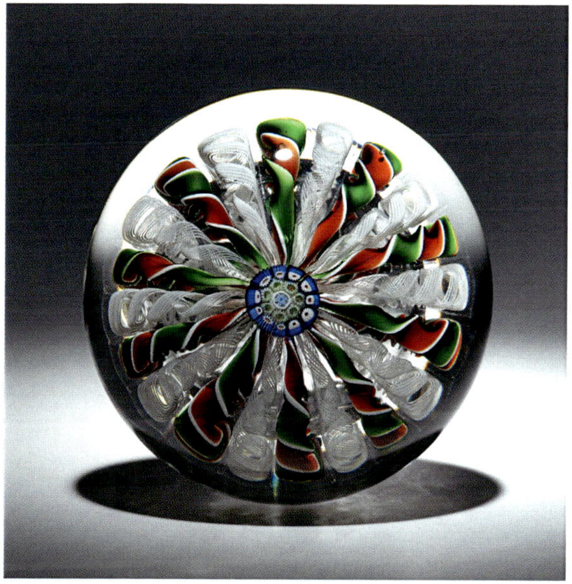

97. Saint-Louis, French, founded 1767
Two Color Crown with Filigree Twists, ca. 1850
Glass, D. 3 $3/16$ inches

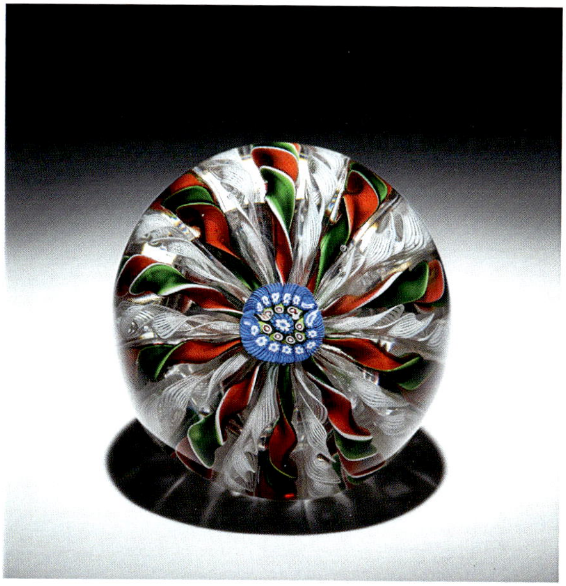

98. Saint-Louis, French, founded 1767
Miniature Crown with White Filigree Ribbons, ca. 1850
Glass, D. 2 inches

Cats. 99 and **100** are unlike any other weights in the Ellis Collection and they are also unique to Saint-Louis. The clear weight was fabricated in the 1850s. The other is a copy of the original design made in 1980. Both contain a coiled lizard created by blowing glass into a reptile shaped mold, which is then gilded. The modern weight has a double overlay of white covered with deep pink glass. When cooled, the weight was engraved with a floral vine pattern revealing the weight's clear interior.

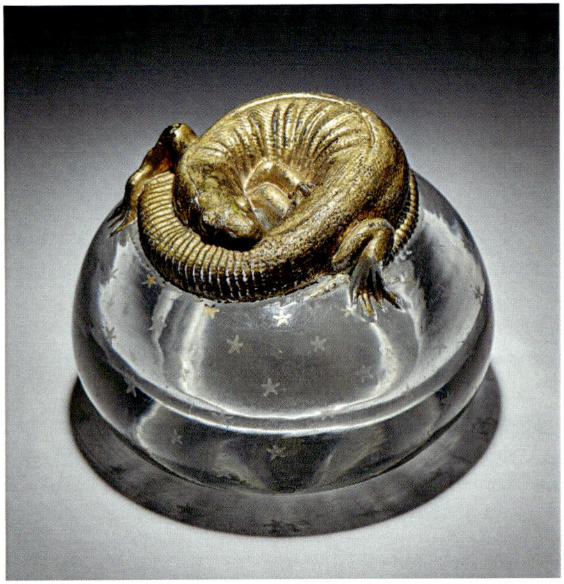

99. Saint-Louis, French, founded 1767
Lizard, ca. 1850
Glass, D. 3 7⁄16 inches

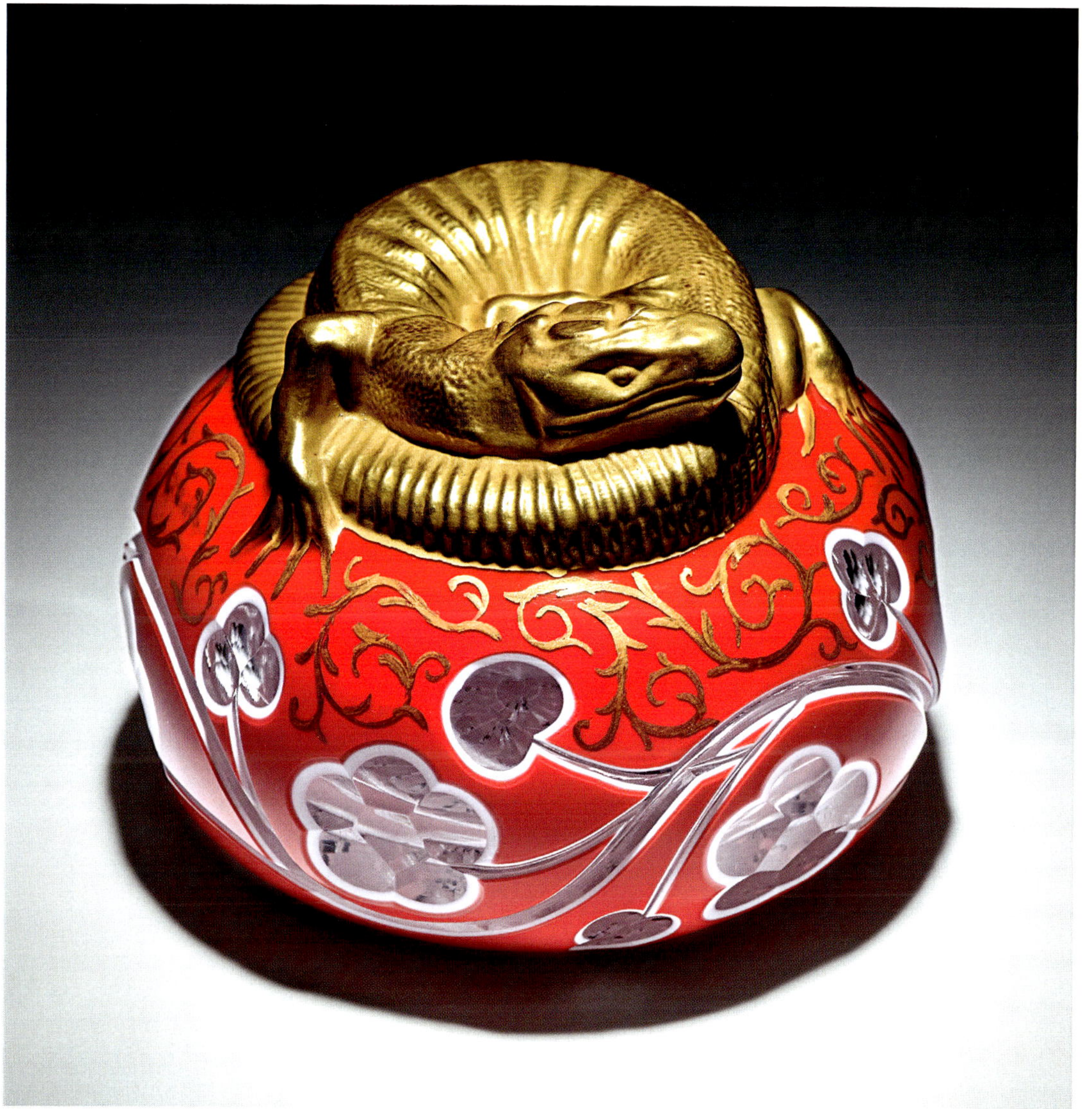

100. Saint-Louis, French, founded 1767
Lizard with Overlay, 1980. Glass, D. 3 ¼ inches

101

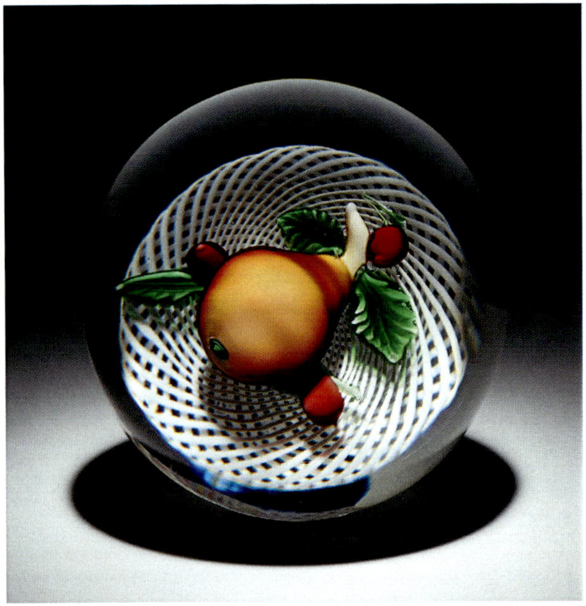

103

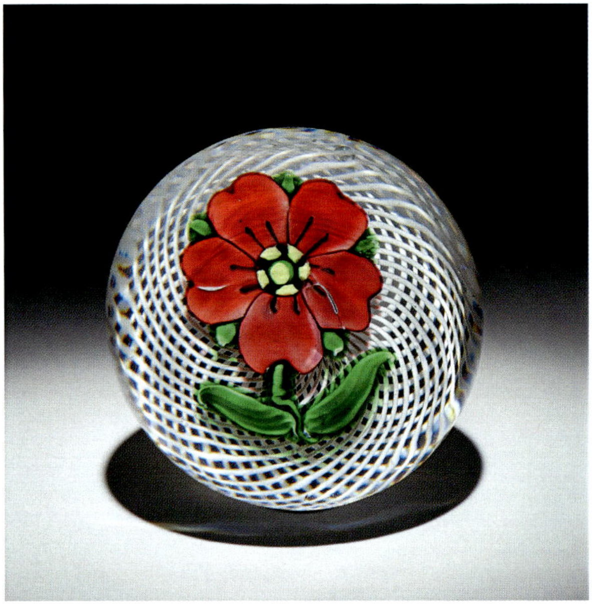

102

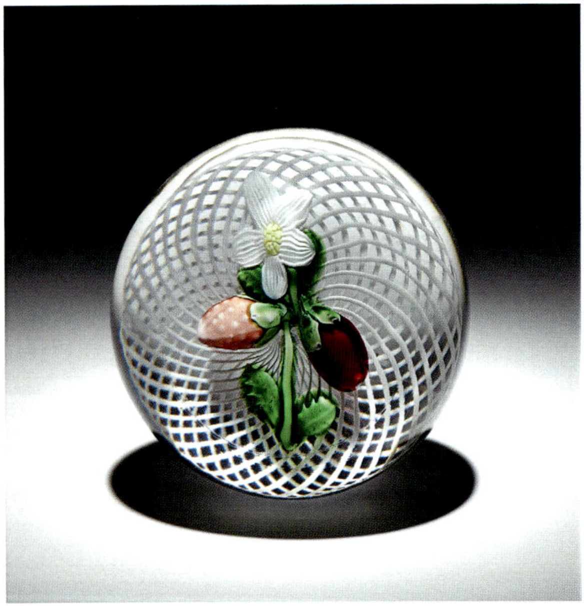

104

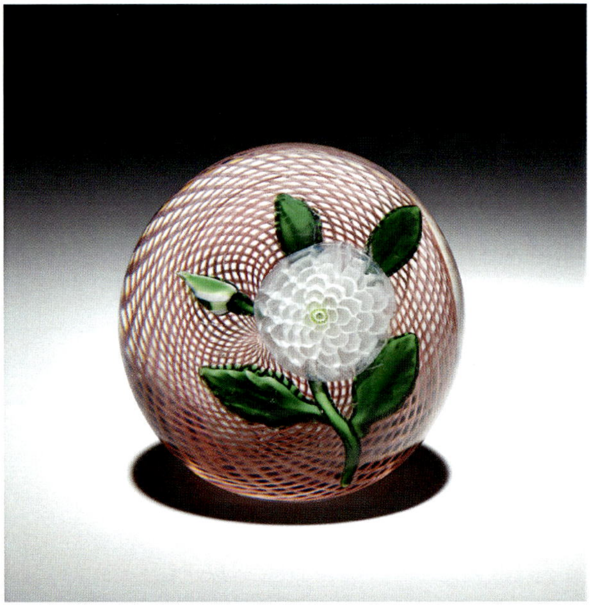

105

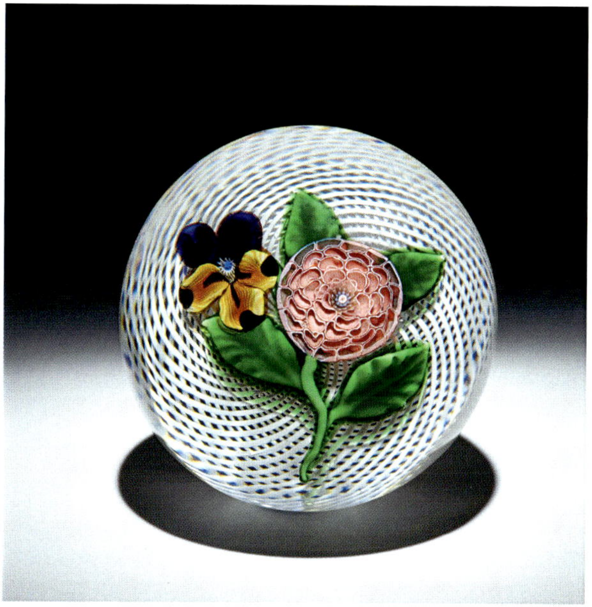

106

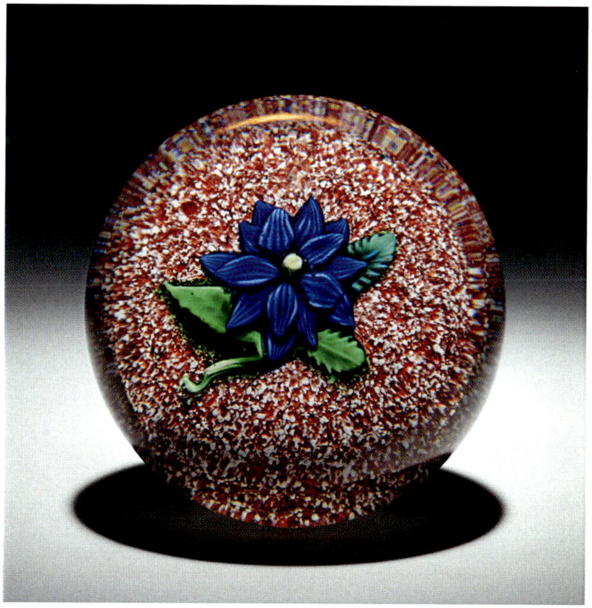

101. Saint-Louis, French, founded 1767
Pear and Cherries on Spiral Filigree Cushion, ca. 1850
Glass, D. 3 ¼ inches

102. Saint-Louis, French, founded 1767
Strawberries and Blossom on Spiral Filigree Cushion, ca. 1850
Glass, D. 2 ⅝ inches

103. Saint-Louis, French, founded 1767
Pelargonium Flower Over Spiral Filigree Cushion, ca. 1850
Glass, D. 2 ⅝ inches

104. Saint-Louis, French, founded 1767
Miniature White Pompon on Pink Spiral Filigree Cushion, ca. 1850
Glass, D. 1 13⁄16 inches

105. Saint-Louis, French, founded 1767
Bouquet Over Spiral Filigree Cushion, ca. 1850
Glass, D. 2 ⅝ inches

106. Saint-Louis, French, founded 1767
Blue Flower on Red and White Jasper Ground, ca. 1850
Glass, D. 3 3⁄16 inches

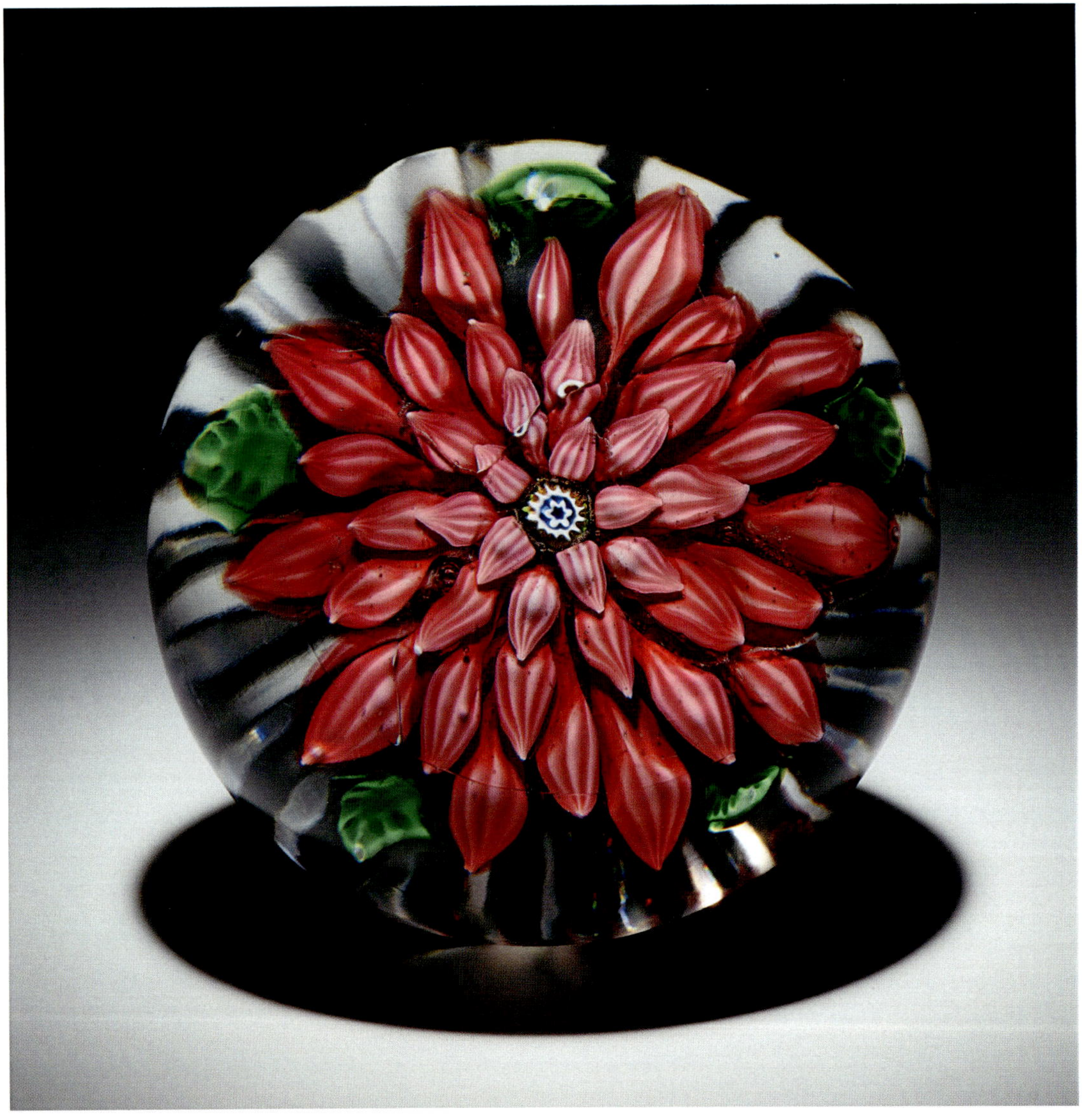

107. Saint-Louis, French, founded 1767
Pink Dahlia, ca. 1850. Glass, D. 3 ⅛ inches

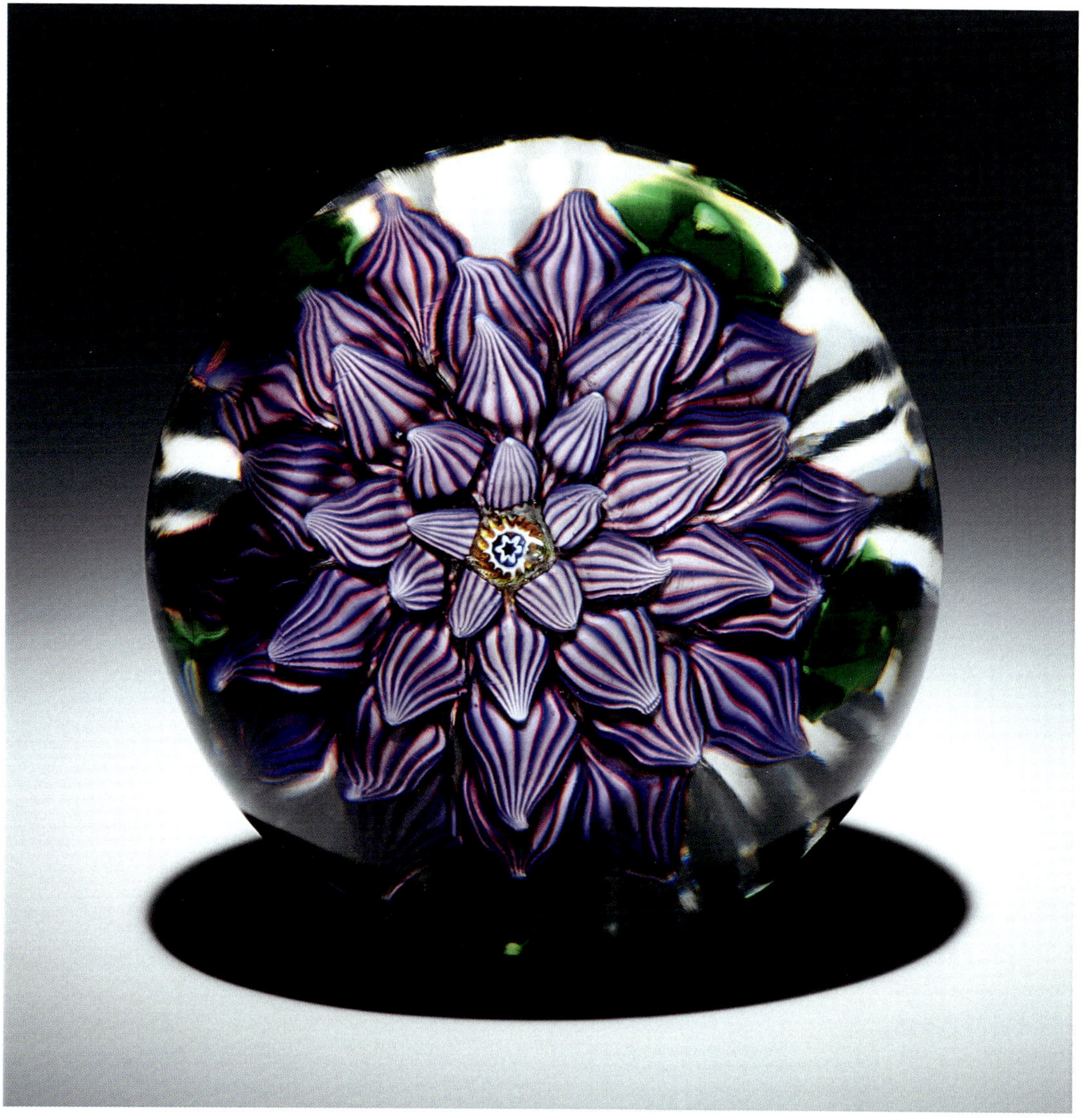

108. Saint-Louis, French, founded 1767
Purple Dahlia, ca. 1850. Glass, D. 3 3/16 inches

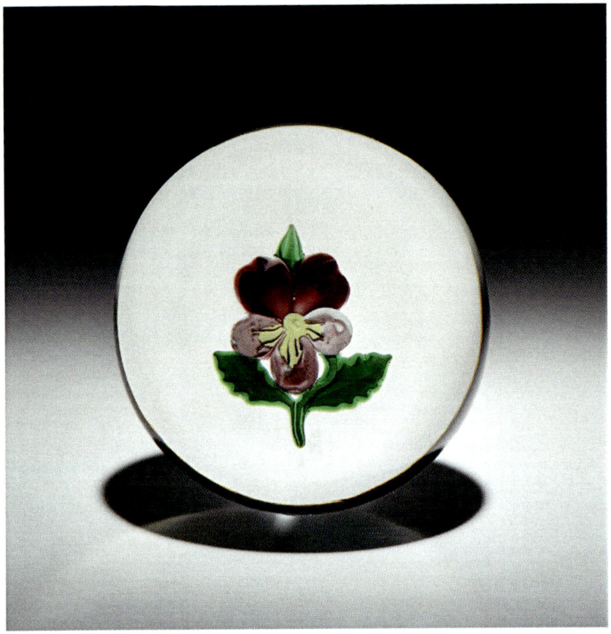

109. Saint-Louis
French, founded 1767
Pansy, ca. 1850
Glass, D. 2 $\frac{7}{16}$ inches

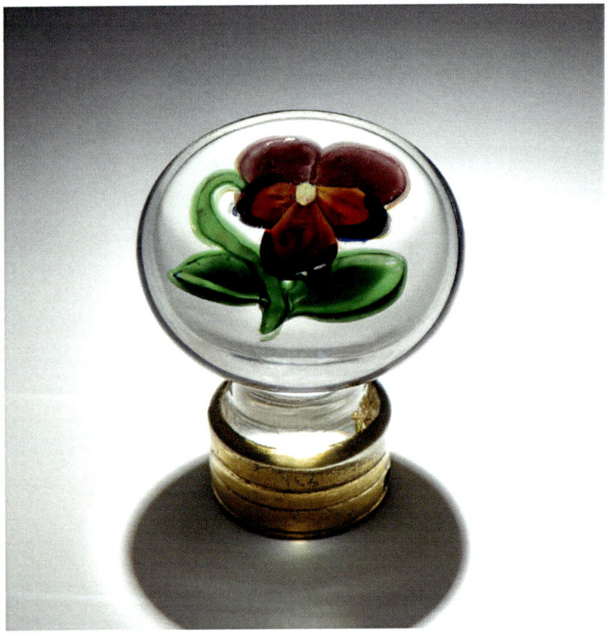

110. Saint-Louis
French, founded 1767
Pansy Knob, ca. 1850
Glass, D. 2, H. 2 $\frac{3}{8}$ inches

Saint Mandé

Saint Mandé was a small glass house founded in 1841 located in the eastern edge of Paris. Only a small number of their weights are known, many of which are millefiori. The factory only operated until 1857.

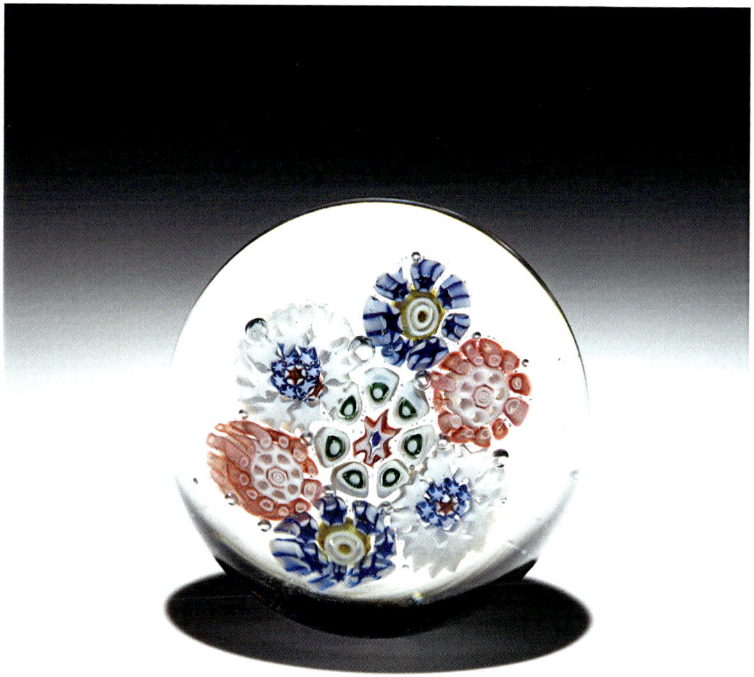

111. Saint Mandé
French, 1841–57
Miniature Millefiori
Glass, D. 1 11/16 inches

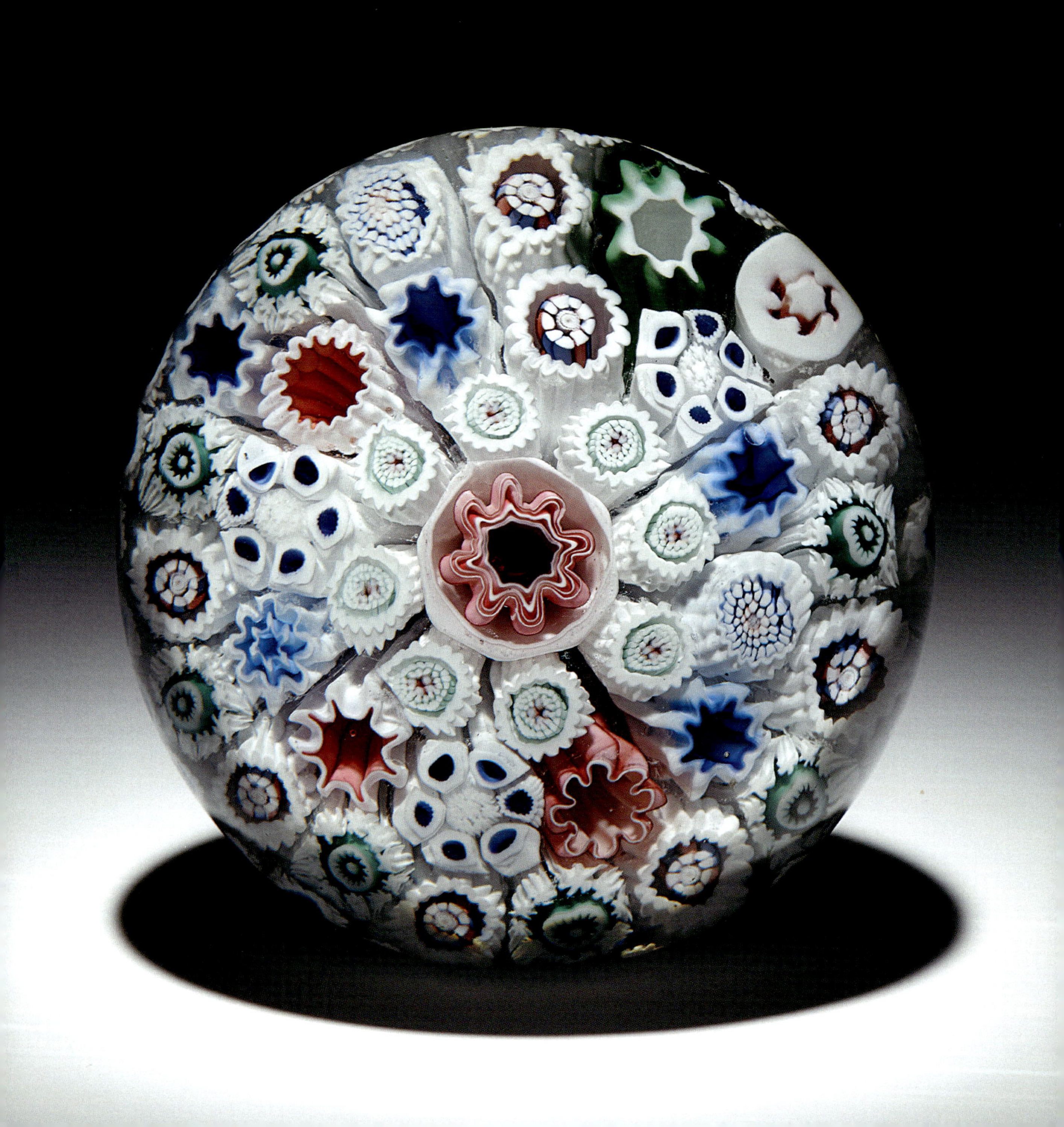

Great Britain *CLASSIC PERIOD*

Bacchus

During the nineteenth century, Birmingham, England, was an area with many manufacturers of glass. Among them was Bacchus, Green & Green founded in 1818. The name was changed to George Bacchus & Sons in 1833 and in 1858 it was renamed Bacchus & Sons. They began making weights in the 1840s. The company was sold in the 1890s, ending work with the Bacchus name.

Bacchus designs are all millefiori, often close concentric with very distinct wide canes. The outer rings of canes, rather than being level with the inner ones, angle and slope down echoing the shape of the weight. Bacchus weights have a unique illusion of a central expanding thrust to their concentric designs as illustrated in **cat. 112.**

112. George Bacchus & Sons, English, founded 1818
Concentric Millefiori with Stave Basket, ca. 1848
Glass, D. 3 inches

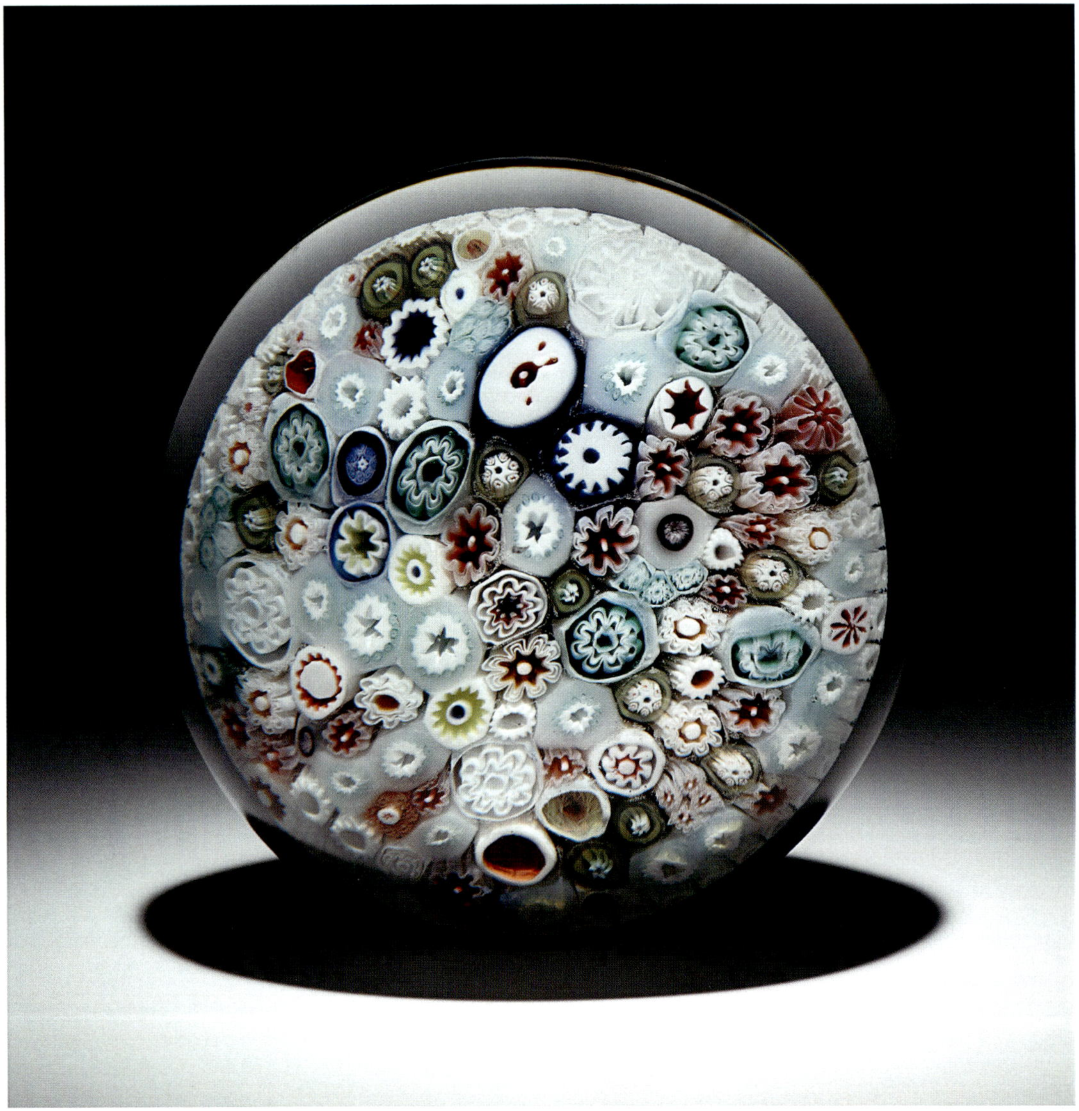

113. George Bacchus & Sons, English, founded 1818
Close Pack Millefiori with Sodden Snow Rings, ca. 1848. Glass, D. 3 5/16 inches

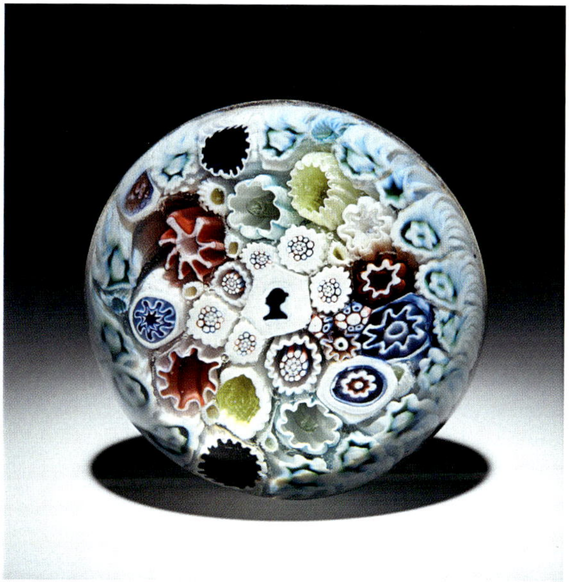

114. English
Close Pack Millefiori with Silhouette Cane, ca. 1848
Glass, D. 3 3/16 inches

Cat. 114 is characteristic of weights created by Bacchus and other English companies during the mid-nineteenth century. The attribution is not definitive. The center of the weight incorporates a silhouette cane which is similar to a portrait cane of Queen Victoria found in weights by Bacchus.

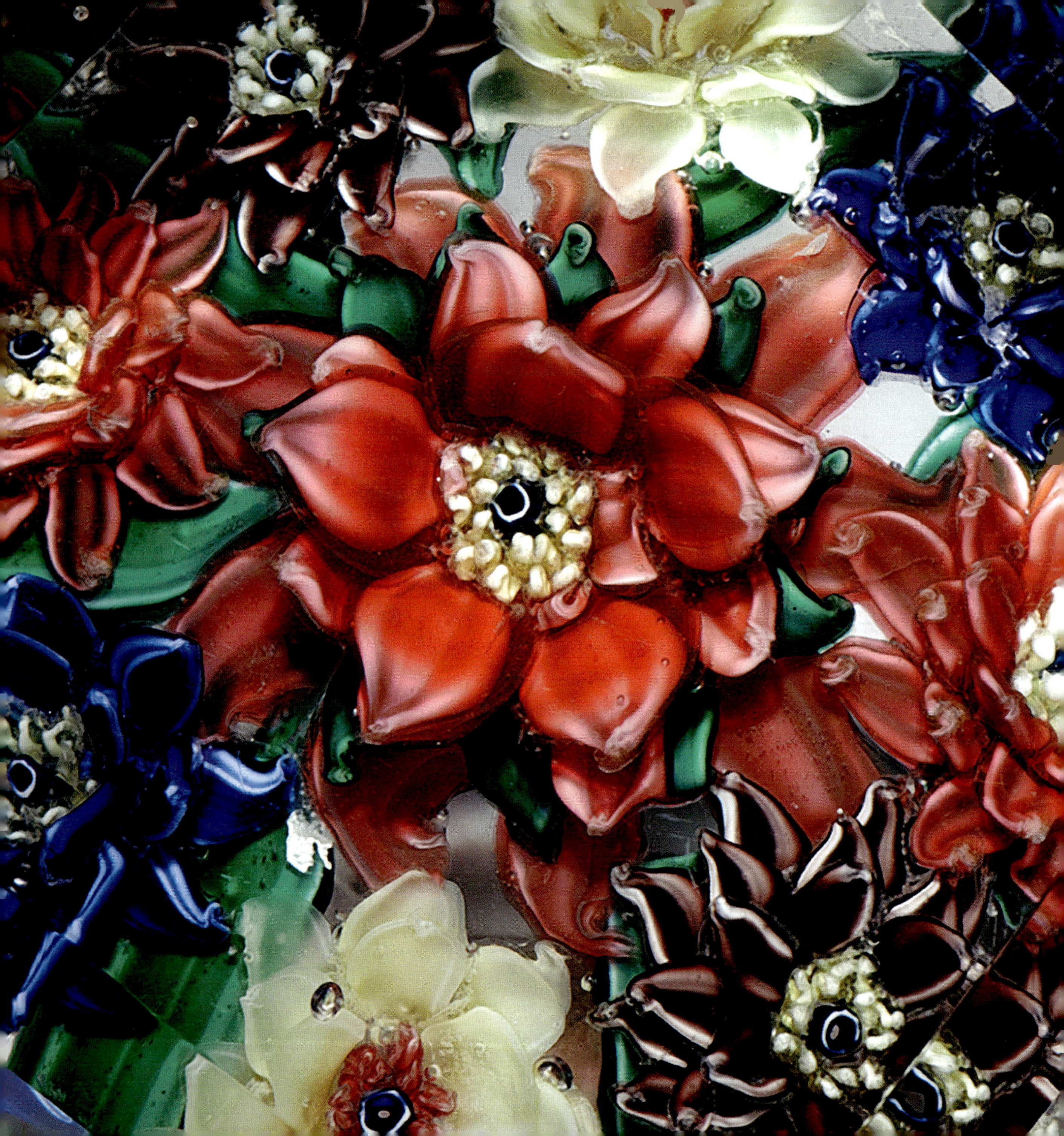

Russia *POST-CLASSIC PERIOD*

Information on Russian paperweight production is limited. Two factories, Dyat'kovo Glass Works and St. Petersburg Glass Works were known to have produced impressive weights displayed at exhibitions in Europe in the 1850s and into the early twentieth century.

Dyat'kovo Glass Works was founded by Marya Vasilyevena Maltsov in 1793, located in the city of the same name 220 miles south-southwest of Moscow. Additional family members became involved in manufacturing glass and by the 1870s the Maltsov family owned sixteen factories. The Maltsov's holdings later became state owned.

The St. Petersburg Glass Works began in 1738 and later became the Imperial Glass Works in 1792. Production of glass weights made in Russia included some in the shape of flat plaques. Primarily the works incorporate intricate, lamp-worked flowers. Perhaps the style of Russian weights was influenced by French weights exported from France to Russia until the Bolshevik Revolution (1917–1923). Russian paperweights are distinctive. Some contain Cyrillic engravings, some have a slight grayish tint to the clear glass, and the motifs within are in deep saturated colors. The flat objects, or plaques, are typically beveled and the weights usually decagonal in shape.

LEFT: Detail of Cat. 121

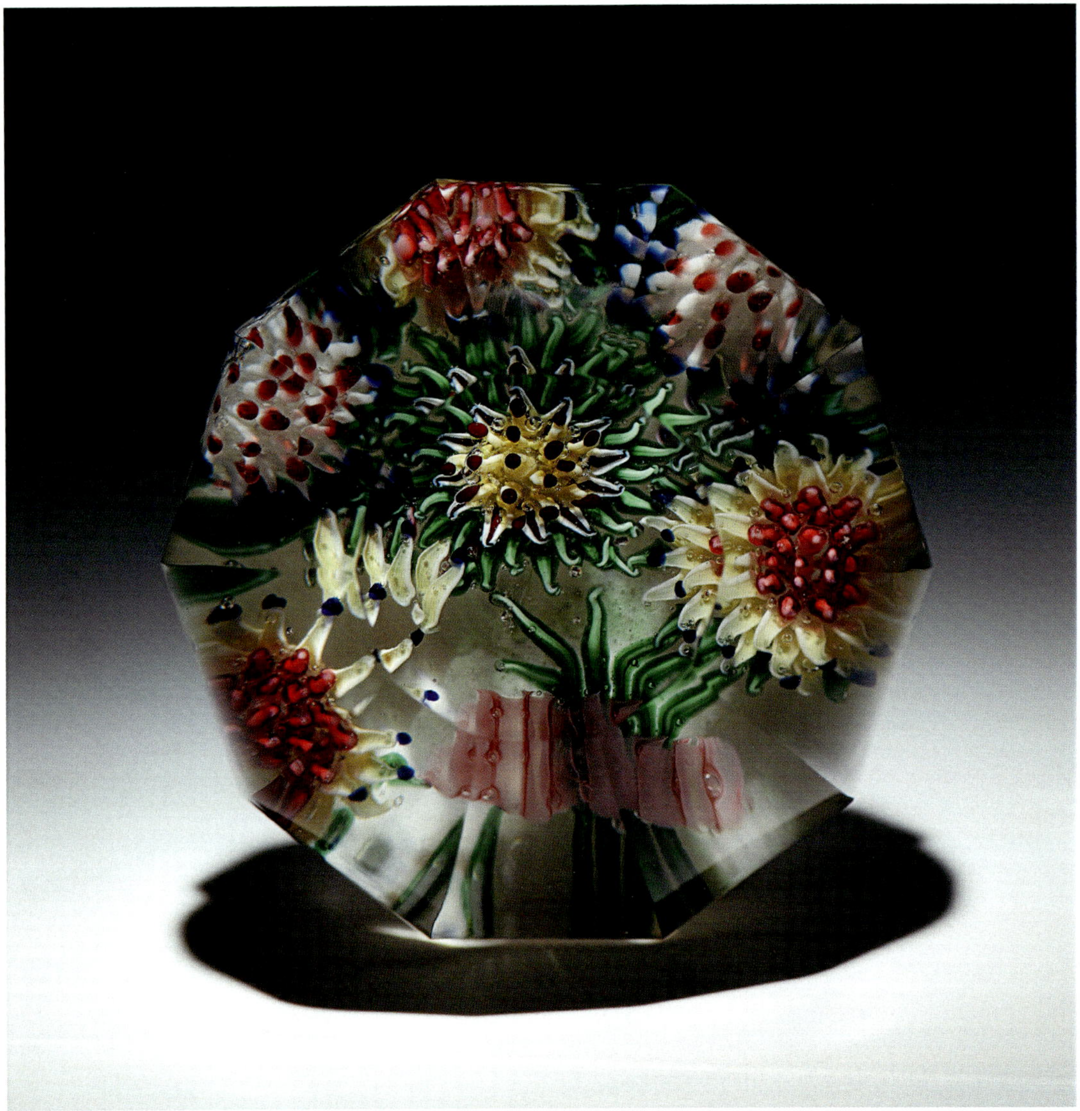

115. Russian
Faceted Bouquet Ring, ca. 1890. Glass, D. 3 inches

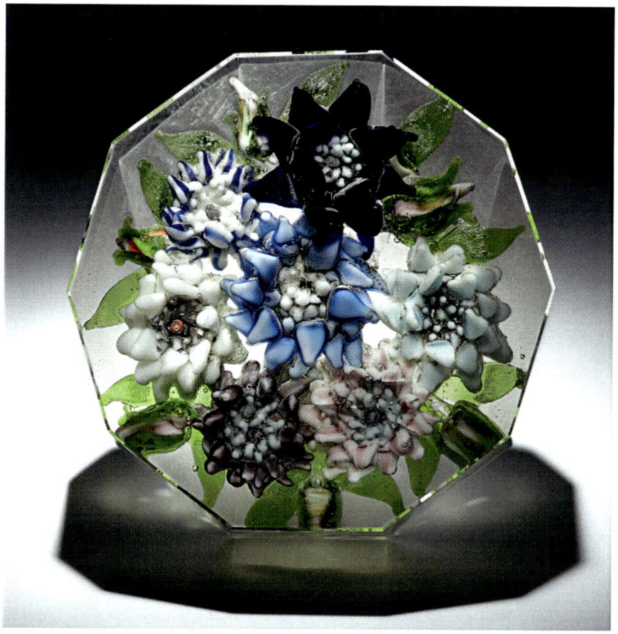

116. **Russian**
Magnum Decagon Dahlia and Flower, ca. 1890
Glass, D. 4 $\frac{3}{16}$ inches

Cat. 116 is a ten-sided form, inset with a central pale blue dahlia within a garland of six assorted dahlias and leaves on a matte-finished base.

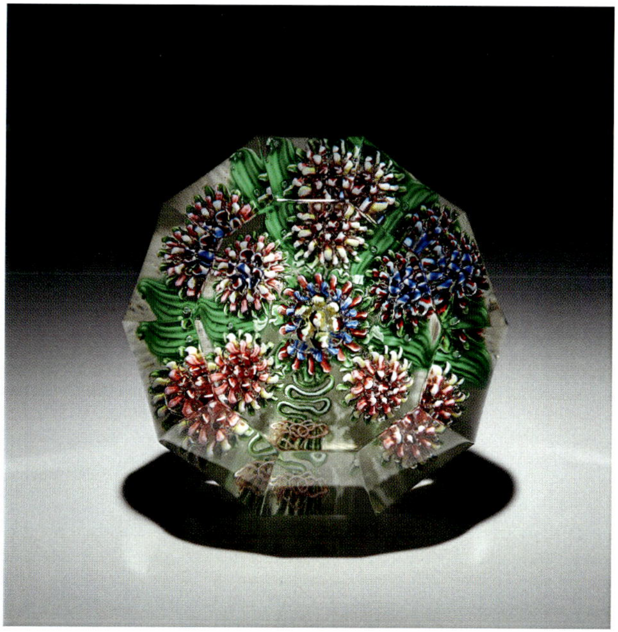

117. **Russian**
Faceted Bouquet, ca. 1890
Glass, D. 2 $\frac{3}{4}$ inches

Cat. 117 is an unusual shape with a large flat top and ten diagonal facets that curve to the smaller diameter base. It includes a colorful variety of flowers with distinct pointed petals.

118

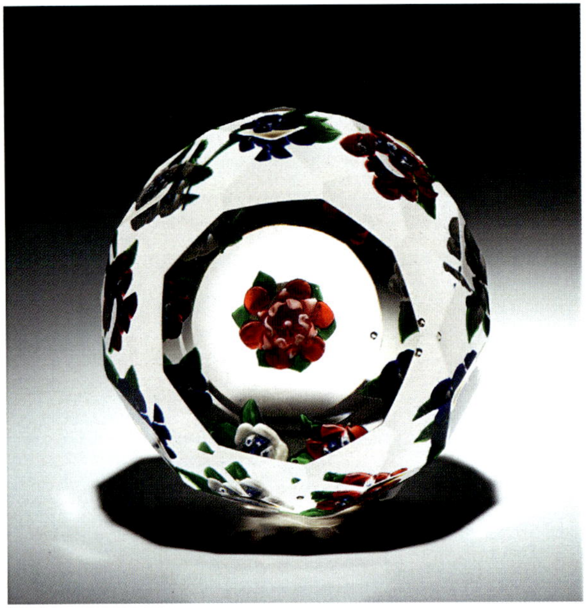

120

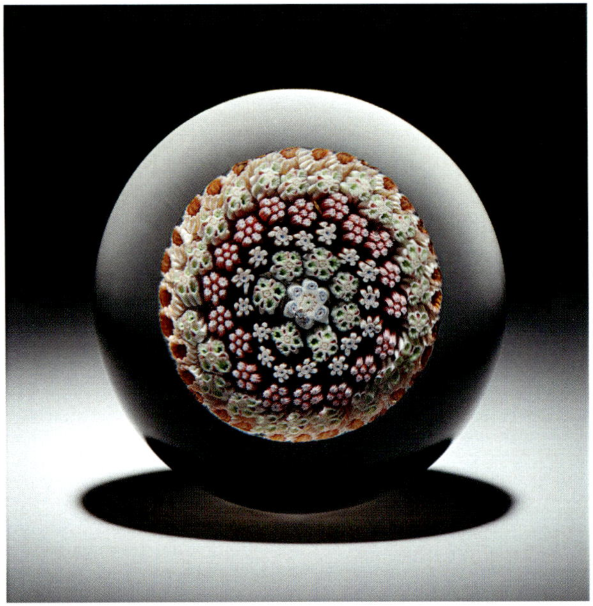

119

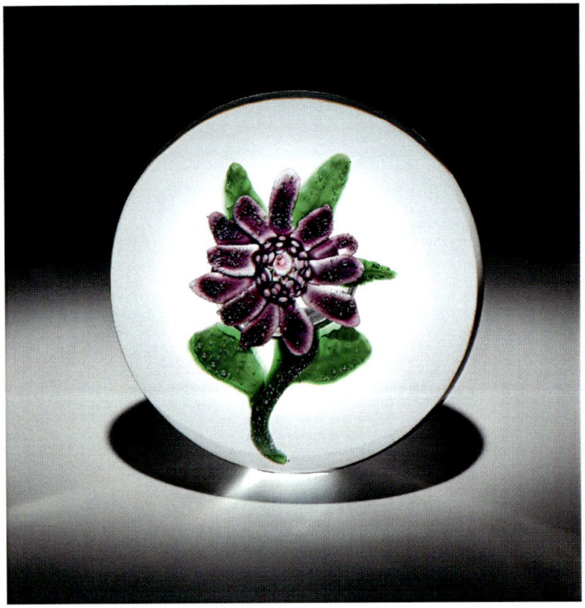

121

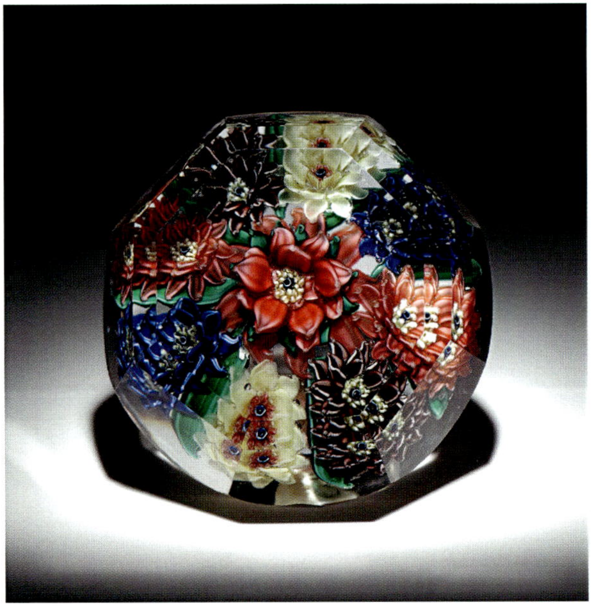

122

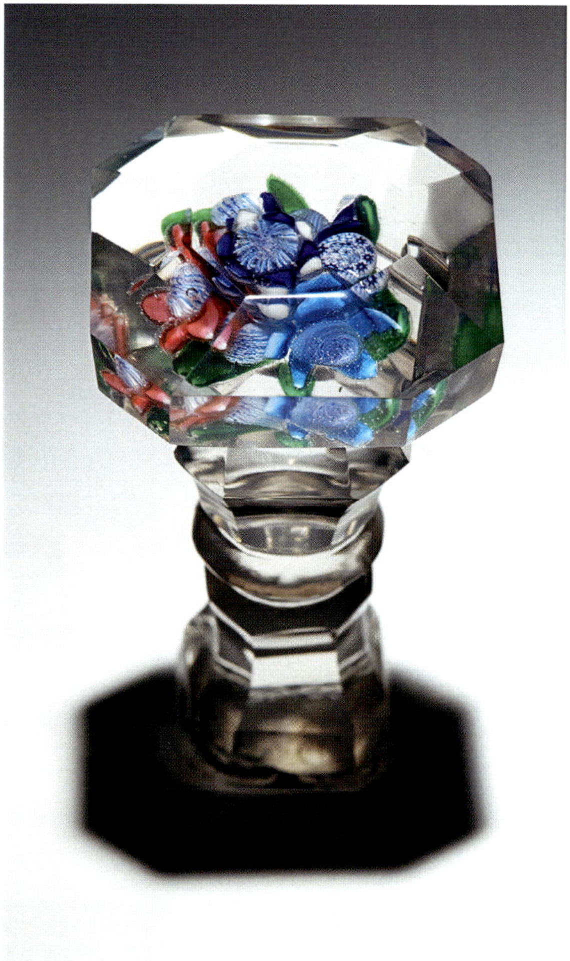

118. Russian
Faceted Pink Flower with Garland, ca. 1890
Glass, D. 2 ¾ inches

119. Russian
Purple Flower, ca. 1890
Glass, D. 2 ⅞ inches

120. Russian
Concentric Millefiori, ca. 1890
Glass, D. 3 ⅛ inches

121. Russian
Magnum Faceted Bouquet Ring, ca. 1890
Glass, D. 3 ¾ inches

122. Russian
Faceted Millefiori Flower Stamp, ca. 1890
Glass, H. 2 5⁄16, W. 1 ¼, L. 1 ¼ inches

Cat. 121 contains a large ruby colored central flower surrounded by a ring of stacked rows each containing two blossoms. The colors are distinctive, pale yellow, royal blue, deep red, and purple. The object is cut with eight inward-leaning panel facets beveled at the top. The top also has a facet with eight sides.

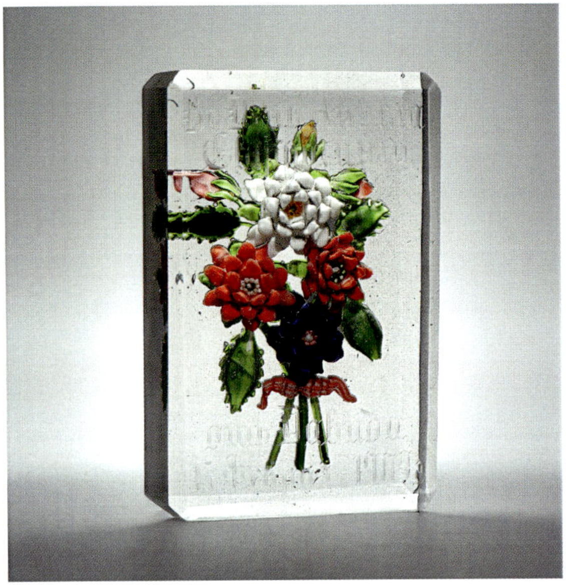

123. **Russian**
Etched and Beveled Bouquet Plaque, ca. 1890
Glass, H. 5 ½, W. 3 ⅝, L. 1 ½ inches

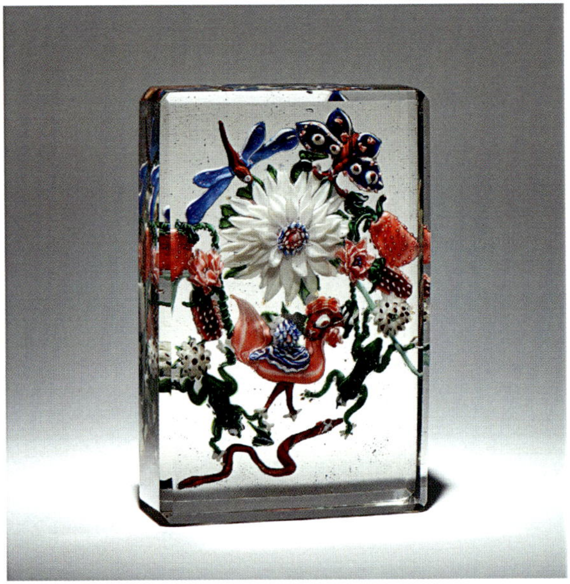

124. **Russian**
Beveled Bouquet with Creatures Plaque, ca. 1890
Glass, H. 5 ⅛, W. 3 ⅞, L. 1 ¼ inches

This plaque illustrates a leafed bouquet of four flowers and eight buds with their stems tied together with a pink bow. The weight has an etched back that appears frosted. The Russian inscription translates as: *On the day of the angel of Euphrosinia.*

Created circa 1890, **cat. 124** displays an abundance of colorful floral elements animated with a blue dragonfly, two green frogs, a red snake, a pink-and-blue rooster, a pink-and-blue butterfly, and other spotted elements.

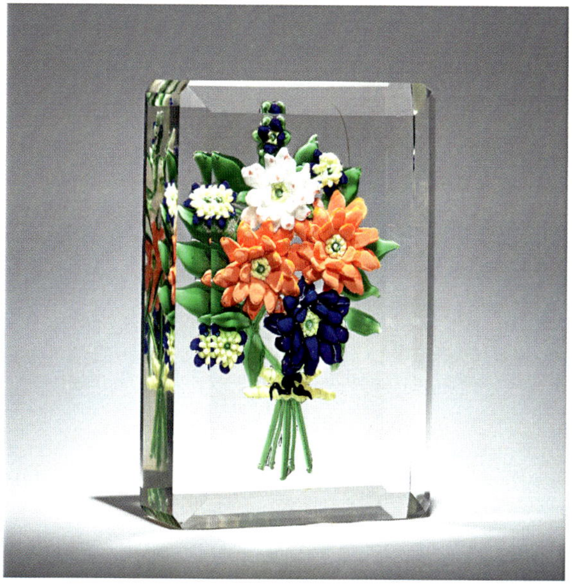

125. **Russian**
Beveled Bouquet Plaque ca. 1890
Glass, H. 5 ½, W. 4, L. 1 $\frac{7}{16}$ inches

This plaque incorporates four dahlias with green stems tied tightly together with thin yellow and blue ribbons. The bouquet contains two orange flowers placed with a deep saturated cobalt blue flower and a bright white blossom surrounded by bright green leaves and smaller yellow and blue blossoms.

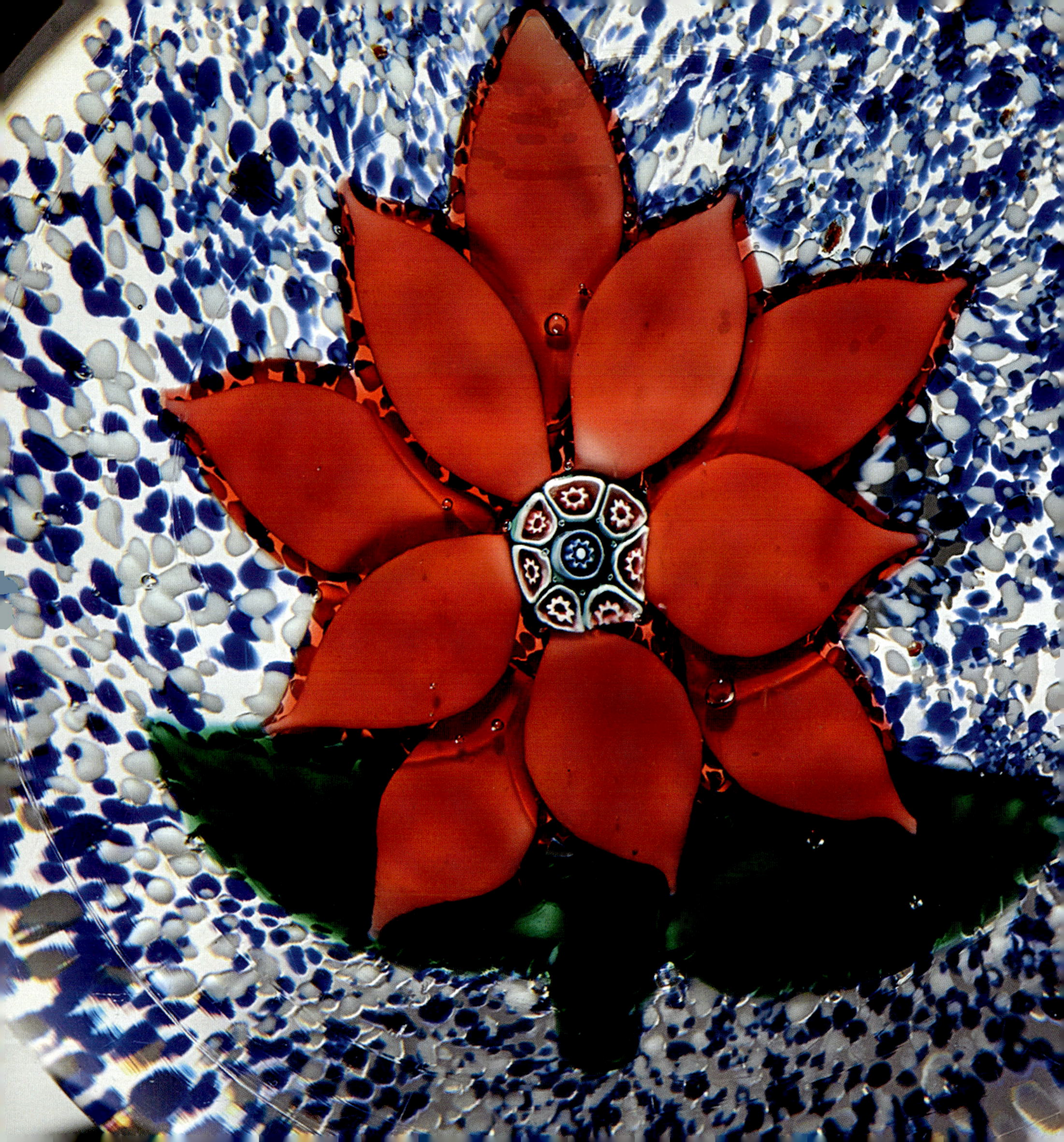

United States *POST-CLASSIC PERIOD*

During the mid-nineteenth century many Americans considered European art and cultural sensibilities as the gold standard. Initiatives to beautify cities with parks, monuments, and public sculptures were fashioned on European models. Growth in American cultural organizations, including museums, libraries, opera houses, and symphonies supported the importance of education and individual expression, and refinement of taste was reflected in the style of European classical architecture used for the buildings. Much of the growth of cultural institutions was through the support of private philanthropists who sought to educate and provide resources for themselves and for the good of their communities.

At the same time, Americans were traveling abroad to tour and study. They took advantage of transatlantic ocean liners and the convenience of the European international railroad. These new modes of transportation allowed easy access to many countries with elegant hotels, historic sites, and fashionable cities. Great industrial exhibitions and world's fairs were popular in Vienna, Paris,

LEFT: Detail of Cat. 126

and London. Pavilions showcased technological, industrial, and cultural achievements of nations from around the world and enticed American manufacturers who were keen on understanding trends that might interest their buyers. These expositions included displays of beautiful objects fabricated by the major glass houses including innovative paperweights. In 1851 American weights were exhibited in London at the Great Exhibition and in 1853 in New York City at the Exhibition of the Industry of All Nations.

Three Massachusetts glasshouses became the first to produce weights in the United States. They were all founded by a Boston merchant named Deming Jarvis. The workers were from a group of skilled craftsmen, many emigrating from Europe where they served as apprentices in glass factories. Each of the three factories had a unique history but the craftsmen shared materials and techniques. Because of this, weights from these companies had similar styles that also resemble their European counterparts.

Boston & Sandwich Glass Company

The Sandwich Manufacturing Company was founded in 1825 in Sandwich, Massachusetts, by Deming Jarvis, one of the former owners of the New England Glass Company. A year later it incorporated and was renamed the Boston & Sandwich Glass Company, where Jarvis remained until 1858. Commonly referred to as simply "Sandwich," the company closed in 1888.

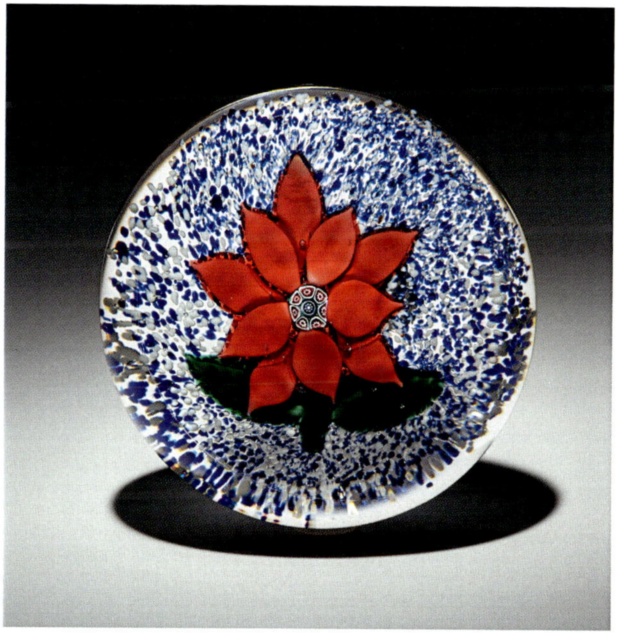

126. **Boston & Sandwich Glass Company**
American, 1826–88
Poinsettia on Blue and White Jasper Ground, ca. 1870
Glass, D. 3 inches

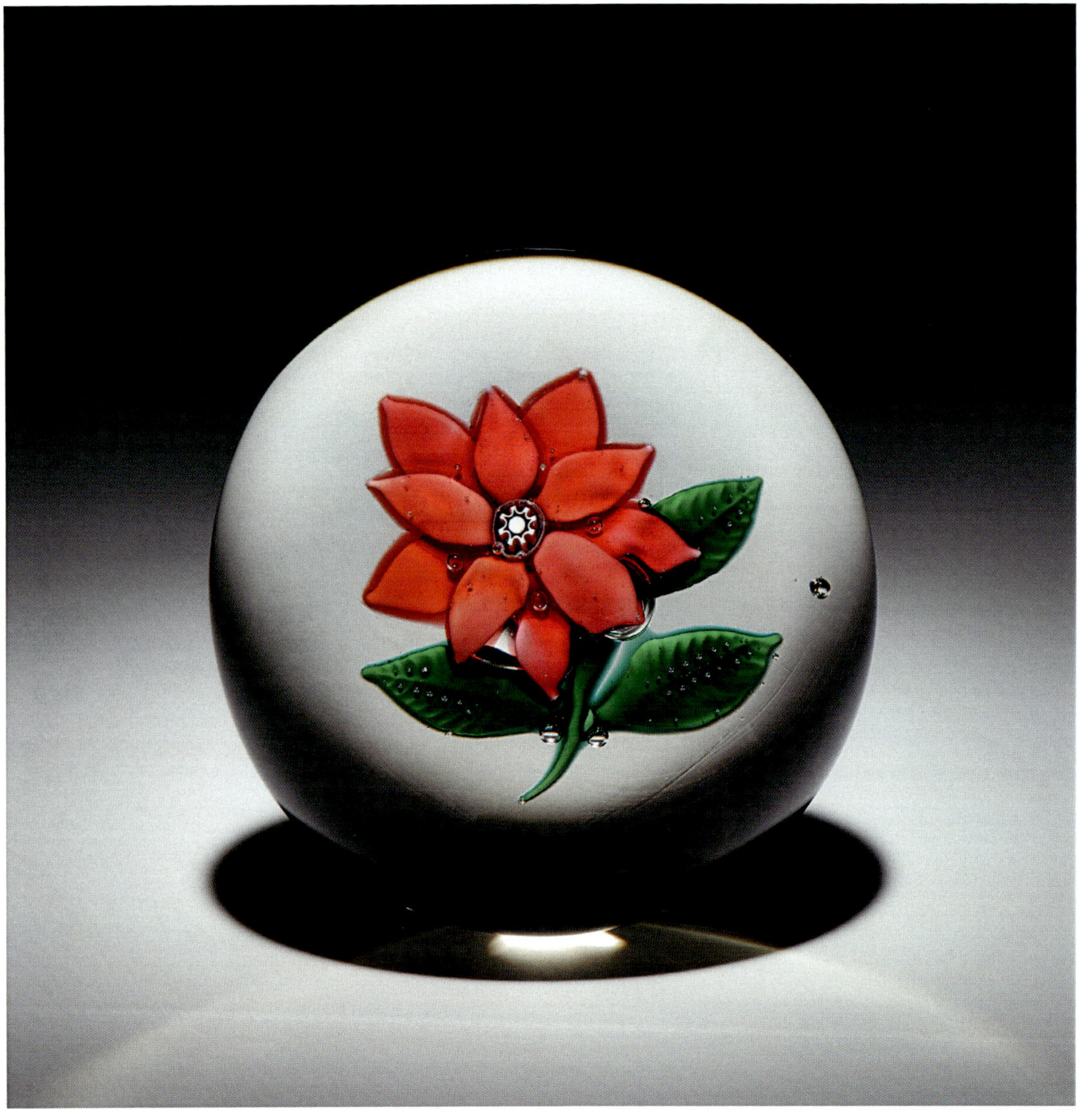

127. Boston & Sandwich Glass Company, American, 1826–88
Poinsettia. Glass, D. 2 ½ inches

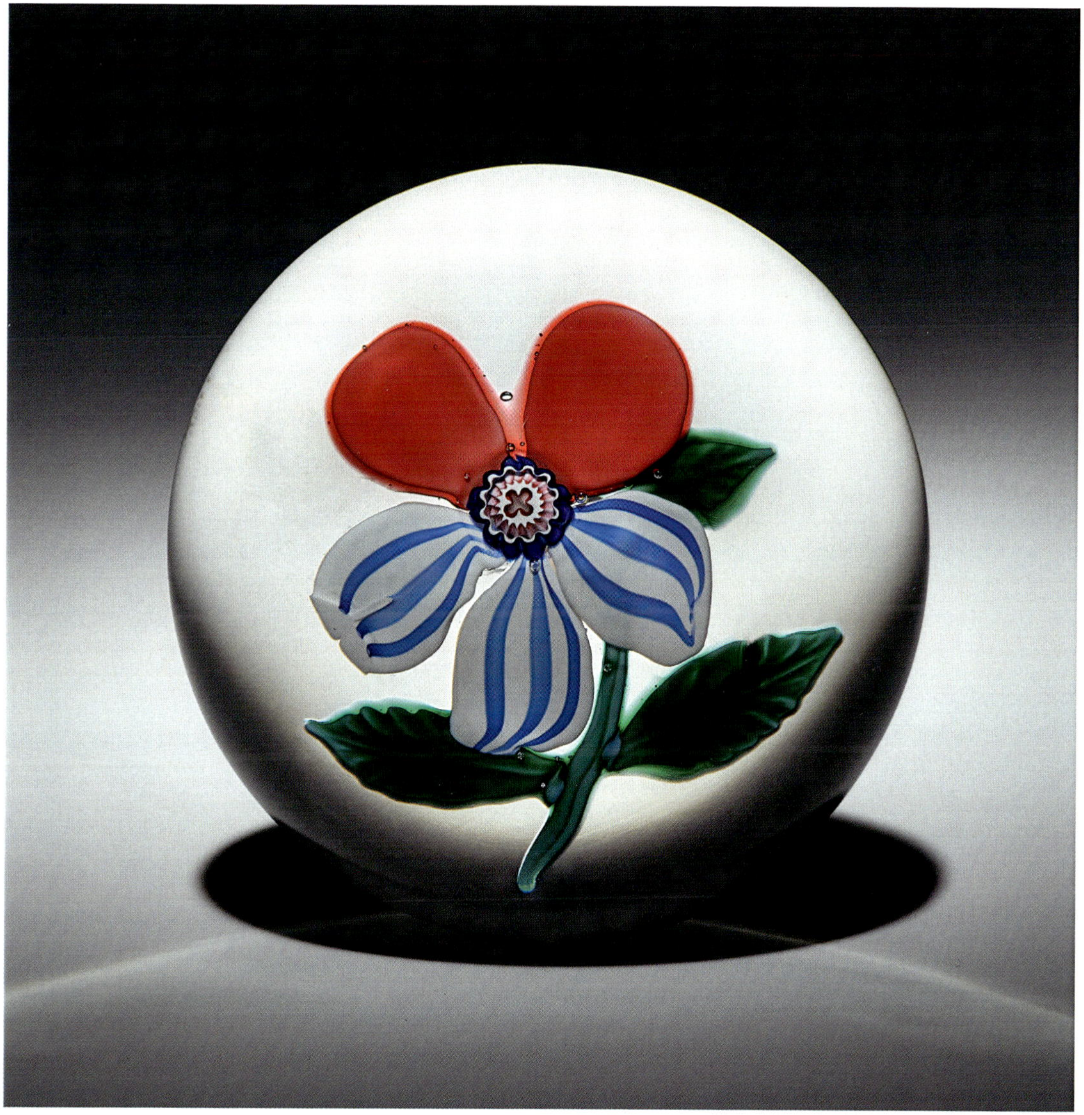

128. Boston & Sandwich Glass Company, American, 1826–88
Red, White, and Blue Weed Flower, ca. 1870. Glass, D. 3 inches

Gillinder & Sons

Gillinder & Sons was founded in 1861 by William T. Gillinder. Gillinder worked in British glass factories from the age of eight until he was in his twenties. The 1850s were difficult for English workers due to a lack of employment in the glass industry so he immigrated to Massachusetts to seek work in the glass industry. He eventually moved to Pittsburgh and then Philadelphia where he found work. In 1861, he opened Philadelphia Flint Glass Works that soon became known as Gillinder & Sons. Between 1861 and 1871 the company created paperweights influenced by George Bacchus & Sons. The majority of Gillinder weights use millefiori. Today, Gillinder Glass is a custom technical molded and filter glass manufacturer located in Port Jervis, New York.

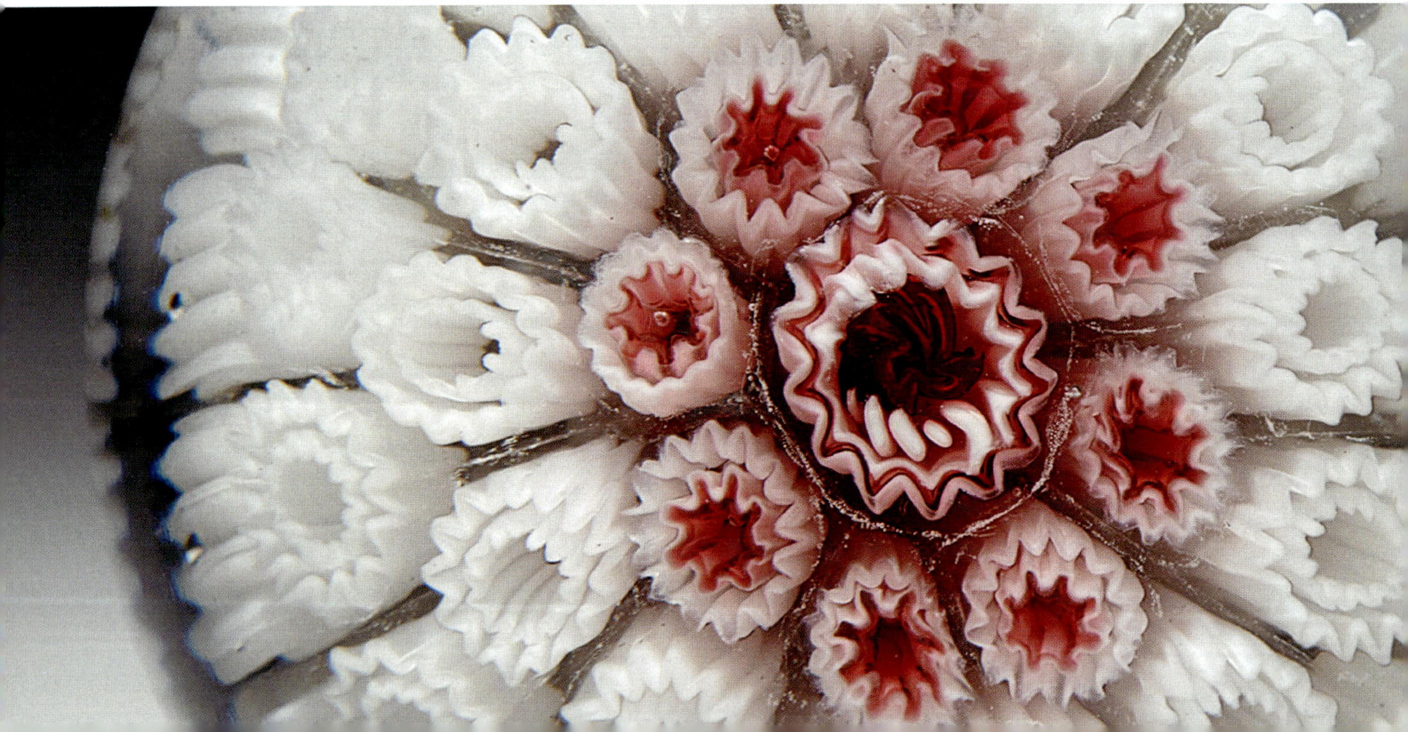

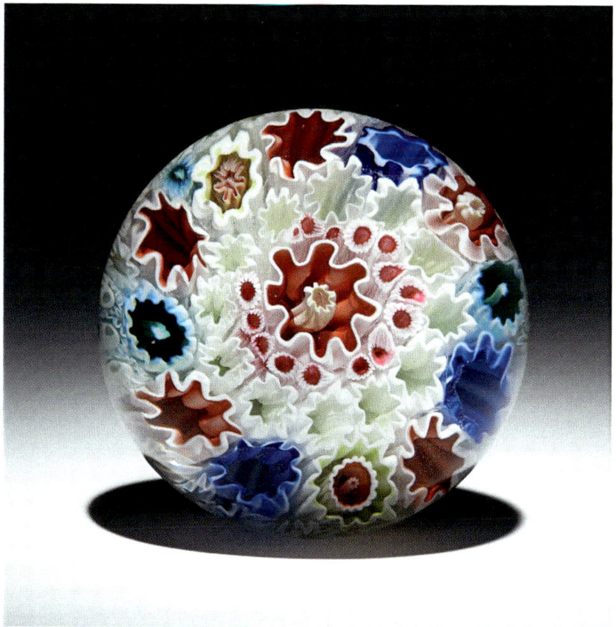

129. **Gillinder & Sons**
American, founded 1861
Concentric Canes with White Stave Basket
Glass, D. 2 ¾ inches

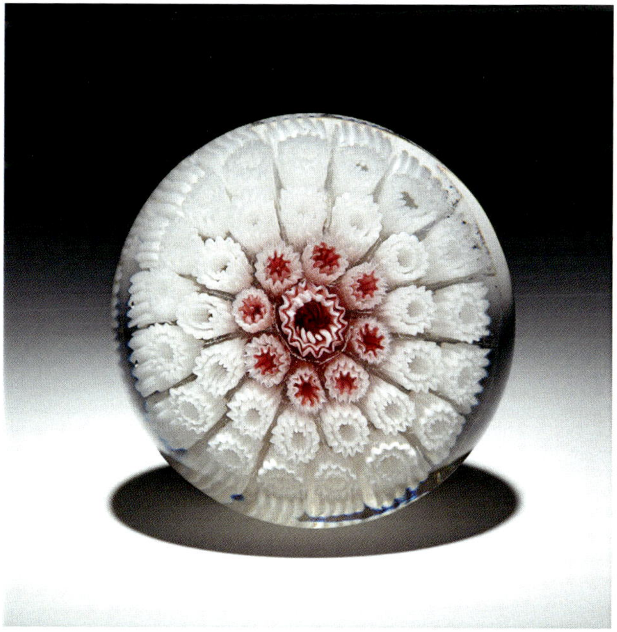

130. **Gillinder & Sons**
American, founded 1861
Concentric Canes
Glass, D. 2 ¼ inches

LEFT: Detail of Cat. 130

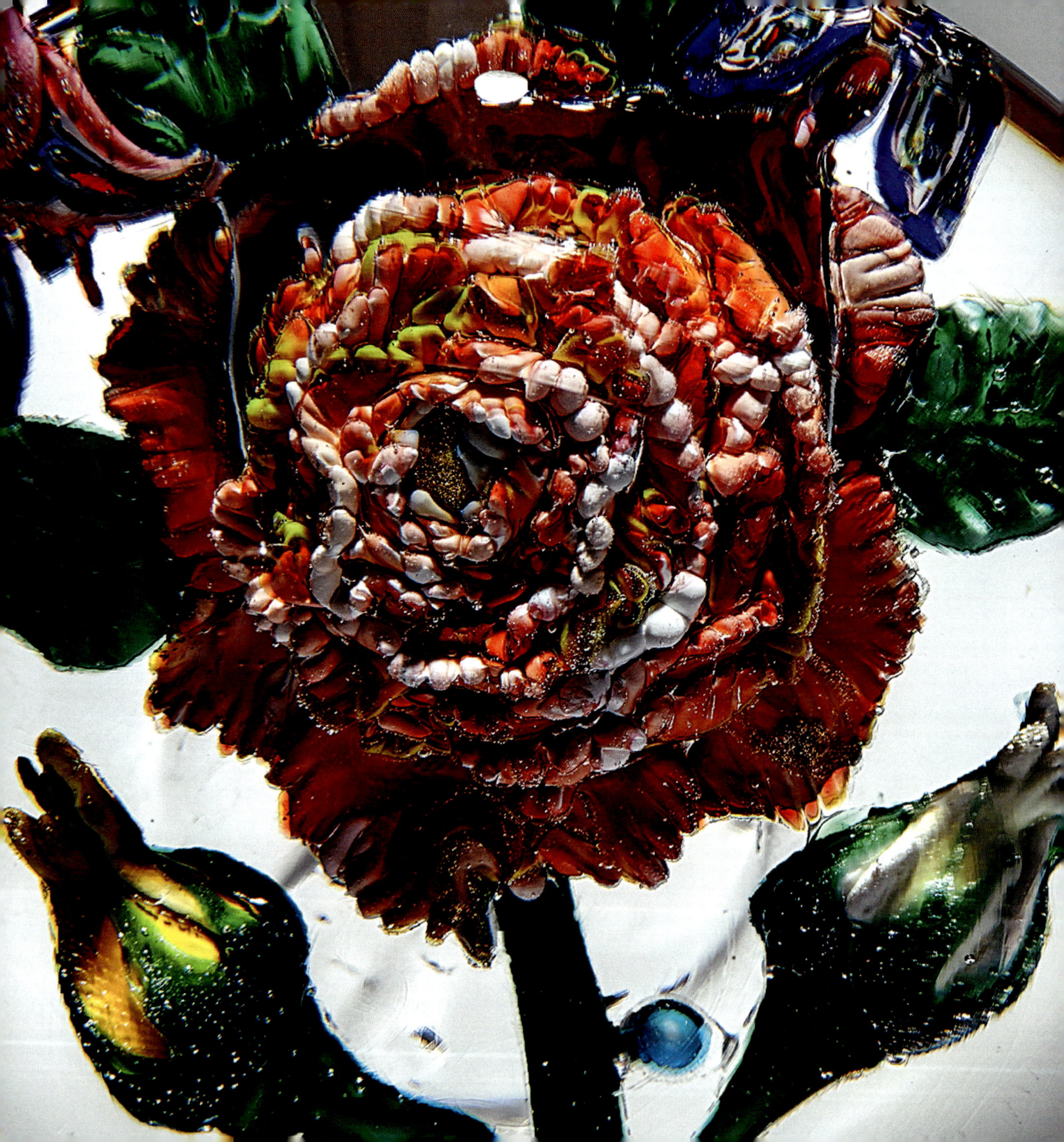

Mount Washington Glass Works

Deming Jarvis's third company, Mount Washington Glass Works, opened in South Boston in 1837. The company moved to New Bedford, Massachusetts, in 1870. In 1880, Thomas J. Pairpoint, an English silversmith, was hired to run another factory, the Pairpoint Manufacturing Company. Mount Washington's owners established Pairpoint to produce ornate silver-plated mounts to incorporate into their glass items. In 1894, the Pairpoint Manufacturing Company absorbed Mount Washington, and in 1900 the company was renamed the Pairpoint Corporation, which remained the company's name until it went out of business in 1938. In 1939, the company reorganized under its new owner, master glassblower Robert Gundersen as Gundersen Glass Works. In 1952, the company became the Gundersen-Pairpoint Glass Works until 1957, when it was renamed a final time to Pairpoint Glass Company. It ceased operations at its New Bedford plant and relocated briefly to East Wareham, Massachusetts. The company moved in 1958 to leased facilities in Spain, exporting limited quantities of stemware, perfume bottles, and paperweights back to the United States. Pairpoint returned to the United States in 1967 and opened a newly built factory in Sagamore, Massachusetts, shortly after, which continues to produce fine glass to this day.

LEFT: Detail of Cat. 131

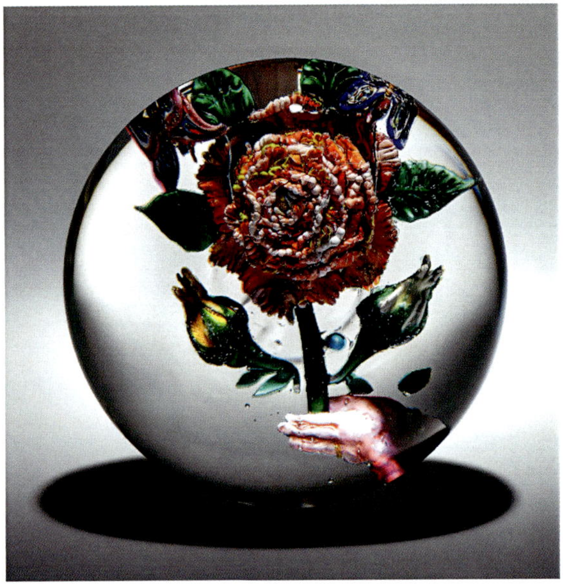

131. Mount Washington Glass Works
American, 1837–94
Magnum Rose with Butterflies, ca. 1890
Glass, D. 4 ½ inches

Cat. 131 is one of the most unusual weights in the Ellis Collection. This fairly large piece features a variegated ruffled pink rose attached to a thick green stem with two parallel buds. Two small colorful butterflies move towards the rose which is held by an enigmatic pink hand. The sentiment, during the time this object was made was that a hand holding flowers could mean that they are being presented in friendship, remembrance, or romance.

New England Glass Company

The New England Glass Company was founded in 1818 in Cambridge, Massachusetts, by four partners including Deming Jarvis. Jarvis left the company in 1825 and the company closed in 1888.

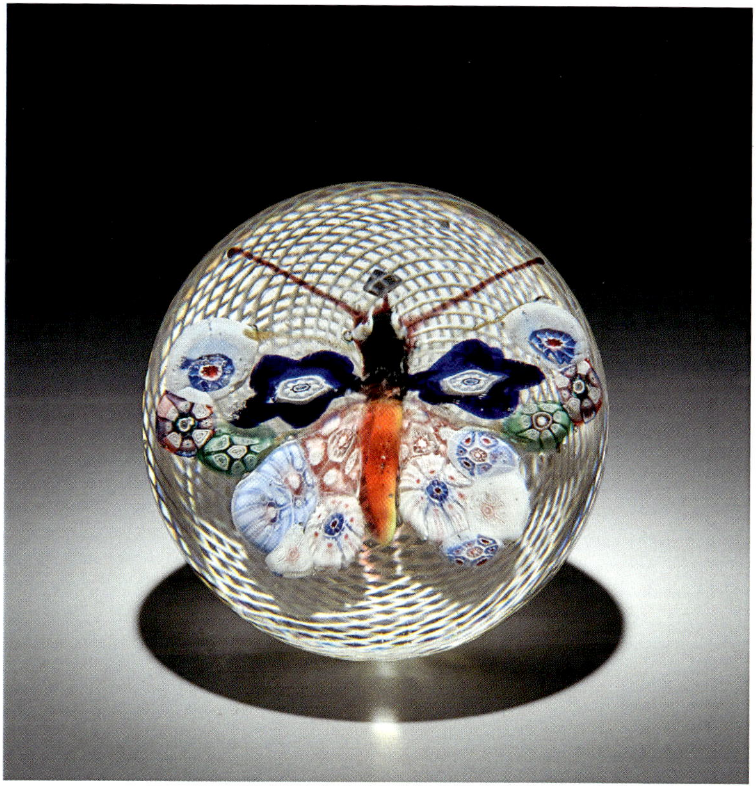

132. New England Glass Company, American, 1818–88
Butterfly with Millefiori Cane Wings on Spiral Filigree Cushion, ca. 1870
Glass, D. 2 ½ inches

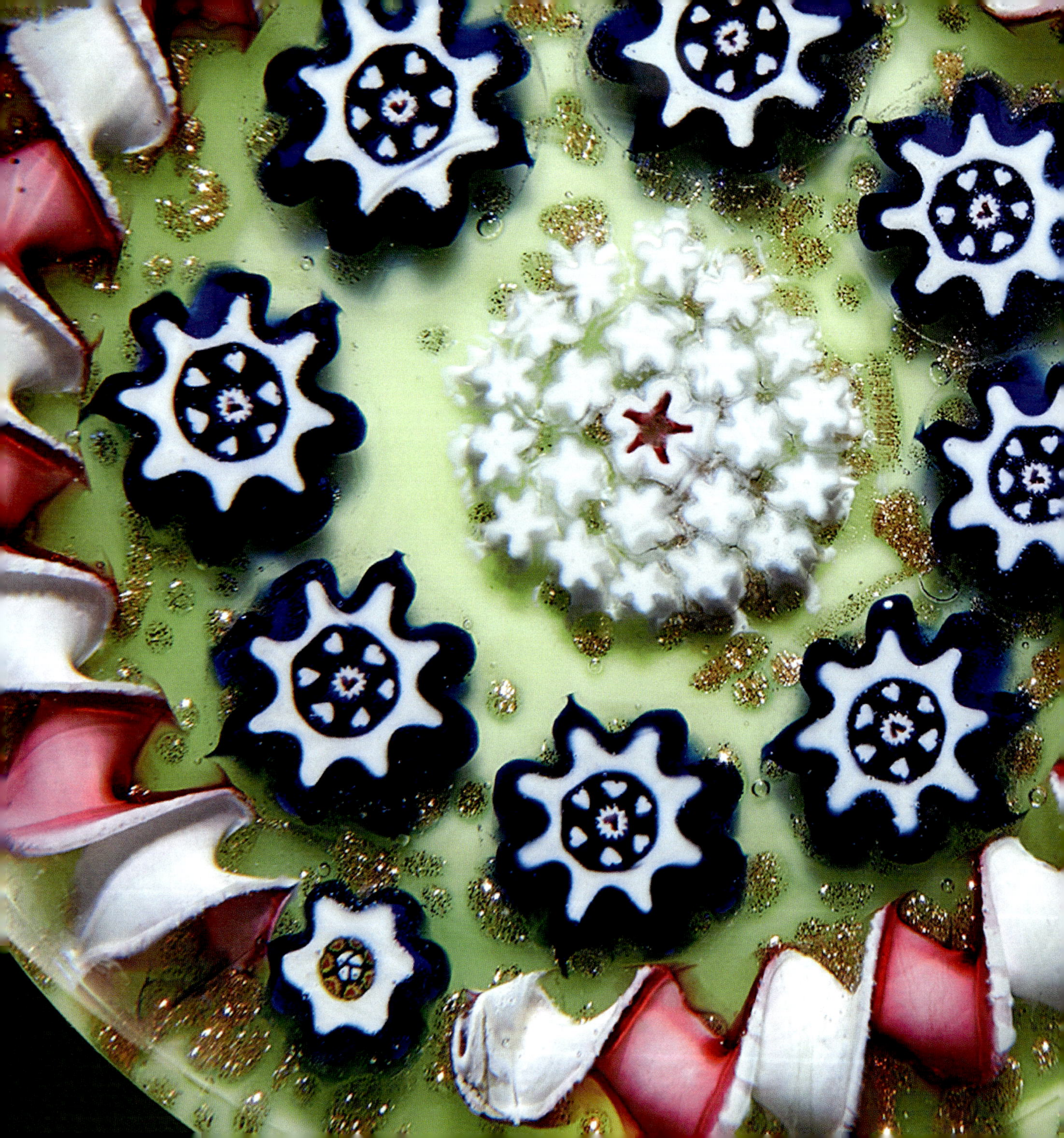

Classic Revival & Transitional *1952–1969*

By the turn of the twentieth century paperweight manufacturing had declined and all but ceased through World Wars I and II. In 1952, the French-American entrepreneur, collector and art dealer, Paul Jokelson, sparked the renaissance of classical French paperweight production. He persuaded the French factories of Baccarat and Saint-Louis to again make paperweights in their classical style of the previous century. The workers in both companies had to learn what had been a common part of the product line nearly 100 years earlier. This period also witnessed the emergence of knowing the names of individual glass workers.

Successfully working in glass requires a team of skilled craftspeople that share knowledge and have the muscle memory and spatial awareness to move safely together in a glass shop—collaboration is required. Because of this trust and in many cases mentorship, the workers learned from one another. Undoubtedly, since factories began, glassworkers have experimented with creating objects in their free time but they were unable to work independently on their own. The economic and creative climate of the twentieth century fostered independence for individuals creating decorative arts and fine crafts. No longer anonymous, the artists were becoming recognized by their signatures both literally and stylistically.

LEFT: Detail of Cat. 153

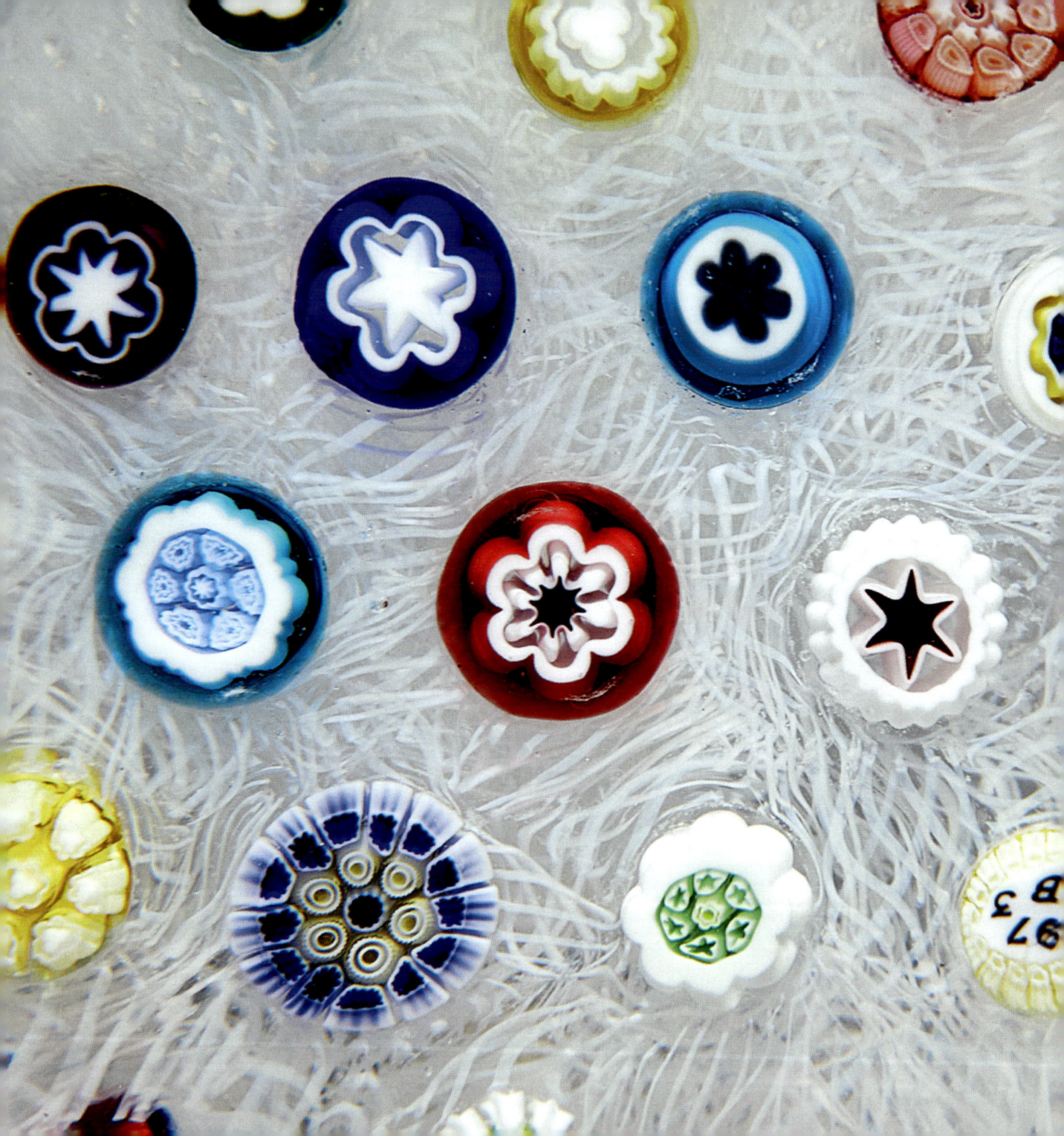

France

CLASSIC REVIVAL & TRANSITIONAL PERIOD

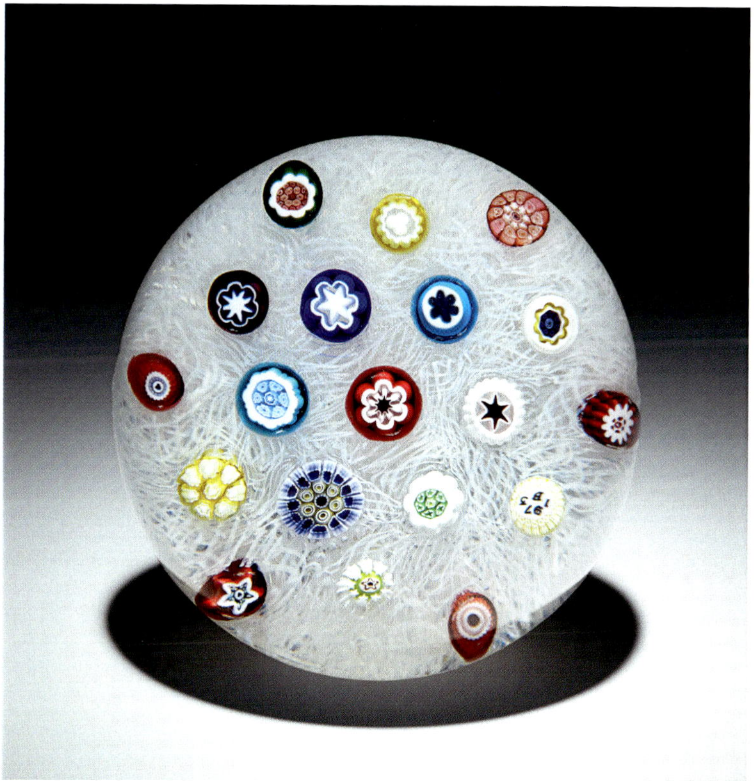

133. Baccarat
French, founded 1764
Spaced Millefiori on Upset Muslin, 1973
Glass, D. 3 inches

Cat. 133 is a fine example of a Classic Revival spaced millefiori weight with picture canes. Upon closer inspection, many of the canes are different from those of the previous century.

LEFT: **Detail of Cat. 133**

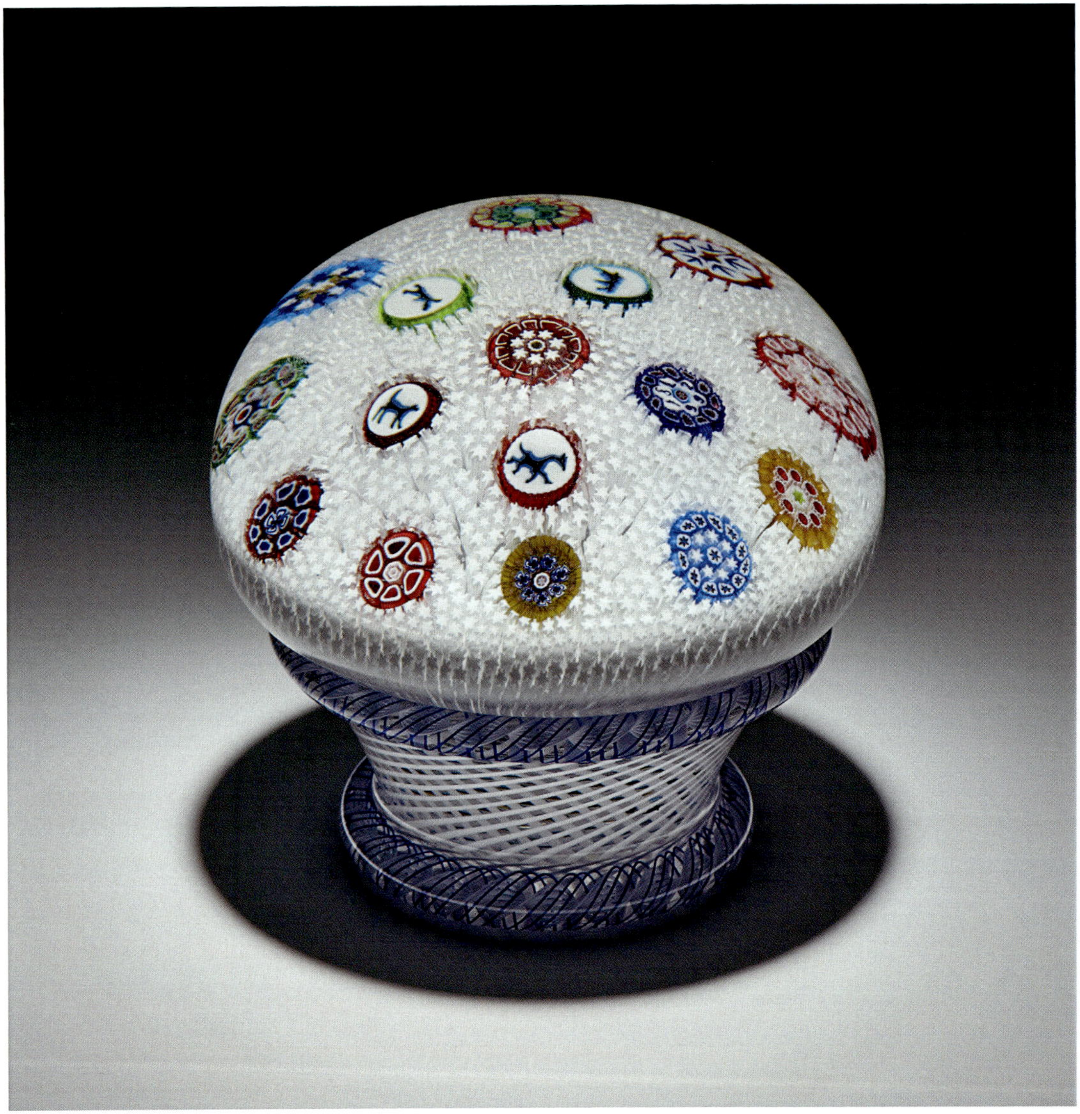

134. Saint-Louis, French, founded 1767
Complex and Silhouette Cane Piedouche, 1992
Glass, D. 3 3/16, H. 3 3/16 inches

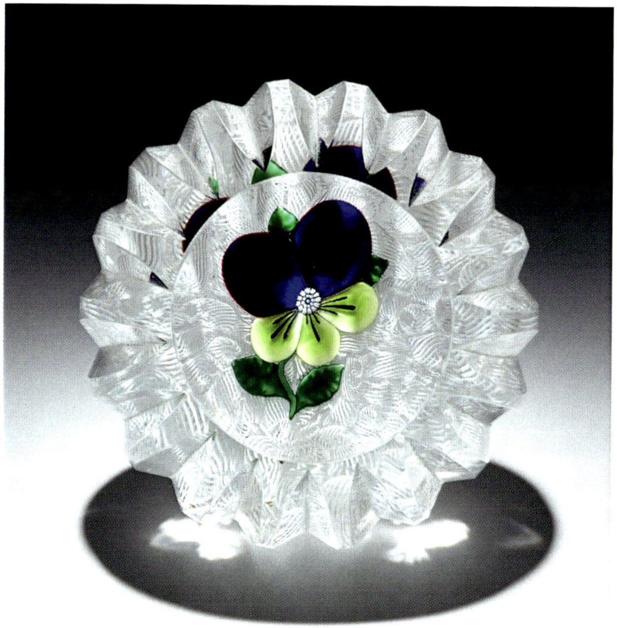

135. Saint-Louis, French, founded 1767
Fluted Pansy on Muslin Ground, 1980
Glass, D. 2 15/16 inches

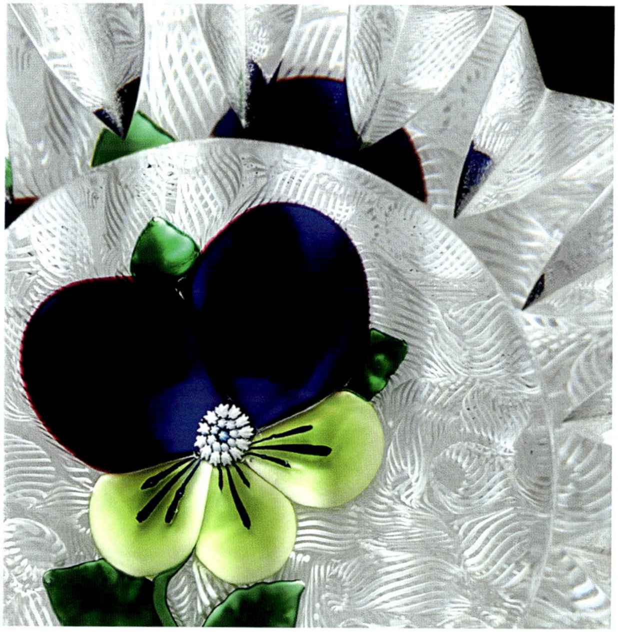

Detail of Cat. 135
Here Saint-Louis revisits the nineteenth-century affection for the pansy placing the flower over a muslin ground with the addition of precision fluting and faceting.

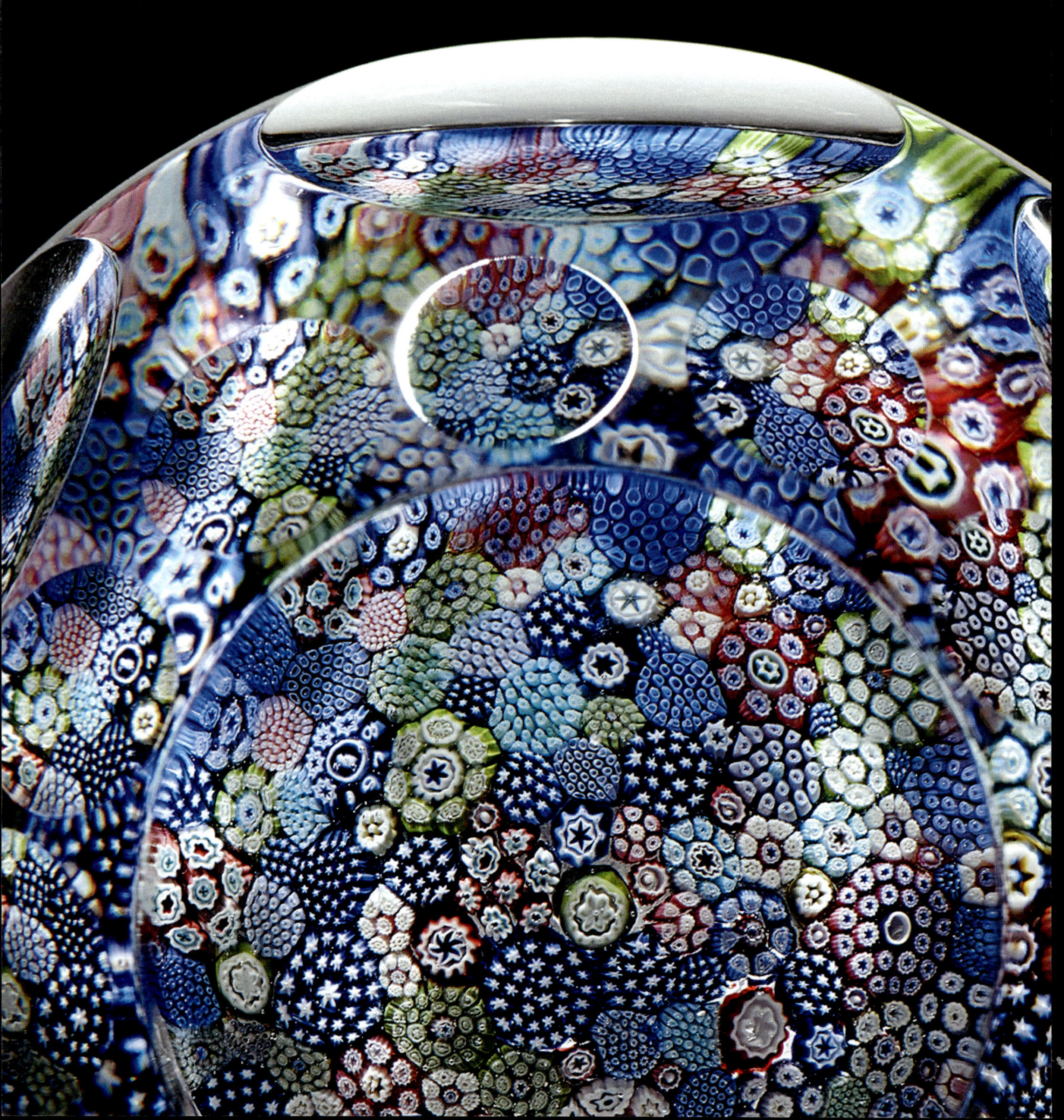

Great Britain

CLASSIC REVIVAL & TRANSITIONAL PERIOD

In Great Britain, glass companies became prevalent in the manufacturing of traditional weights. Whitefriars Glass Ltd. (1680–1980) located in Middlesex, England fabricated classical millefiori styles in the 1950s. The company sold the rights to their name in 1980 to Caithness Glass (founded 1961–2004) in Scotland. **Cat. 136** is an example of Whitefriars' style. The revival also prompted the establishment of other manufacturers in Scotland including Edinburgh, Perthshire, Selkirk, Strathearn, and Ysart.

A third-generation glass maker, Salvador Ysart (1878–1955), moved his family from Spain to Crieff, Scotland, in 1922. He worked for John Moncrieff Ltd. (est. 1865). His son Paul (1904–1991) apprenticed as a glassblower from his early teens. Independent of his family in 1963, Paul worked as a master glassblower at Caithness until opening his own glassworks in 1971 until 1975. For more than fifty years Ysart experimented with the creation of paperweights.

LEFT: Detail of Cat. 136

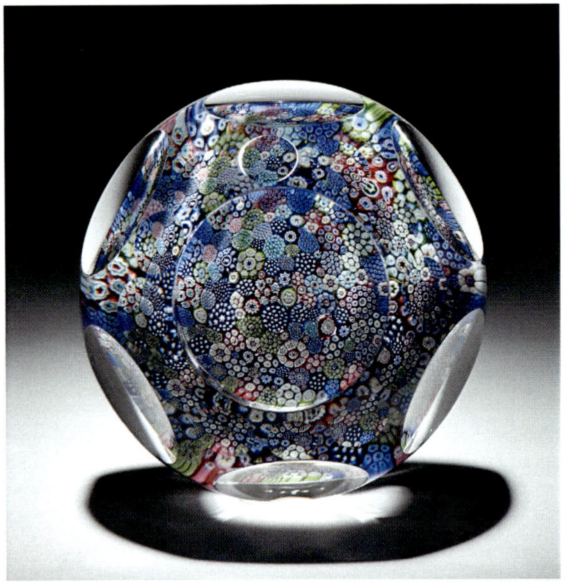

136. **Whitefriars Glass Ltd.**
English, 1680–1980
Faceted Close Pack Millefiori, 1978
Glass, D. 3 inches

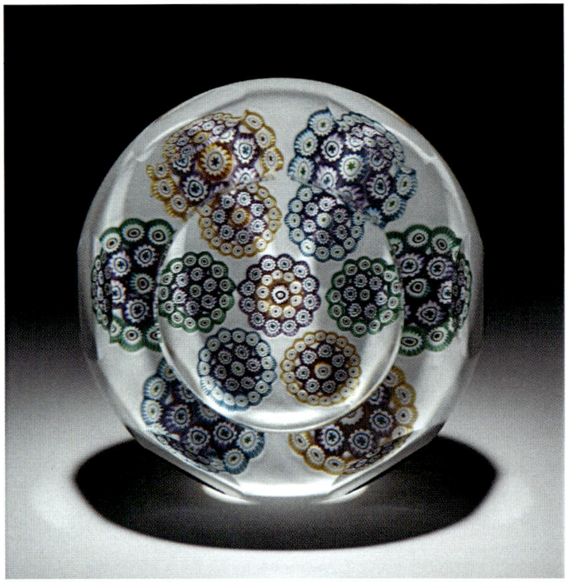

137. **Edinburgh Crystal**
Scottish, ca. 1820–2006
Faceted Millefiori Circles on White Ground, 1985–86
Glass, D. 2 ⅞ inches

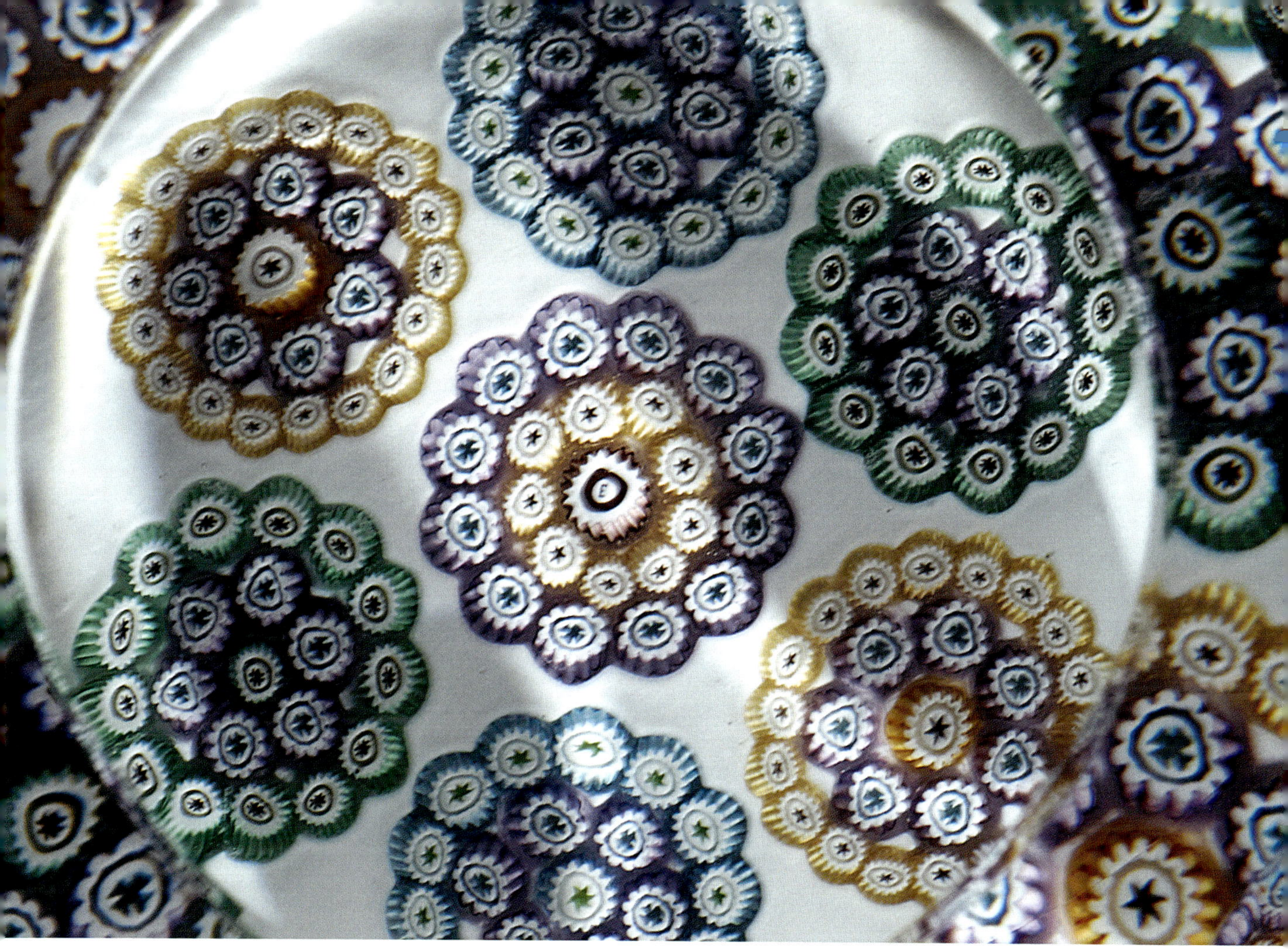

Detail of Cat. 137

This is the first purchase that was made for the Ellis Collection from Edinburgh Crystal. The weight was fabricated as part of a limited edition marked with an "E" cane produced by Caithness Glass in 1985–86 commissioned by Edinburgh.

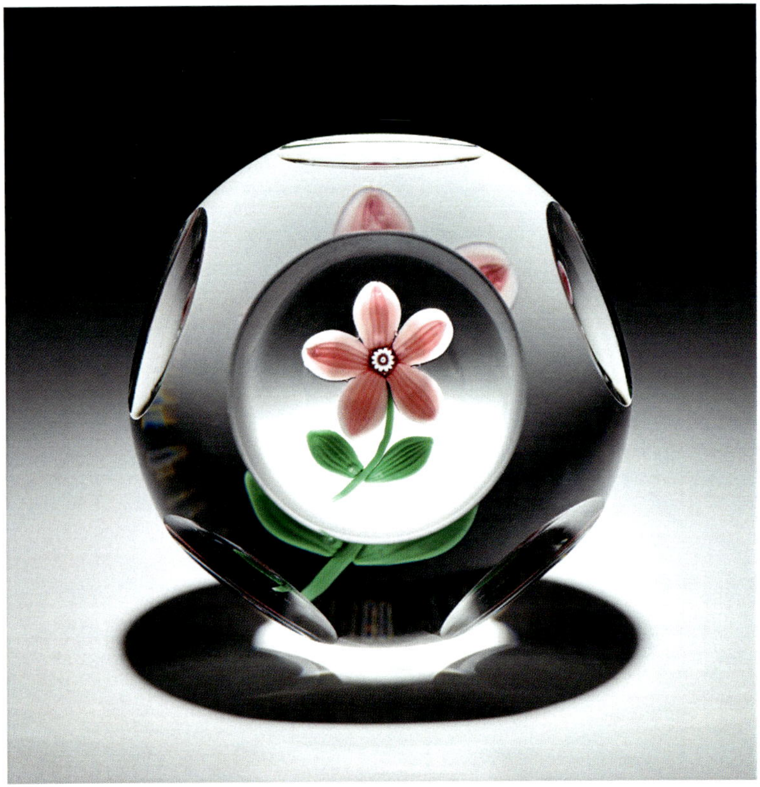

138. Selkirk
Scottish, 1977–2006
Faceted Pink Daisy, 1984
Glass, D. 2 $^{9}/_{16}$ inches

Selkirk Glass (est. 1977) produced faceted single lampwork flowers in the Classic tradition as seen in **cat. 138.**

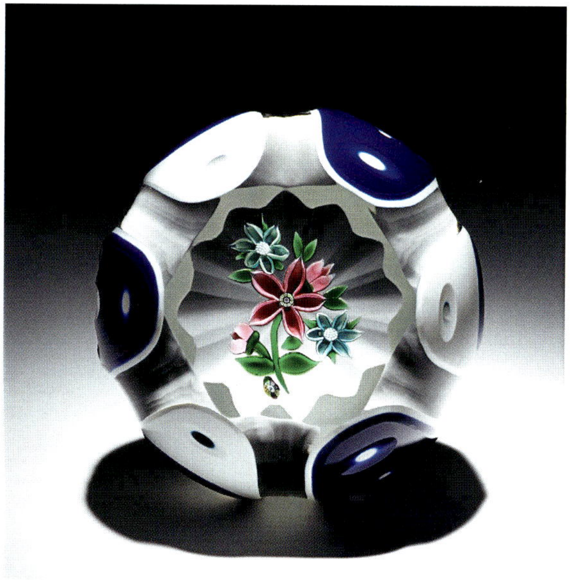

139. Perthshire, Scottish, 1968–2002
Floral Bouquet with Double Overlay
Glass, D. 2 ¾ inches

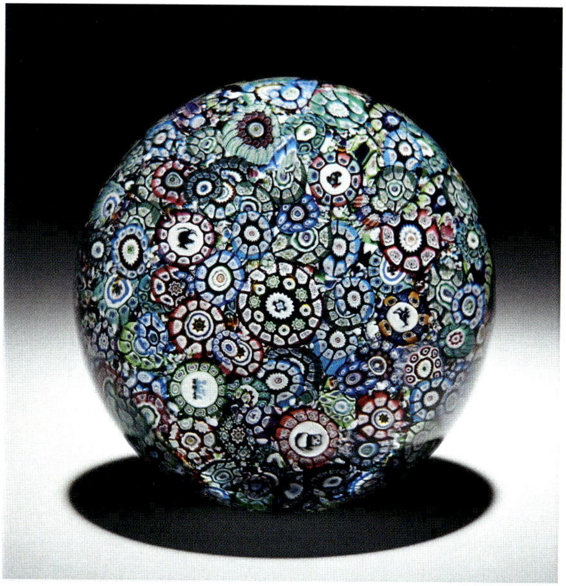

140. Perthshire, Scottish, 1968–2002
Close Pack Millefiori, 1994
Glass, D. 2 ⅝ inches

It is notable that there are a wide variety of weights by Perthshire (1968–2002) in the Ellis Collection. The company was formed when Strathearn Glass (1965–1980) workers left Strathearn because the company did not produce classical weights. Perthshire's intent was to faithfully reference many historical nineteenth-century styles while also using many new color combinations and shapes. One of the company's strengths was understanding the market, distribution, and pricing of their product. Perthshire created limited editions as well as annual pieces. Technically, they also mastered complex overlays and faceting.

141

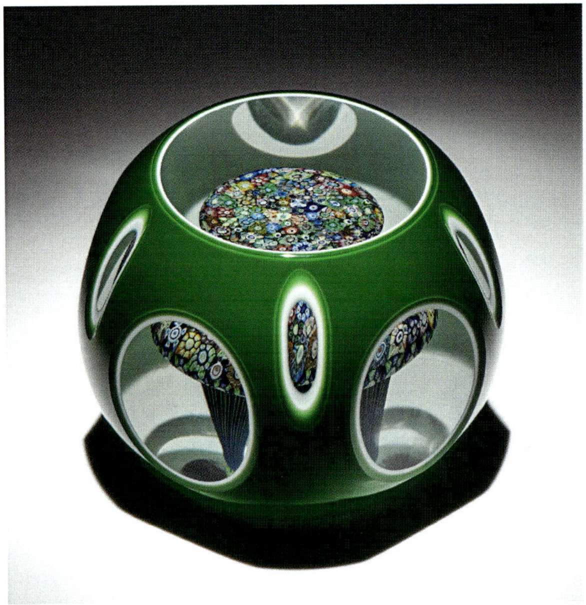

143

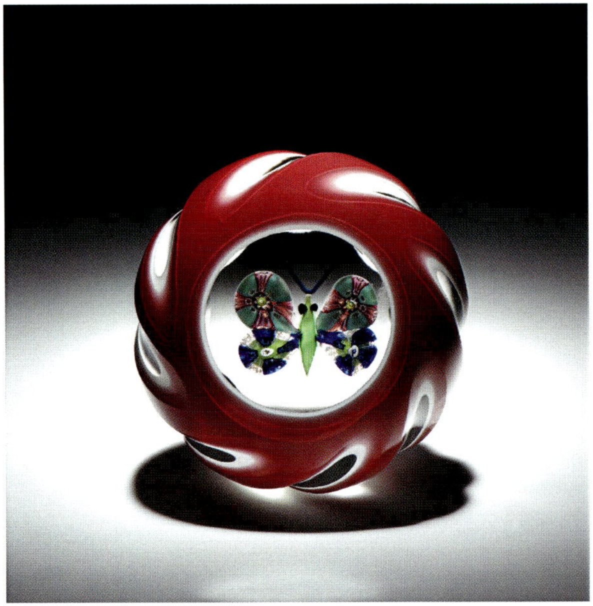

142

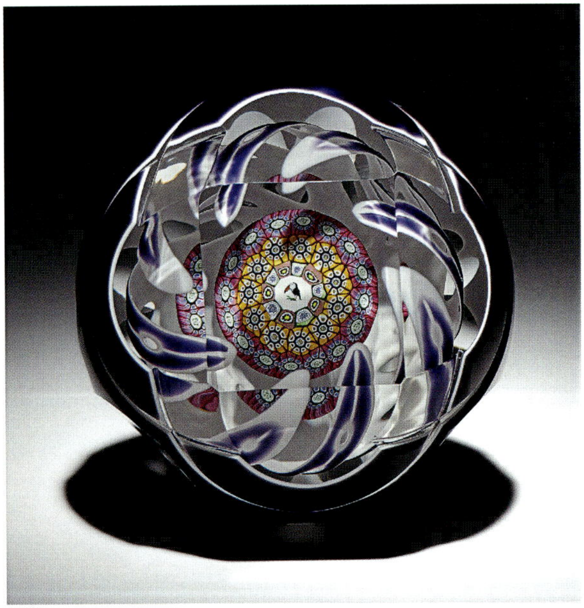

141. Perthshire, Scottish, 1968–2002
Close Pack Millefiori Mushroom with Double Overlay
Glass, D. 3 3/16 inches

142. Perthshire, Scottish, 1968–2002
Double Overlay with Millefiori Ground, 1980
Glass, D. 3 inches

143. Perthshire, Scottish, 1968–2002
Miniature Double Overlay Butterfly
Glass, D. 1 7/8 inches

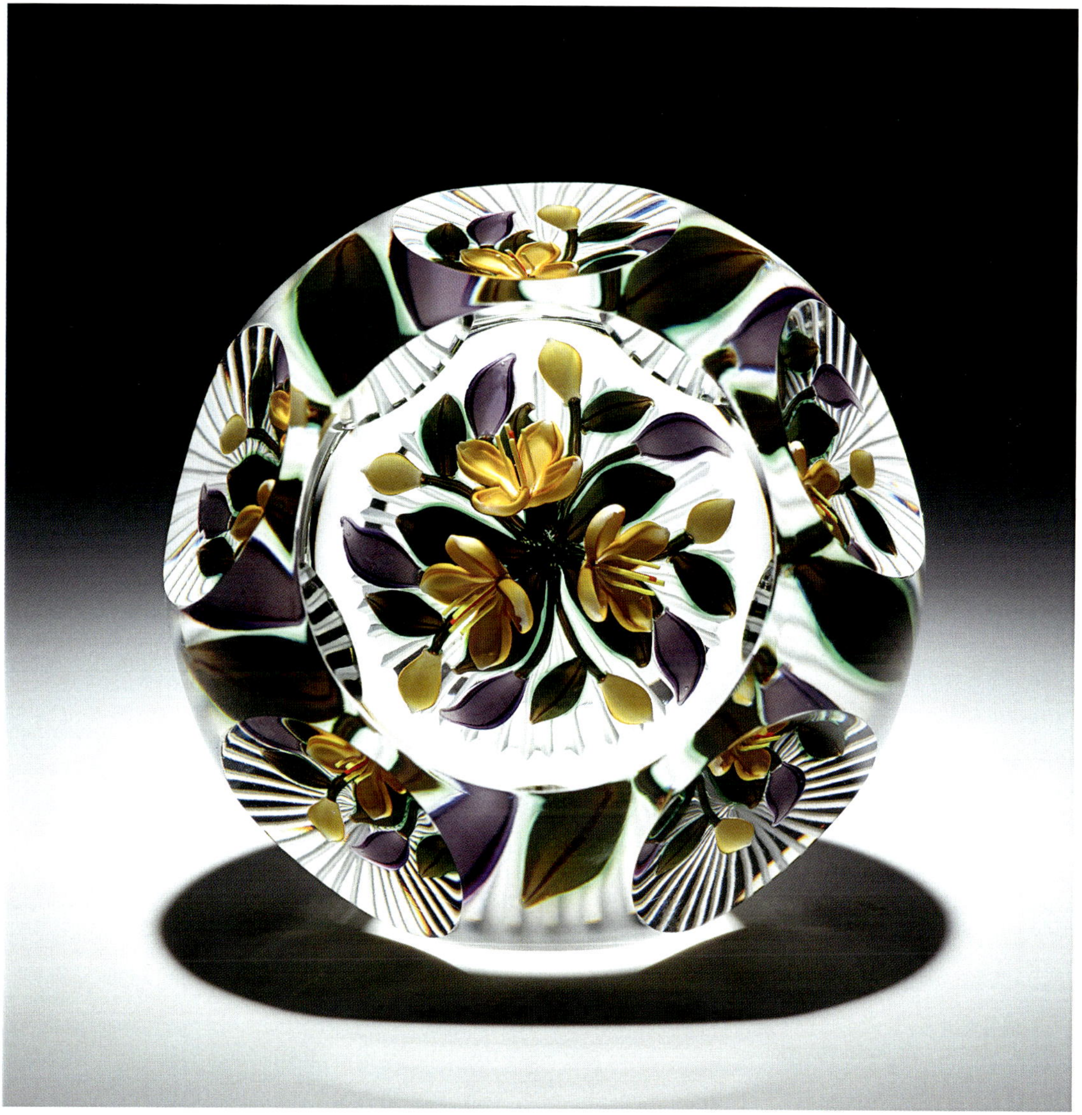

144. Perthshire, Scottish, 1968–2002
Faceted Upright Flowers. Glass, D. 2 13⁄16 inches

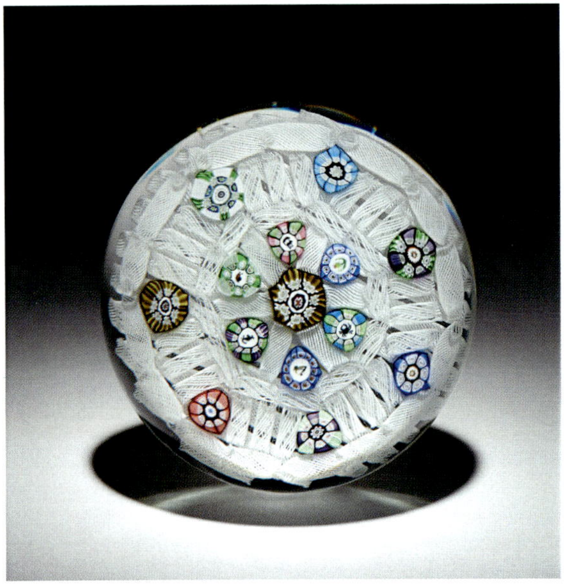

145. Perthshire, Scottish, 1968–2002
Spaced Millefiori with Silhouette Canes on White Filigree Ground, 1991
Glass, D. 3 ¼ inches

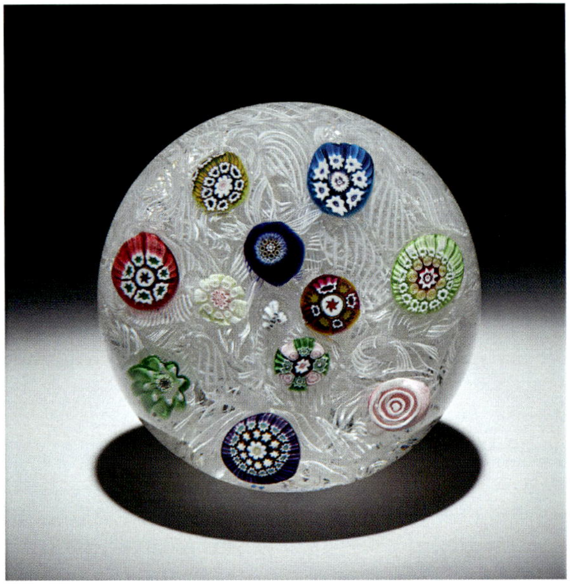

146. Perthshire, Scottish, 1968–2002
Spaced Millefiori on Upset Muslin, 1971
Glass, D. 2 ¾ inches

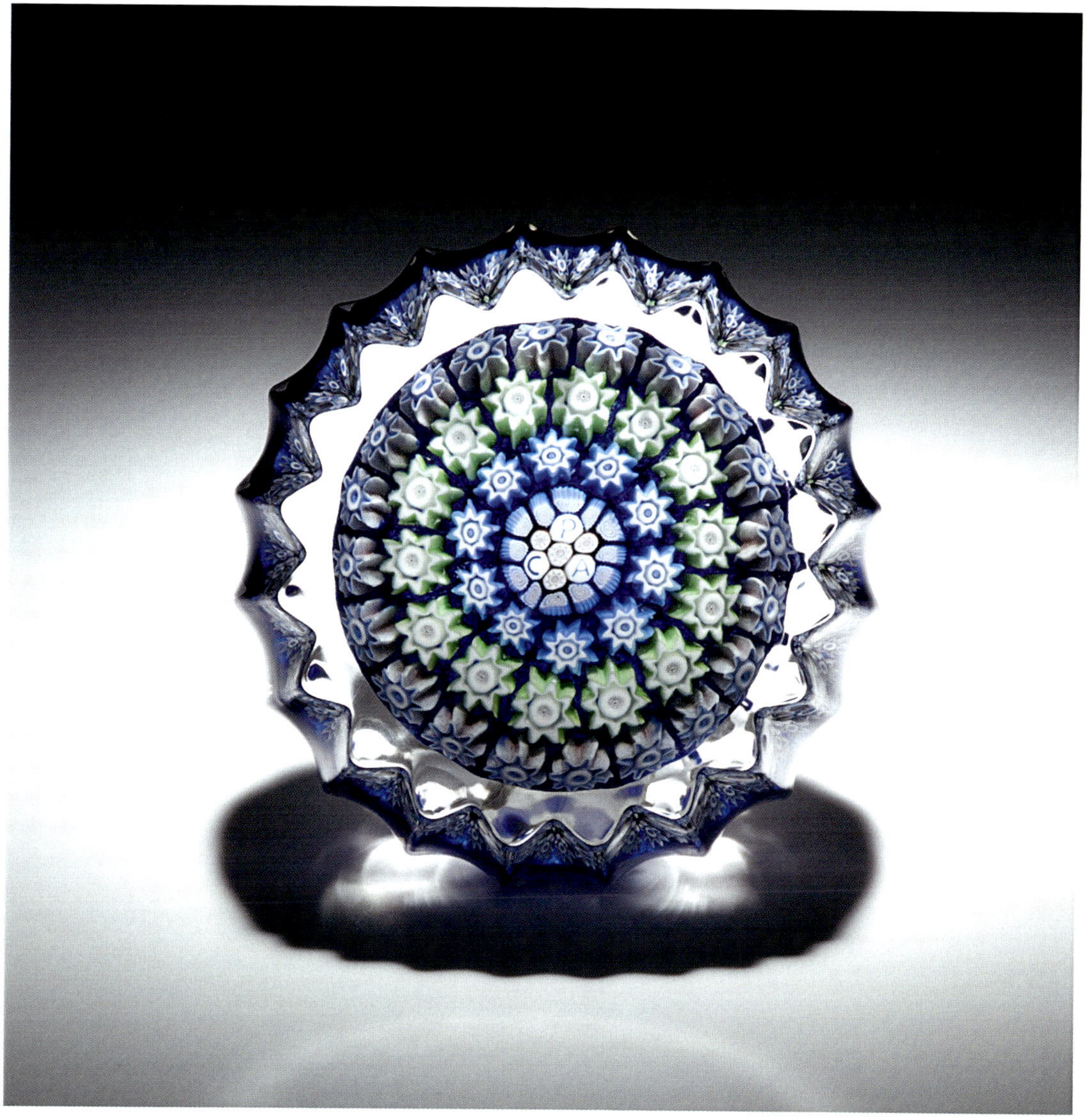

147. Perthshire, Scottish, 1968–2002
Miniature Fluted Concentric Millefiori, 1997. Glass, D. $1\frac{13}{16}$ inches, H. $1\frac{1}{2}$ inches

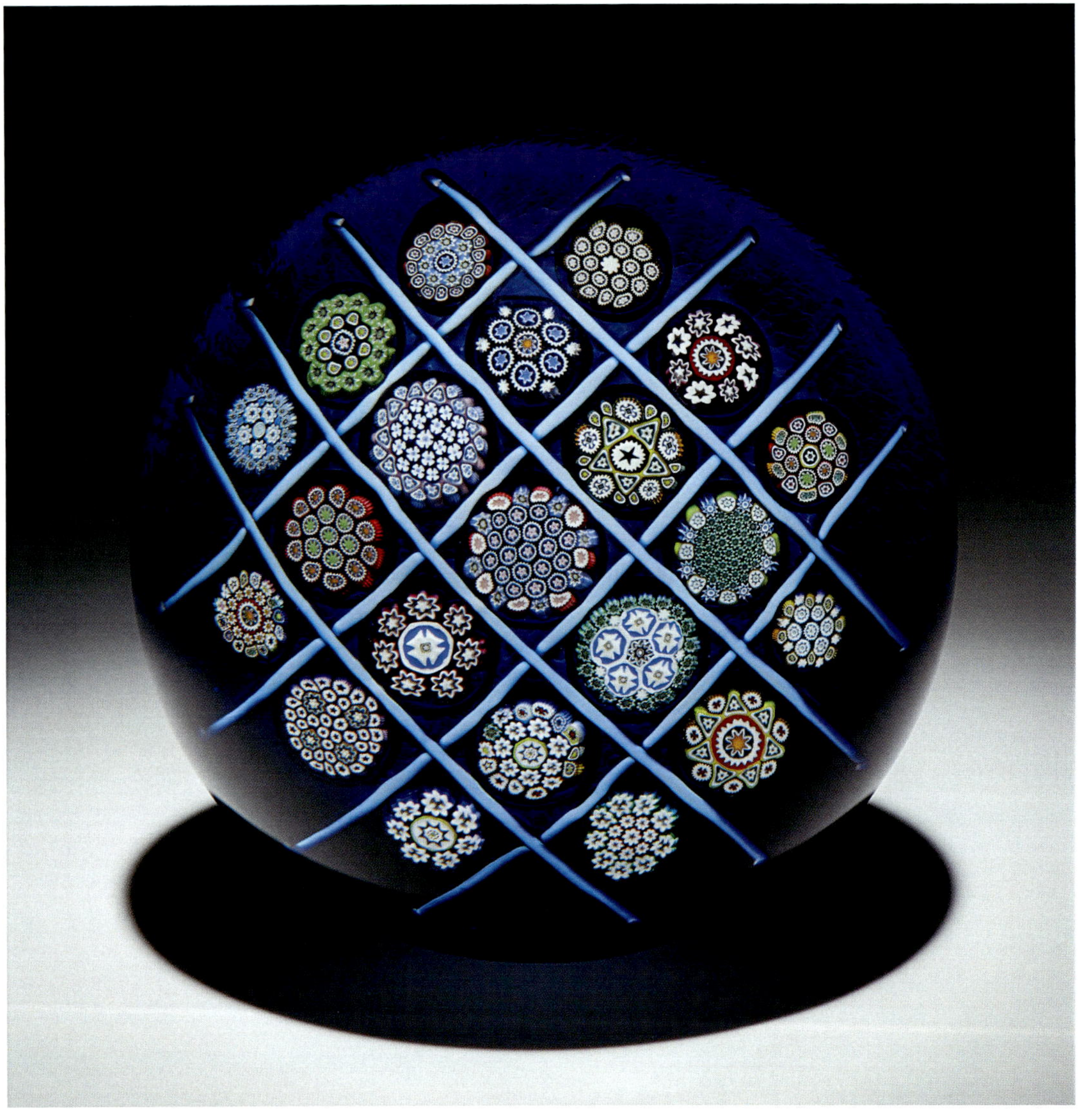

148. Peter McDougall, Scottish, born 1952
Chequerboard with Complex Canes and Sapphire Ground, 2006. Glass, D. 3 inches

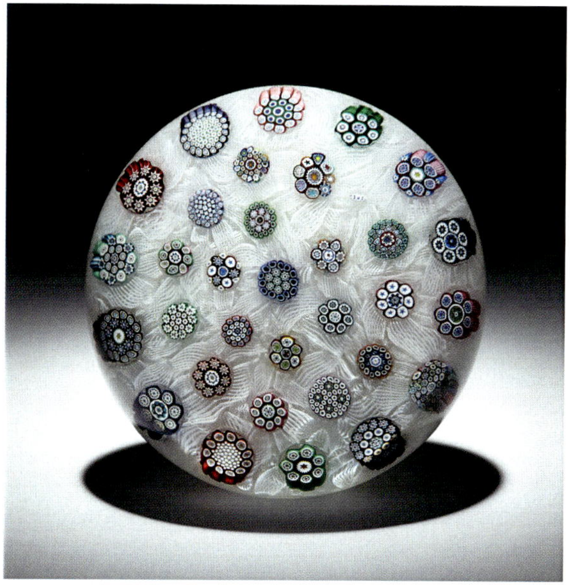

149. Peter McDougall, Scottish, born 1952
Spaced Millefiori on Upset Muslin, 2006
Glass, D. 3 ¼ inches

Peter McDougall was one of the workers that left Strathearn Glass when Perthshire formed. He was the manager of the company through 2002. Currently, McDougall's glass studio, PMcD Glass Studio Ltd. is in Crieff, Scotland. **Cats. 148** and **149** meticulously echo the approach of the Classic Period.

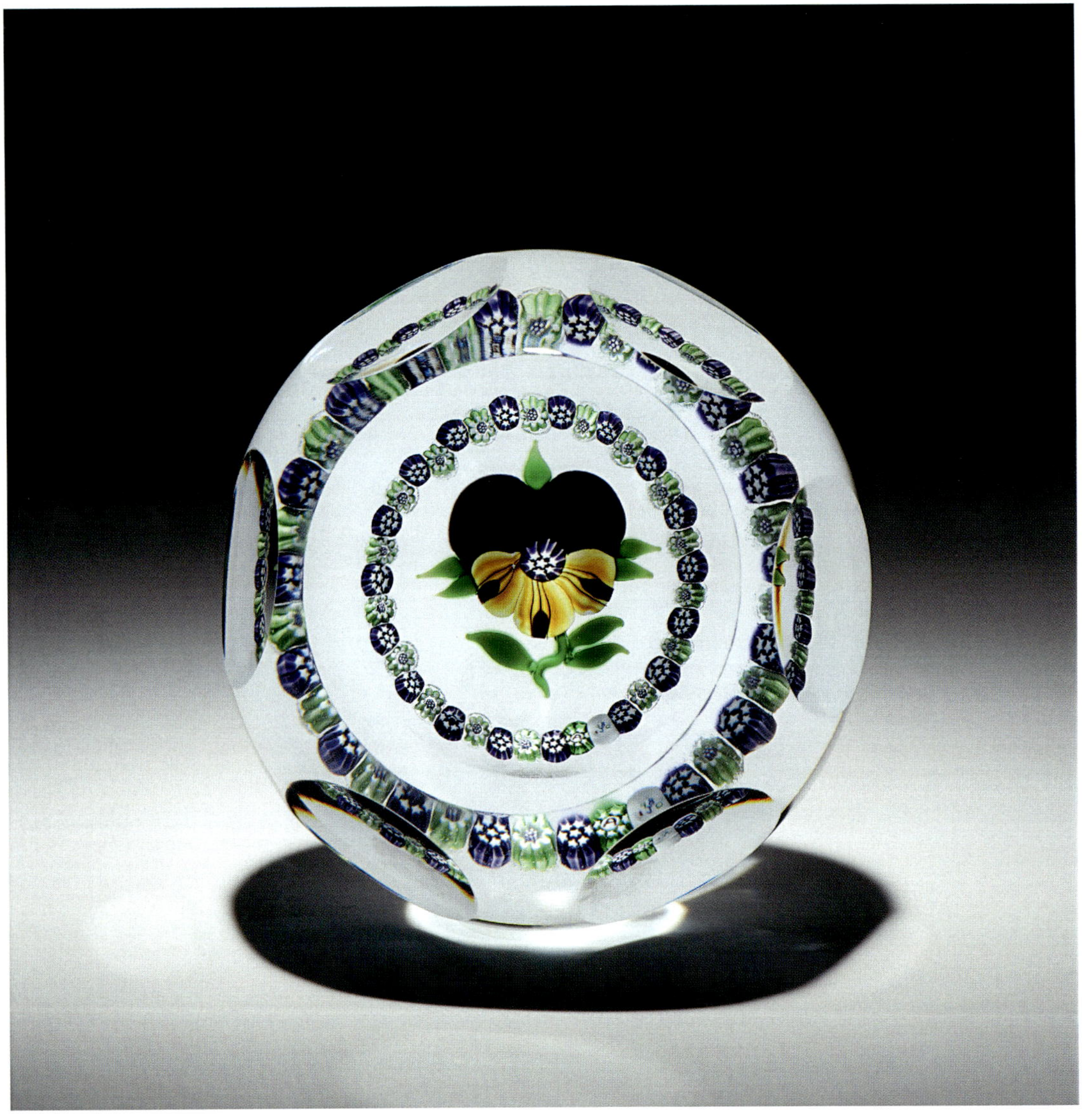

150. John Deacons, Scottish, b. 1950
Faceted Pansy with Garland, 1980. Glass, D. 2 11⁄16 inches

John Deacons started his glassmaking career at Strathearn Glass leaving to work at Perthshire until 1978 when he started Jay Glass. In 1983 he changed the company to John Deacons. **Cats. 150, 151,** and **152** exhibit his technical expertise and knowledge of historical weights.

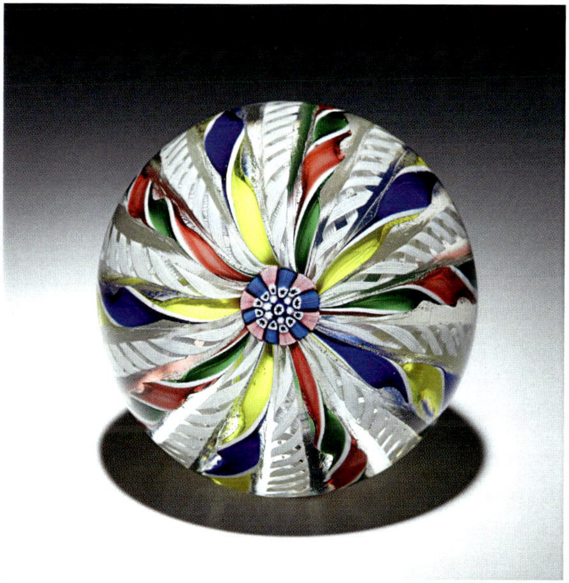

151. John Deacons, Scottish, b. 1950
Multi-Colored Crown, 1993
Glass, D. 2 ½ inches

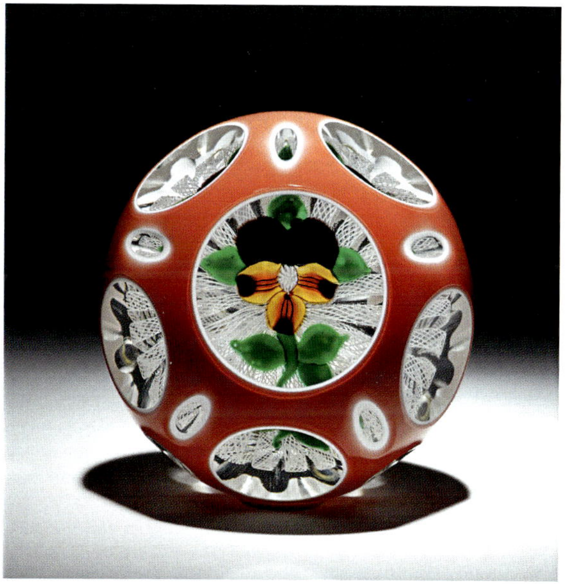

152. John Deacons, Scottish, b. 1950
Double Overlay Pansy, 2000
Glass, D. 3 3⁄16 inches

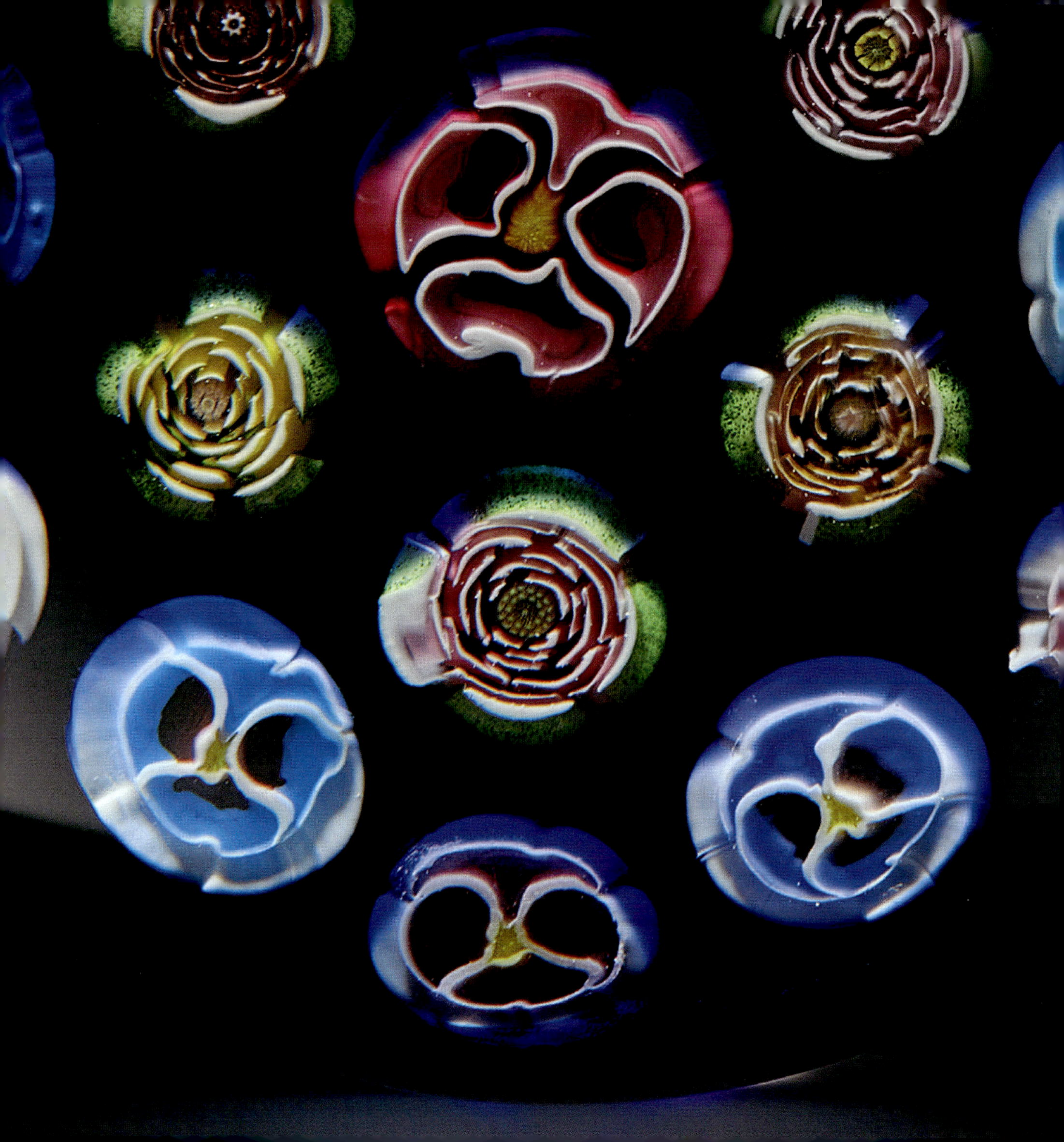

United States

CLASSIC REVIVAL & TRANSITIONAL PERIOD

In the United States new technology radically changed the production of weights. Charles Kaziun, Jr. from Brockton, Massachusetts, was briefly employed as a technical glassblower. Inquisitive and independent, he was determined to learn techniques from experienced glass workers and become a successful weight maker independent of a manufacturer. He spent his free time producing objects in the classic French style in a small studio. He made millefiori and lampwork weights using a furnace he designed, becoming one of the first "studio artists" in the United States.

A few other glass artists were successful in working on their own, using equipment they personally fabricated in makeshift studios. In 1962, a seminal event at the Toledo Museum of Art in Toledo, Ohio, quickly changed the future of the art form. Two groundbreaking workshops were led by artist and faculty member of the University of Wisconsin, Harvey K. Littleton and Ohio glass scientist Dominick Labino. They introduced artists to the material of

LEFT: Detail of Cat. 168

glass as a medium for artistic expression. Littleton and Labino presented their development of a small, portable furnace and glass that had a melting point at a lower temperature than industrial formulas. These discoveries allowed artists to work outside of the industry in glass and glassblowing for the first time. These workshops were the spark that ignited the Studio Glass movement, which emphasized the artist as designer and maker, with a focus on making one-of-a-kind objects.

153

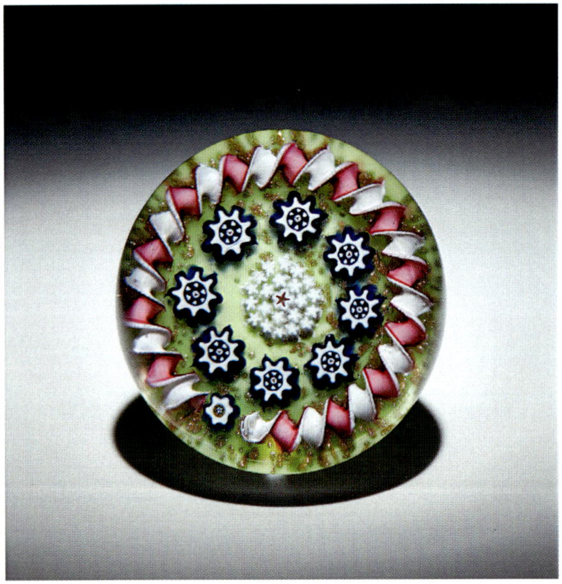

154

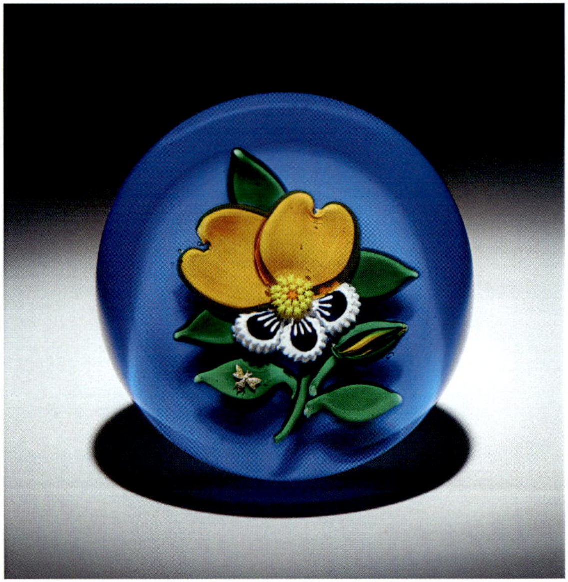

155

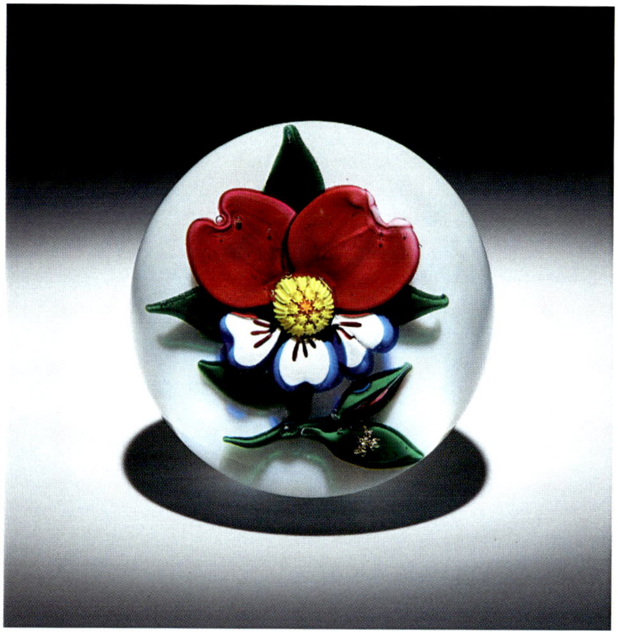

153. Charles Kaziun, Jr.
American, 1919–92
Miniature Concentric Millefiori with Torsade on Green Ground
Glass, D. 2 inches

154. Charles Kaziun, Jr.
American, 1919–92
Orange Pansy with Bee
Glass, D. 2 3/16 inches

155. Charles Kaziun, Jr.
American, 1919–92
Pansy with Bee
Glass, D. 2 1/16 inches

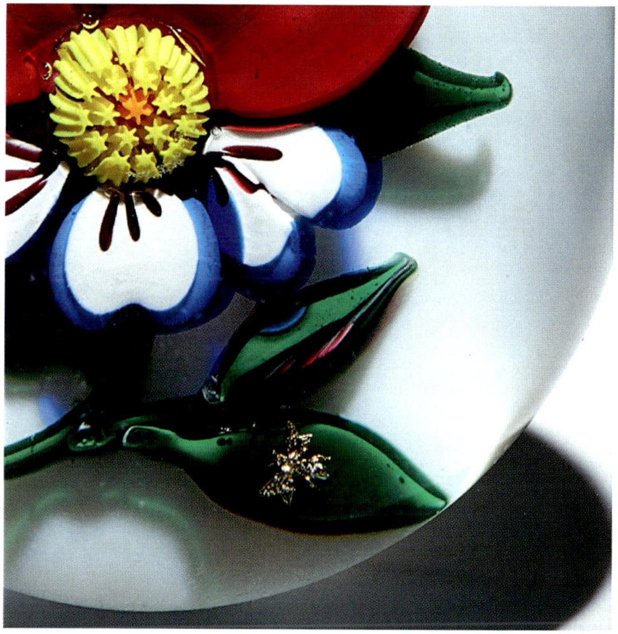

Detail of Cat. 155

Kaziun's works included in the collection feature a few distinctive elements. **Cat. 153** contains a "K" signature cane. **Cats. 153, 154,** and **155** each contain a tiny 14-karat gold foil butterfly or bumblebee, a characteristic signature of the artist.

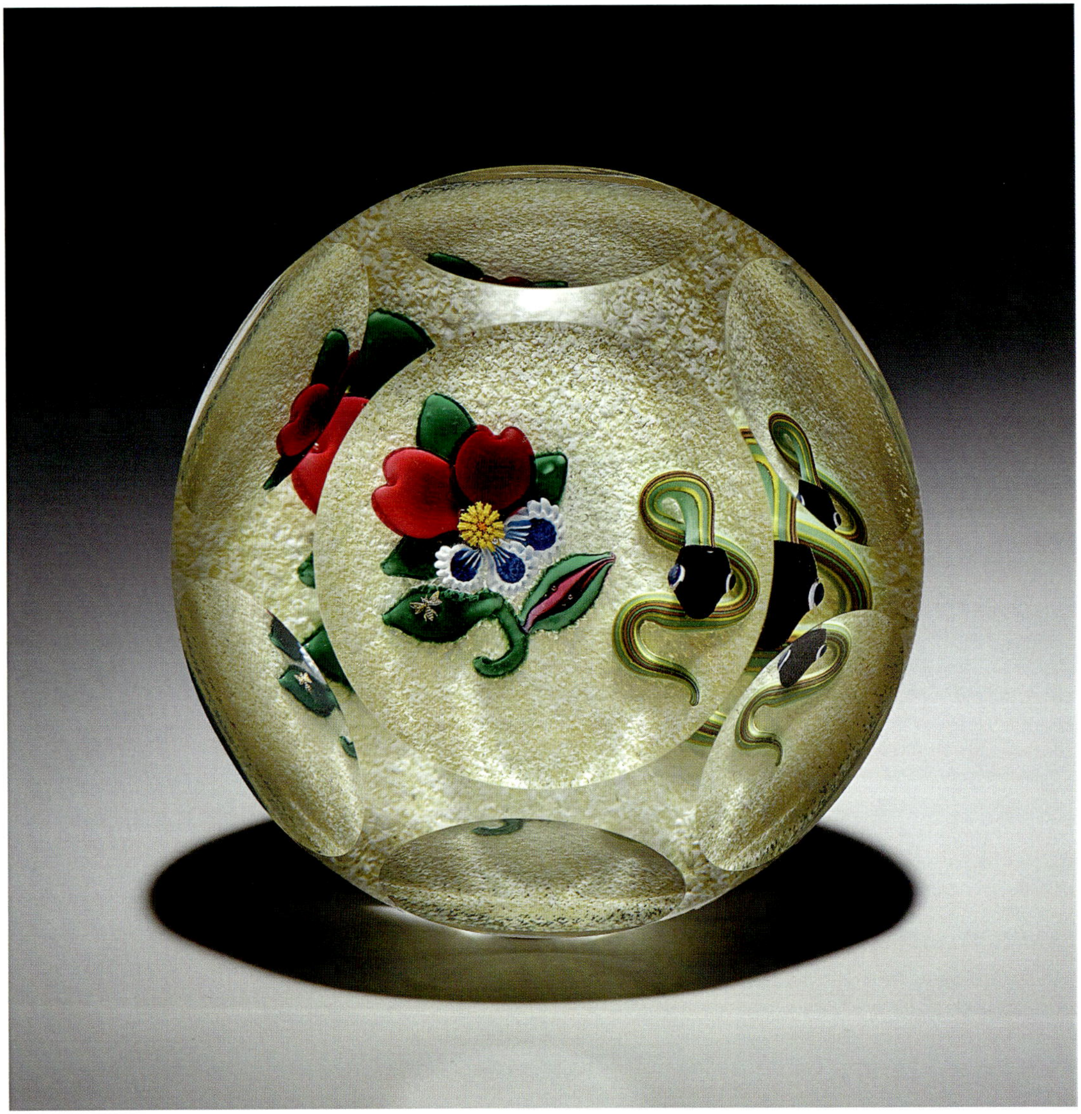

156. **Charles Kaziun, Jr.,** American, 1919–92
Faceted Snake and Pansy. Glass, D. 2 ½ inches

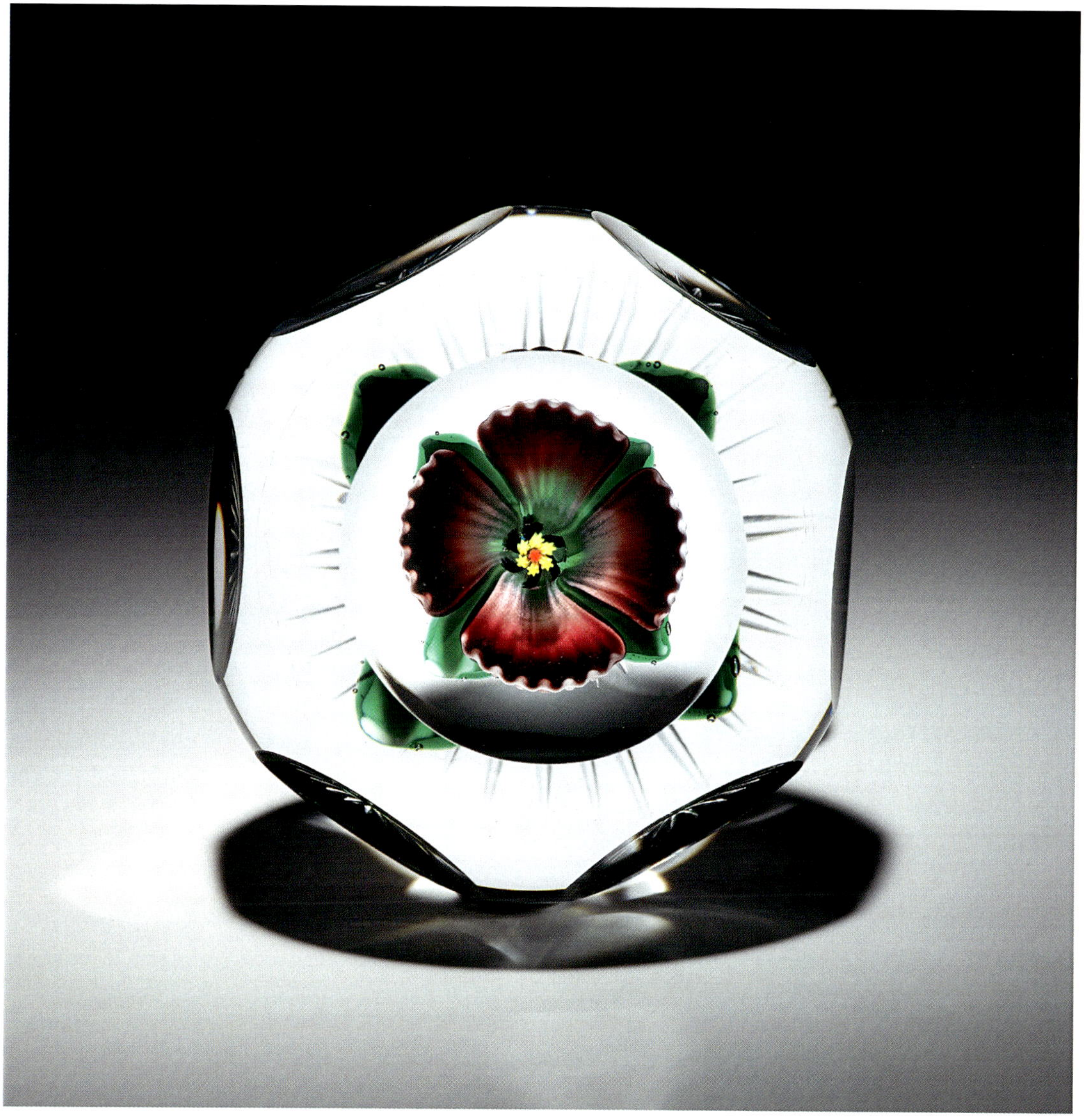

157. **Charles Kaziun, Jr.**, American, 1919–92
Faceted Pleated Petal Dogwood. Glass, D. 2 $\frac{7}{16}$ inches

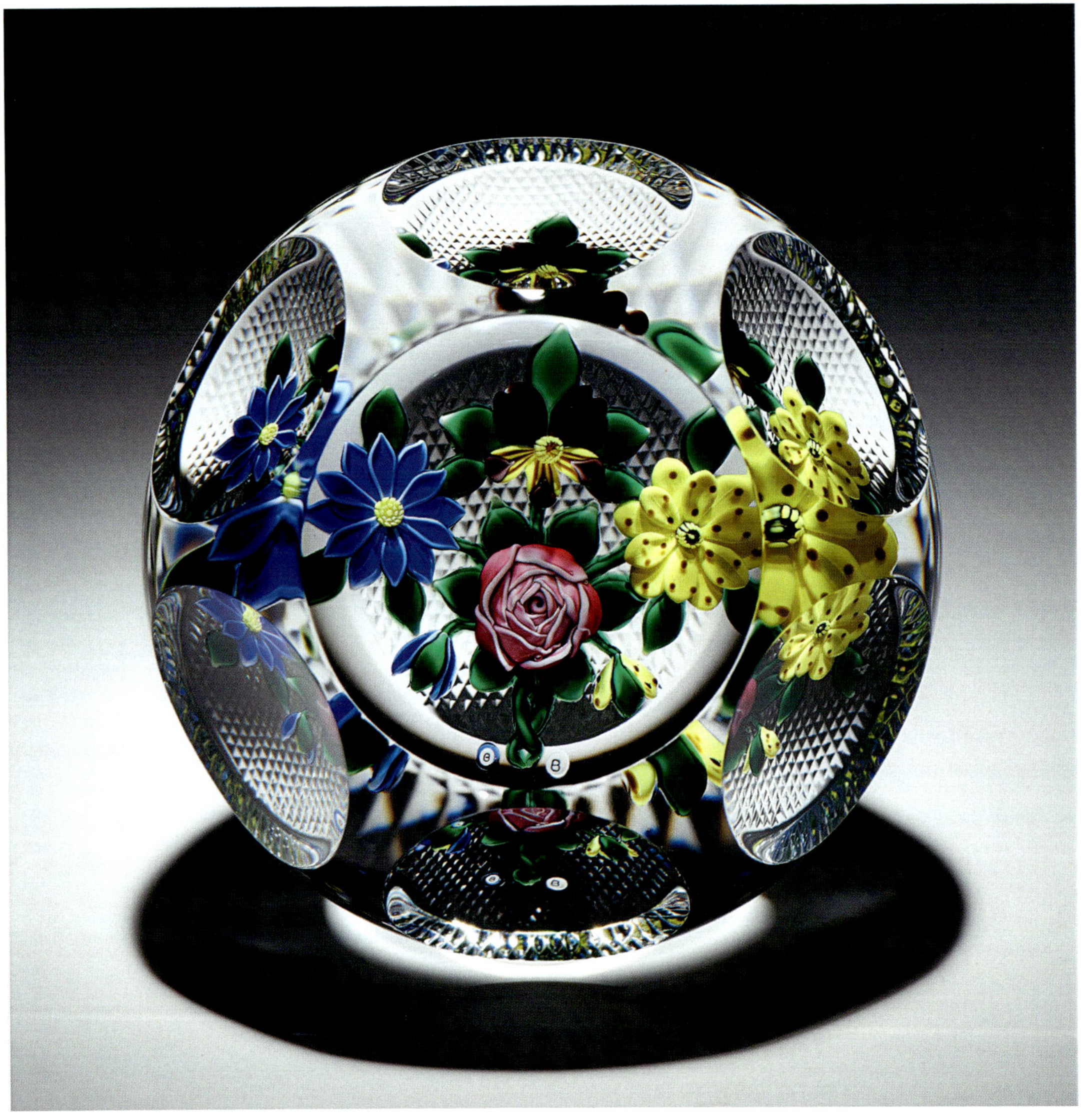

158. Bob Banford, American, b. 1952; **Ray Banford,** American, 1918–2003
Faceted Bouquet. Glass, D. 3 ⅛ inches

Ray Banford of Camden, New Jersey, and his son Bob produced weights in the mid 1970s. The Classic Period was their inspiration. Their skill and interest in intense colors and coldwork is evidenced in their weights. They each used a distinctive initial cane. Ray's is a black "B" in a white field and Bob's cane is a red "B" in a white field with a cobalt blue ring. The artists worked collaboratively on **cat. 158** so it contains both of their signature canes.

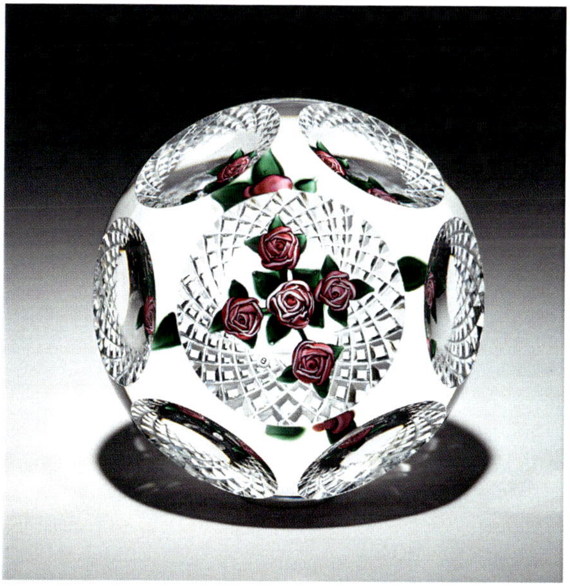

159. Ray Banford, American, 1918–2003
Faceted Cabbage Rose Bouquet
Glass, D. 2 ⅞ inches

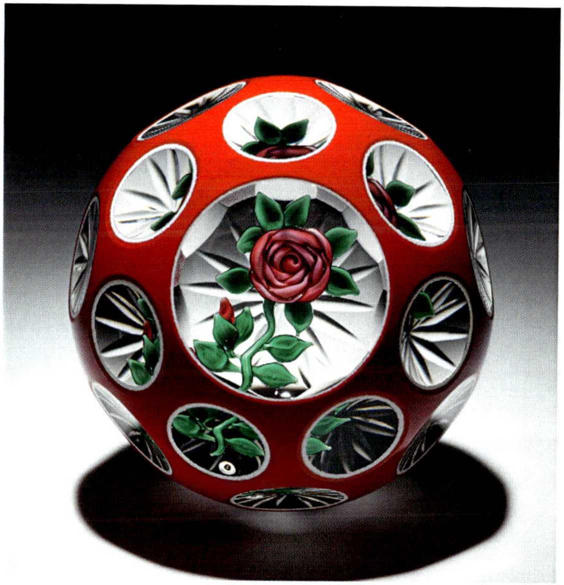

160. Ray Banford, American, 1918–2003
Magnum Red Rose with Overlay
Glass, D. 3 ⅞ inches

161

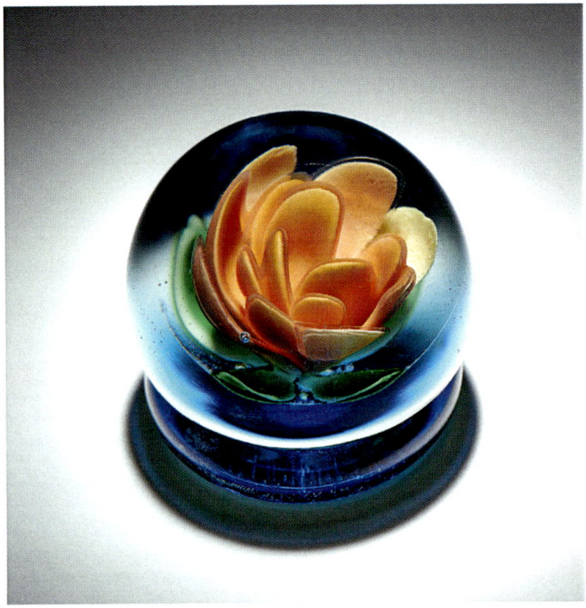

161. Ronald Hansen
American, 1913–87
Miniature Peach Crimp Rose
Glass, D. 1 ⅞ inches, H. 1 ¾

162. Ronald Hansen
American, 1913–87
Blue and White Flower
Glass, D. 2 ¼ inches

162

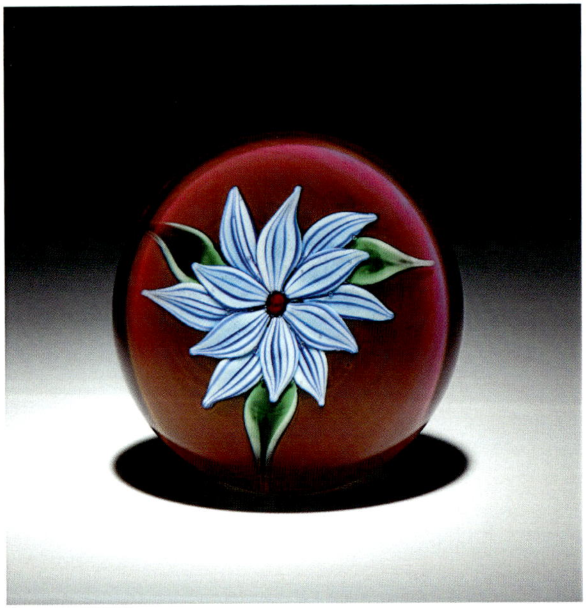

Ronald Hansen began using a torch to fabricate weights in 1962. He established a shop in Mackinaw City, Michigan. Examples of Hansen's weights are a crimp rose **cat. 161** and a singular flower in **cat. 162.**

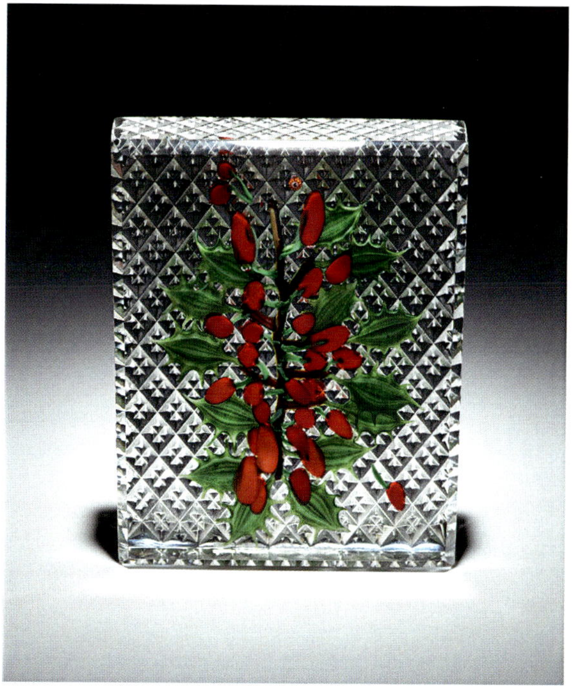

163. Nontas Constantine Kontes
American, 1921–2020
Cut Plaque with Bouquet
Glass, H. 3 13/16, W. 3, L. 7/8 inches

In 1936 Nontas Constantine Kontes worked in a small glass factory with his brother Jim in New Jearsey. In 1942, they established the Kontes Glass Company specializing in blowing scientific glass (the company was sold in 1982). In 1975, Jim and Nontas started making paperweights as a hobby. At that time they set up a small personal studio in a corner of their factory. They noted that they were inspired by the work of their friend Charles Kaziun, Jr., working in the Classic style. This plaque has multiple sharp diamond cuts which animate the encased floral motif.

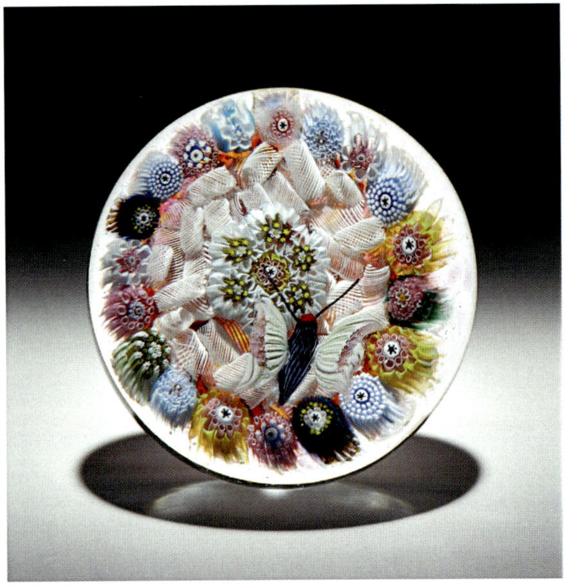

164. **Del Tarsitano**
Italian-American, 1921–90
Butterfly on Latticino and Millefiori Ground
Glass, D. 2 ¾ inches

Adelmo Joseph "Del" Tarsitano grew up in Queens, New York. In the late 1960s he became interested in antiques, becoming a paperweight dealer in 1971. He also studied glassblowing with an interest in making weights. His daughter, Debbie, shared his interest. In 1976, Del became a full-time weight maker.

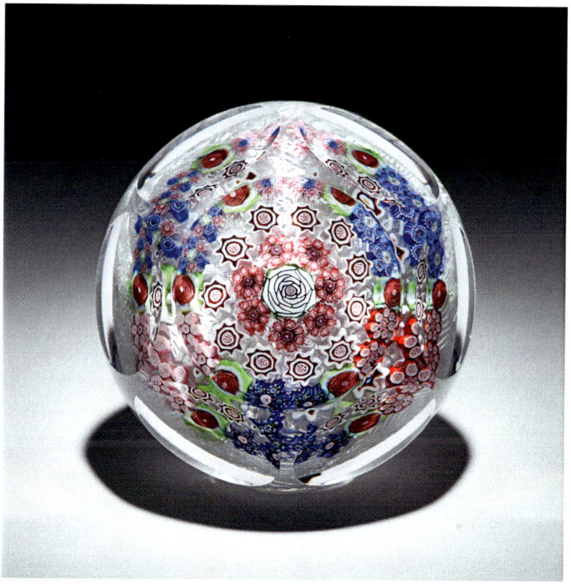

165. Cape Cod Glass Works
American, 1976–2000
Faceted Concentric Millefiori with Central Rose, 1993
Glass, D. 2 5/8 inches

Cape Cod Glass Works was founded by William Burchfield. He started working for Pairpoint Glass Company in 1970 and began making weights in 1972. In 1976, he left Pairpoint to start Cape Cod Glass Works. He created small objects including Classic style weights. Characteristic of his weights was a millefiori rose fashioned after the nineteenth-century signature Clichy rose as exhibited in the central cane of **cat. 165.**

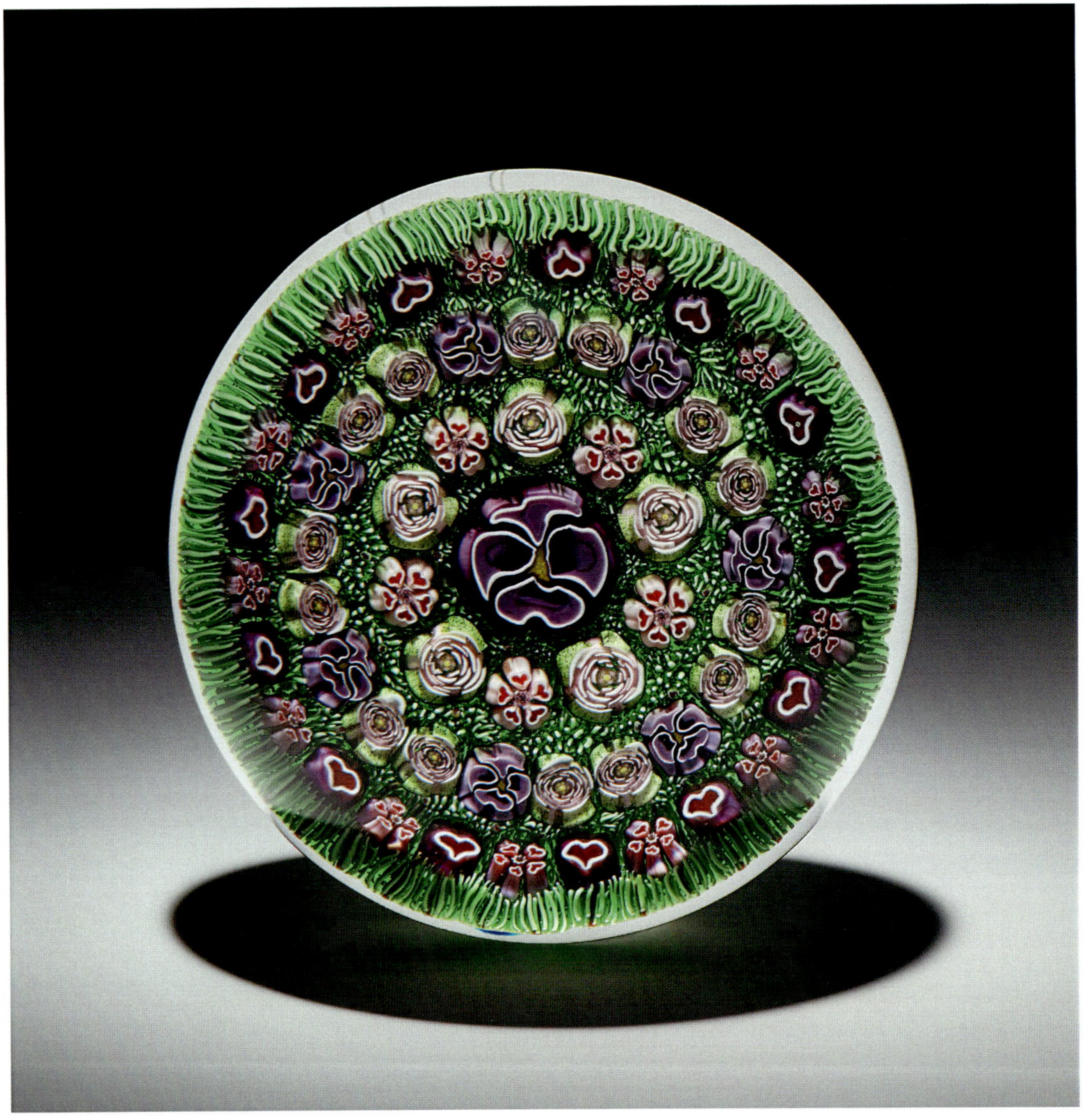

166. Parabelle Glass, American, 1981–98
Concentric Millefiori with Central Pansy on Moss Ground, 1998
Glass, D. 3 ⅛ inches

Working in the style of Classic Revival, Parabelle Glass was founded by Gary Scrutton in 1981. The studio located in Portland, Oregon, produced distinctive weights until 1998. Influenced by Clichy's use of its signature Clichy rose, Parabelle also created a signature flower, a pansy millefiori cane that was incorporated in a wide variety of styles and colors. The Ellis Collection has many works by Parabelle Glass.

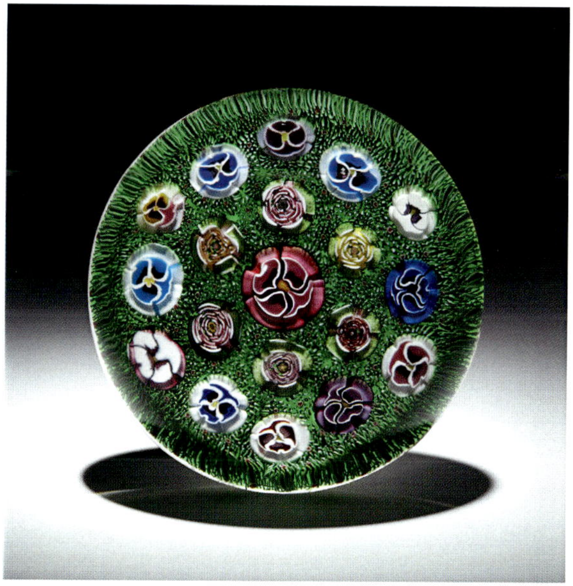

167. Parabelle Glass, American, 1981–98
Pansy on Moss Ground, 1998
Glass, D. 3 ⅛ inches

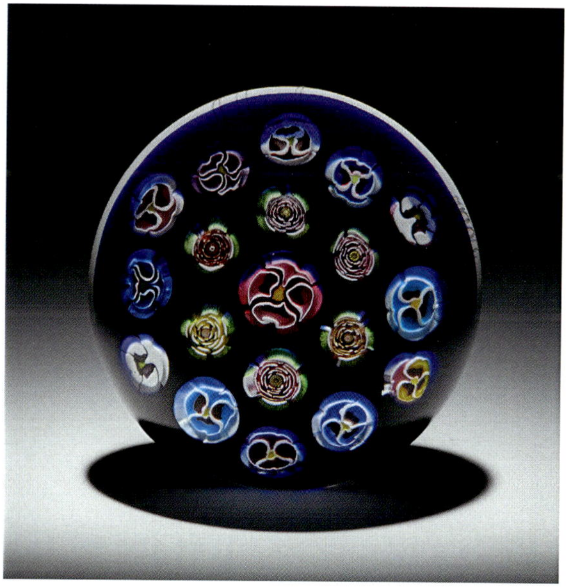

168. Parabelle Glass, American, 1981–98
Pansy on Cobalt Ground, 1998
Glass, D. 3 inches

169

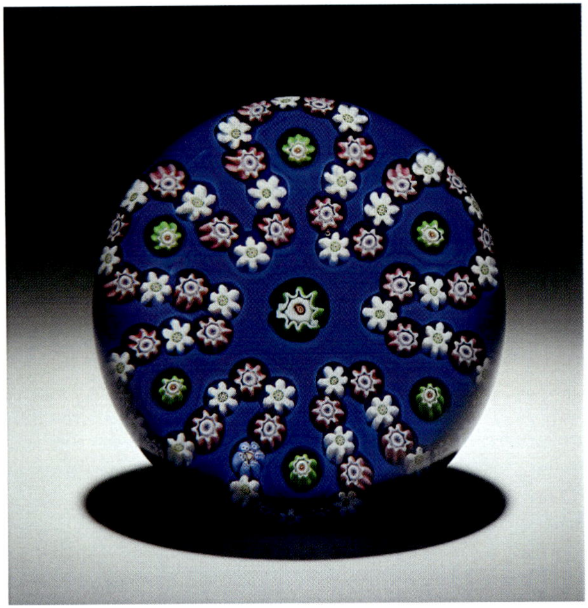

171

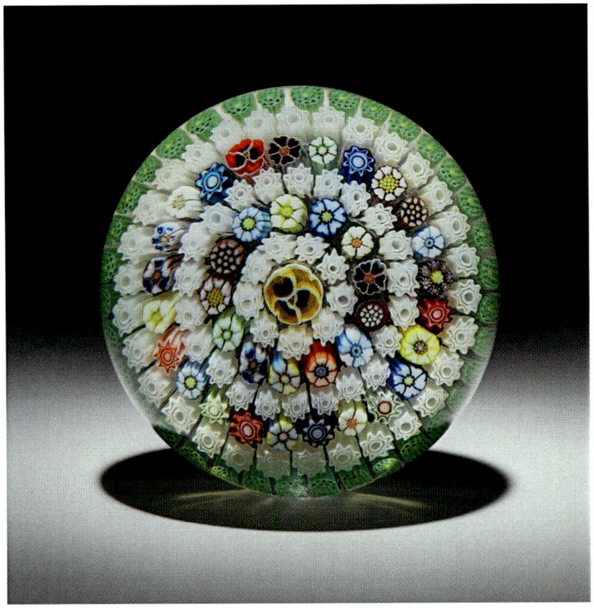

170

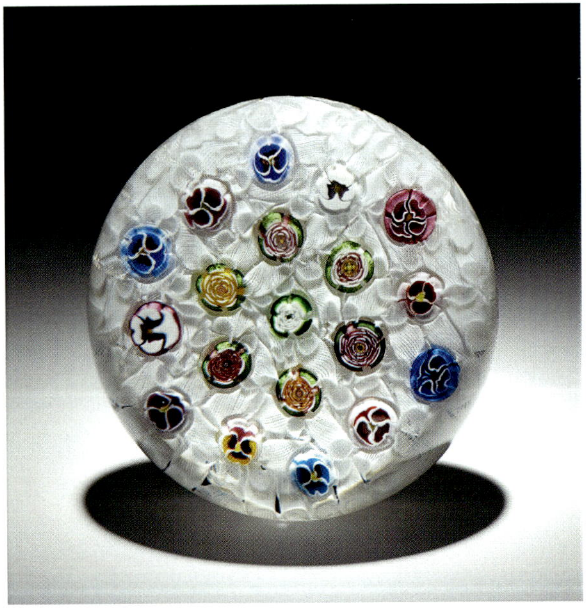

172

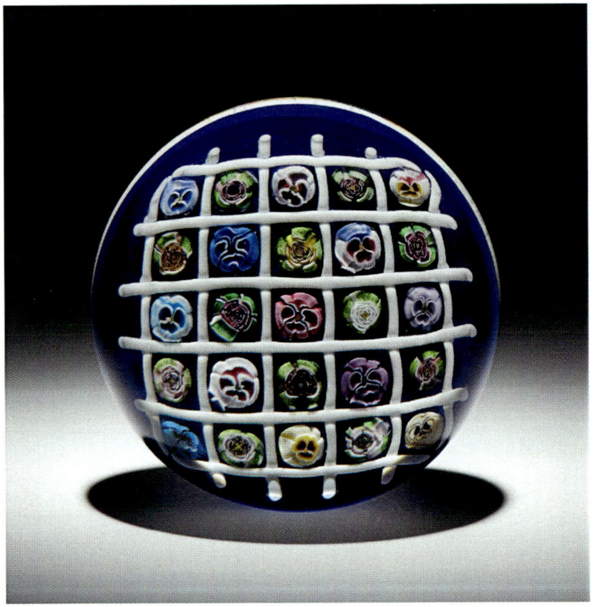

173

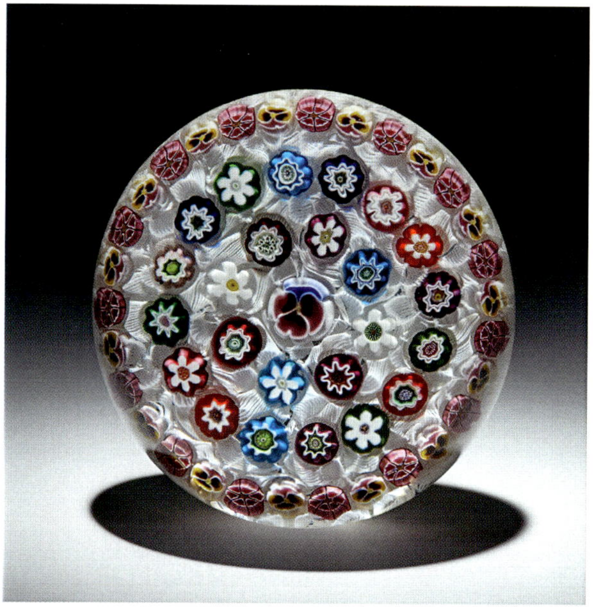

174

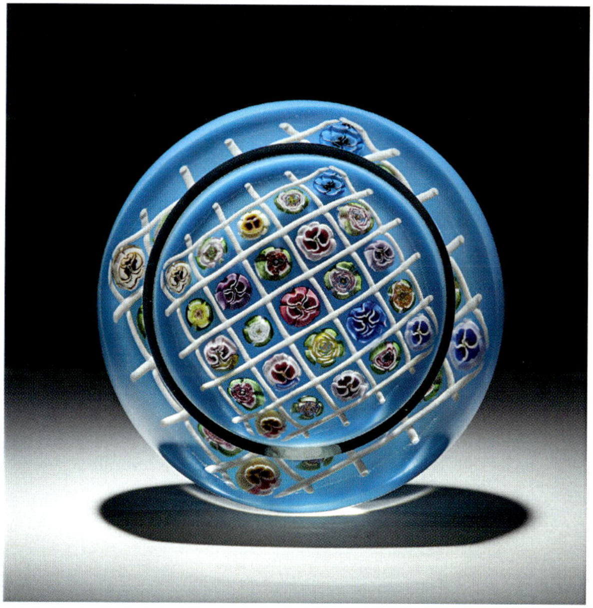

169. Parabelle Glass,
American, 1981–98
Millefiori Garland on Blue Ground, 1990
Glass, D. 2 ⅞ inches

170. Parabelle Glass,
American, 1981–98
Spaced Millefiori with Pansy and Rose Silhouette Canes on Upset Muslin, 1998
Glass, D. 3 ⅛ inches

171. Parabelle Glass,
American, 1981–98
Concentric Millefiori, 1985
Glass, D. 2 $^{15}/_{16}$ inches

172. Parabelle Glass,
American, 1981–98
Pansy and Rose Quadrille on Cobalt Ground, 1998
Glass, D. 3 ⅜ inches

173. Parabelle Glass,
American, 1981–98
Open Concentric Millefiori on Upset Muslin, 1997
Glass, D. 3 ¼ inches

174. Parabelle Glass,
American, 1981–98
Chequer on Blue Ground, 1998
Glass, D. 3 $^{5}/_{16}$ inches

175

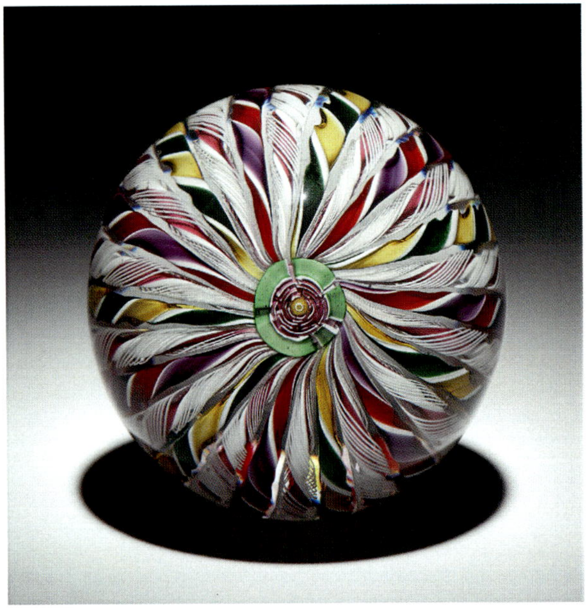

177

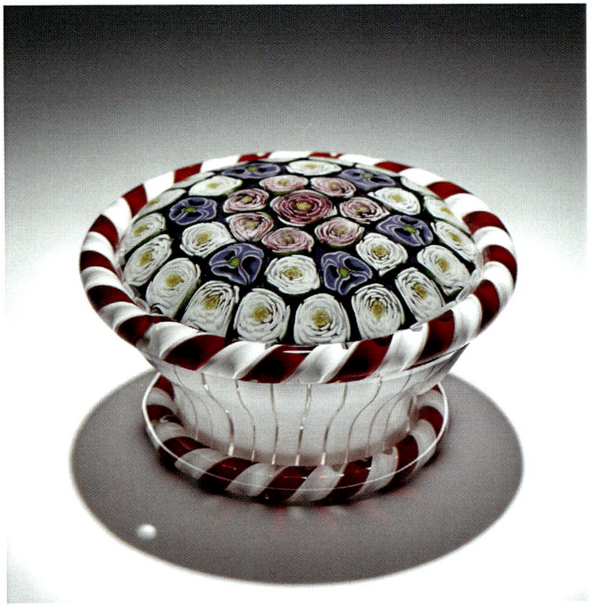

176

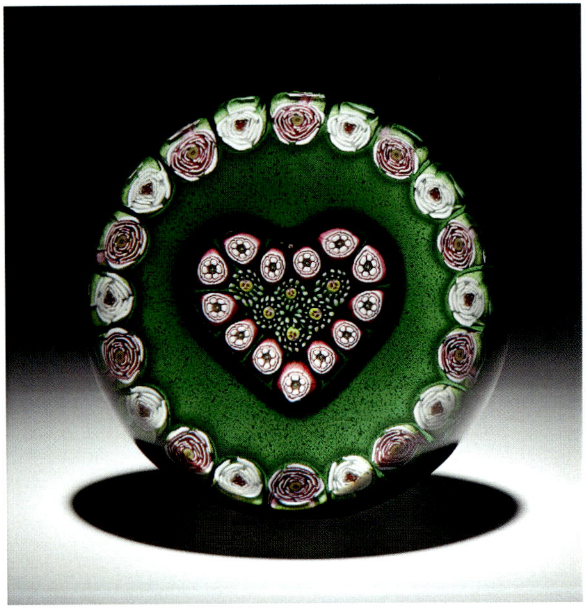

175. Parabelle Glass, American, 1981–98
Crown with Central Rose
Glass, D. 2 13/16, H. 1 11/16 inches

176. Parabelle Glass, American, 1981–98
Pink and Green Millefiori Heart with Garland of Roses, 1996
Glass, D. 3 3/8 inches

177. Parabelle Glass, American, 1981–98
Concentric Millefiori Piedouche, 1998
Glass, D. 2 15/16 inches

RIGHT: **Top view of Cat. 177**

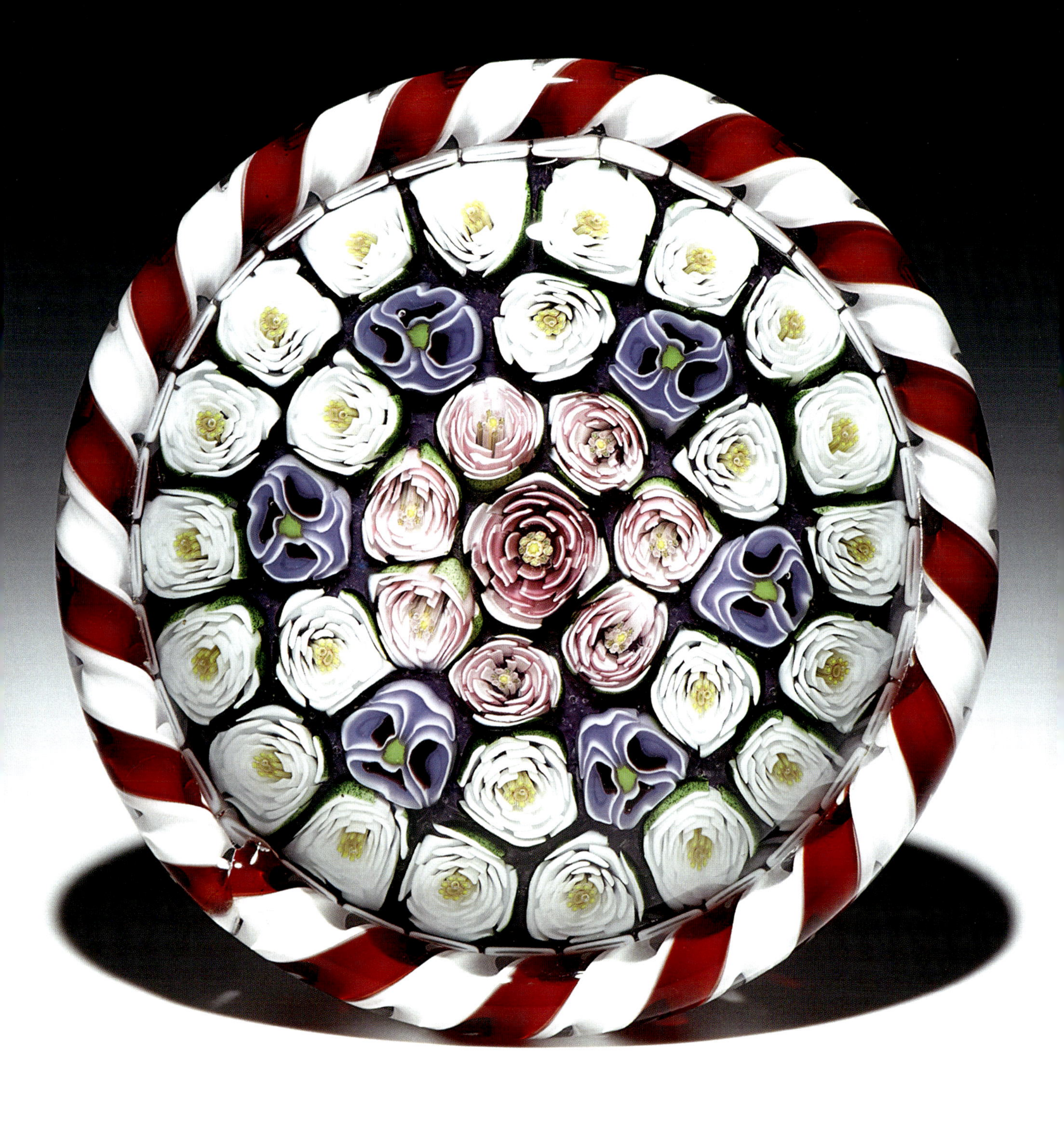

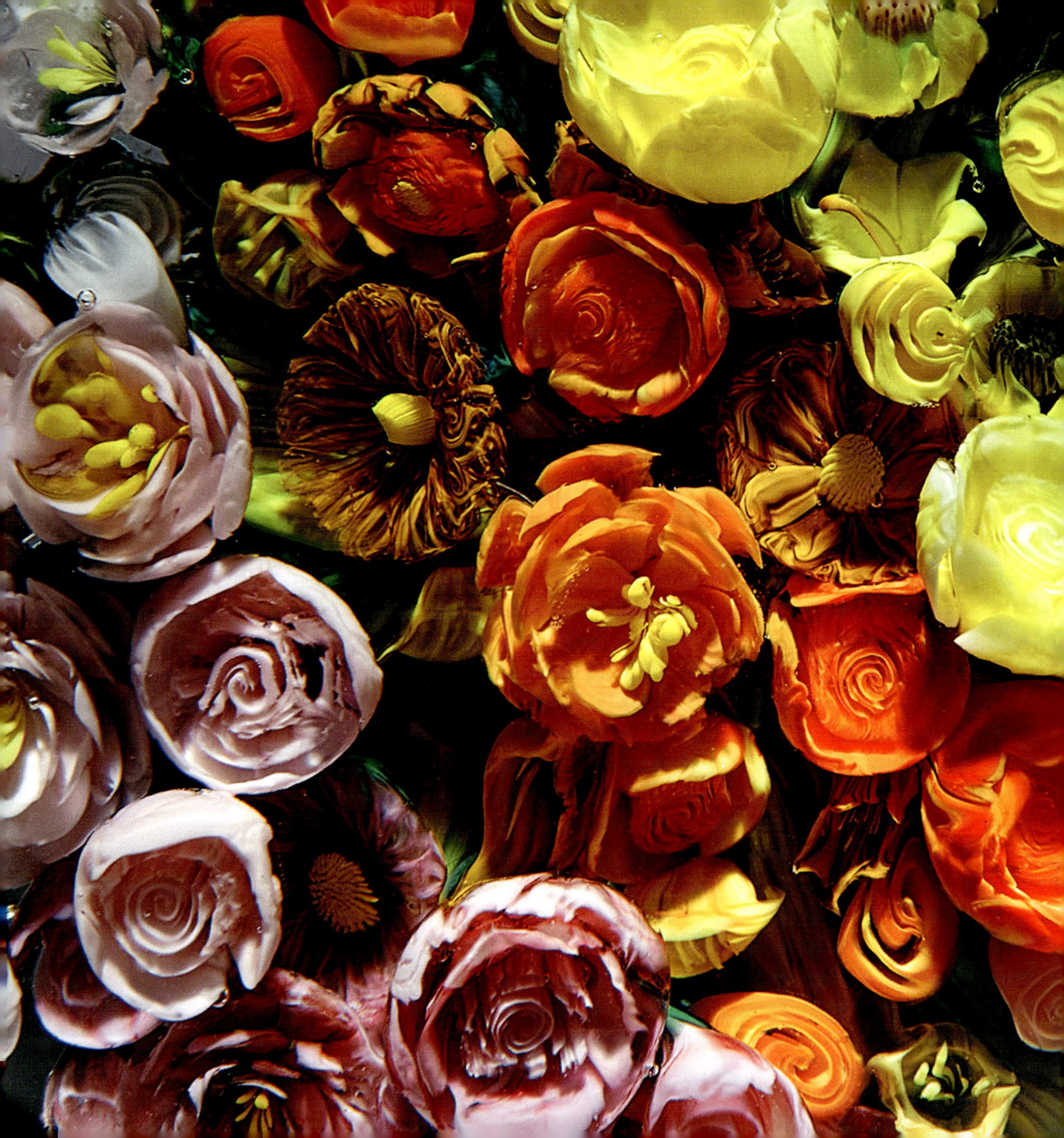

Studio Glass Movement

1962 to Present

Contemporary Artists

Originally an American art phenomenon of the mid-twentieth century, the Studio Glass movement spread quickly to Great Britain, throughout Europe and, eventually, around the world. Focused on individual artists, making one-of-a-kind objects, the Studio Glass movement stands apart from the earlier art glass movements of the century. Its primary difference is the open access to studios, college classes, and workshops, which fostered peer support. This access allowed people the ability to share knowledge and ideas among a community of artists, which was not possible before in a commercial, industrial setting. Another difference was the availability of portable and affordable technical equipment.

Contemporary glass artists have modified some of the technical definitions that describe working in glass. The term *lampwork* is used to describe the process of making elements for the interior of antique weights, while the term *flamework* is

LEFT: Detail of Cat. 179

used contemporarily. Today powerful gas torches are used rather than oil lamps, which were used prior to the invention of the torches. The term *murrine* is used to describe the individual slices of canes that are incorporated into weights, while the term *millefiori* is generally used by collectors to describe the canes and especially the designs incorporating canes.

Each artist included in the Ellis Collection has demonstrated their singular vision and virtuosity. Although they are contemporary, it is evident that they honor and continue to explore the genre that was created more than 175 years ago. Brief biographies of the artists are listed alphabetically by last name with eldest before youngest if related.

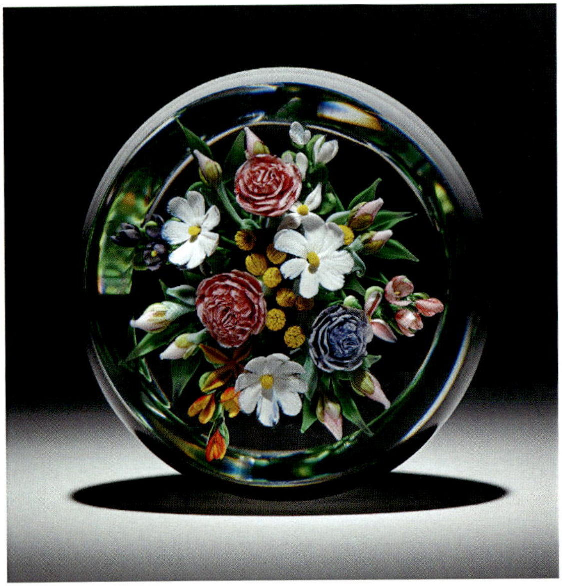

178. Rick Ayotte, American, b. 1944
Sweet Summer Bouquet, 1994
Glass, D. 3 ½ inches

Roland "Rick" Ayotte

Rick Ayotte began a lifelong interest in ornithology during childhood. He studied at Lowell Technological Institute followed by a ten-year career as a scientific glassblower, working for the Macalaster Scientific Corporation (with fellow glass worker, Paul Stankard) and Scientific Specialties. In 1970 he started his own company making glass items to sell in gift shops that incorporated birds and animals placed in natural habitats. By 1979, he exclusively focused on fabricating weights full time. He cites the spherical form, rich colors, optical magic and scale of Classical weights as part of his artistic influence. His weights represent the world around him—living with nature. They are painterly, placing species in a three-dimensional context of seeing them in the habitat in which they live. He creates depth with water beneath or branches above them. His studies of flowers and bouquets are abundant with rich detail and uncanny lifelike accuracy. The weight titled *Sweet Summer Bouquet* (**cat. 178**), is one of the first weights in the Ellis Collection. Glass artist Melissa Ayotte collaborated with her father producing a gradient colored bouquet in *Flowers that Clothe the Meadow* (**cat. 179**).

179

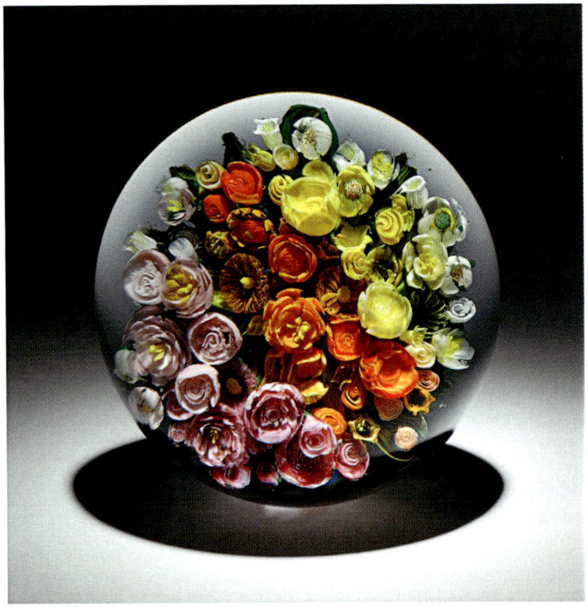

181

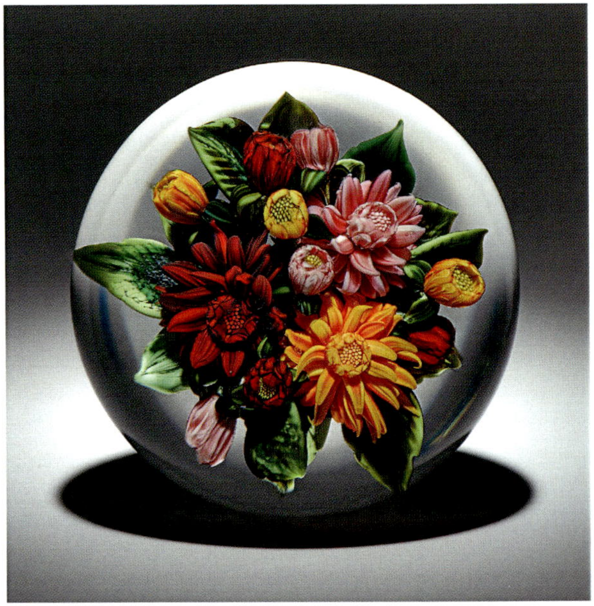

180

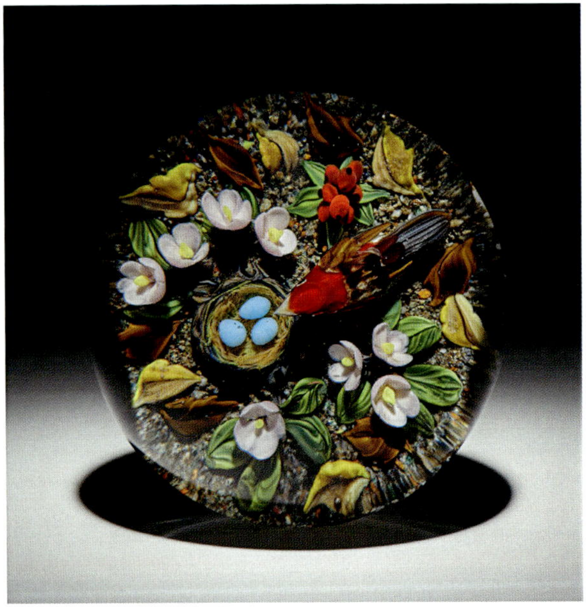

182

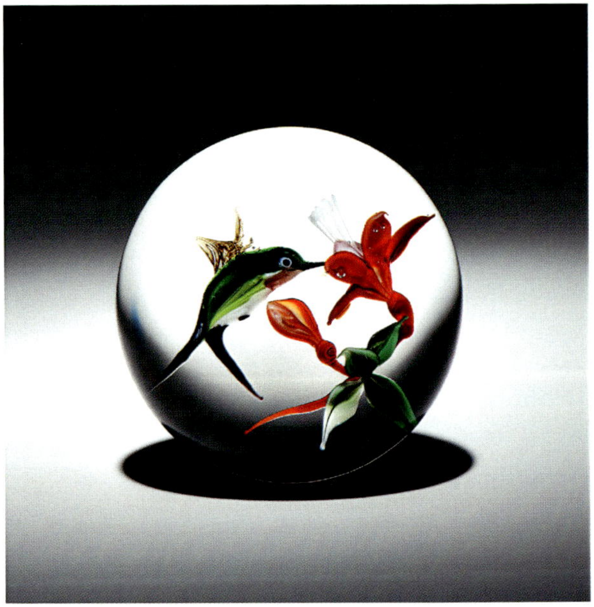

183

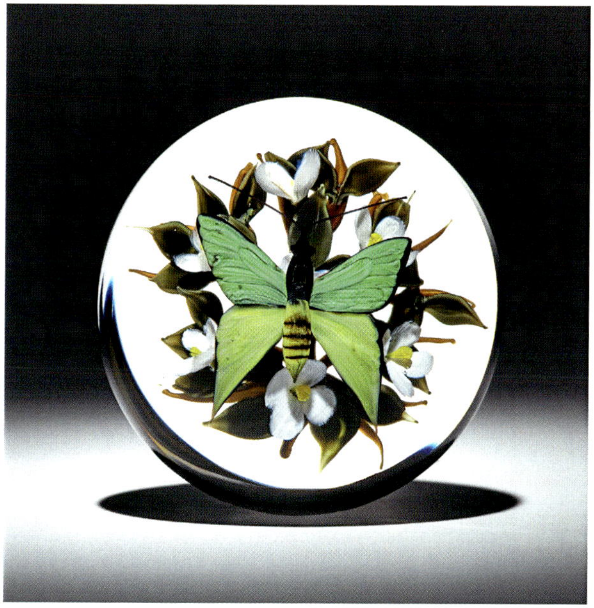

184

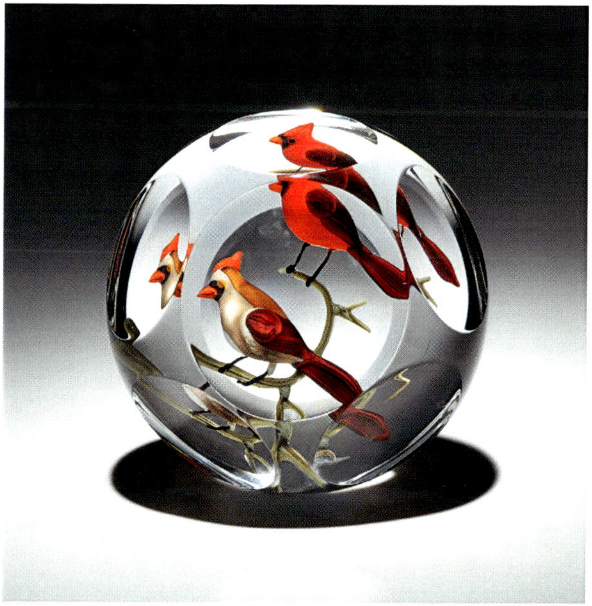

179. Rick Ayotte, American, b. 1944
Melissa Ayotte, American, b. 1971
Flowers that Clothe the Meadow, 2014
Glass, D. 3 inches

180. Rick Ayotte, American, b. 1944
Springtime in New Hampshire, 1986
Glass, D. 3 ¾ inches

181. Rick Ayotte, American, b. 1944
Magnum Dahlia Bouquet, 2003
Glass, D. 4 ¼ inches

182. Rick Ayotte, American, b. 1944
Hummingbird with Fuchsia, 1987
Glass, 2 D. inches

183. Rick Ayotte, American, b. 1944
Paradisea, 1993
Glass, D. 3 ½ inches

184. Rick Ayotte, American, b. 1944
Faceted Pair of Cardinals, 1979
Glass, D. 2 ½ inches

185

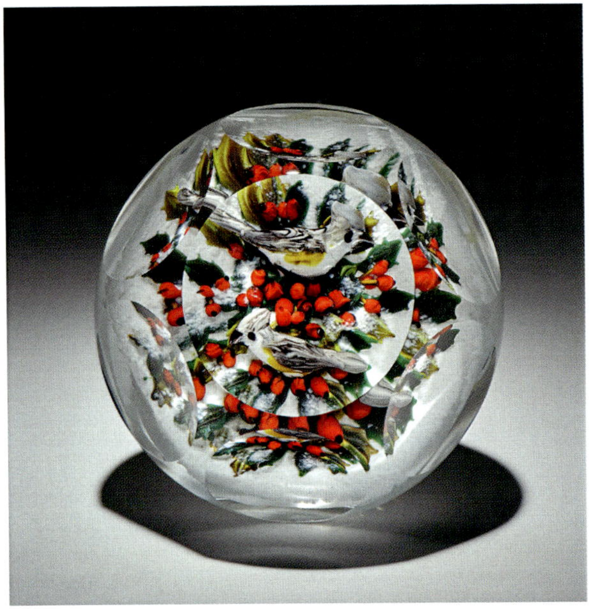

187

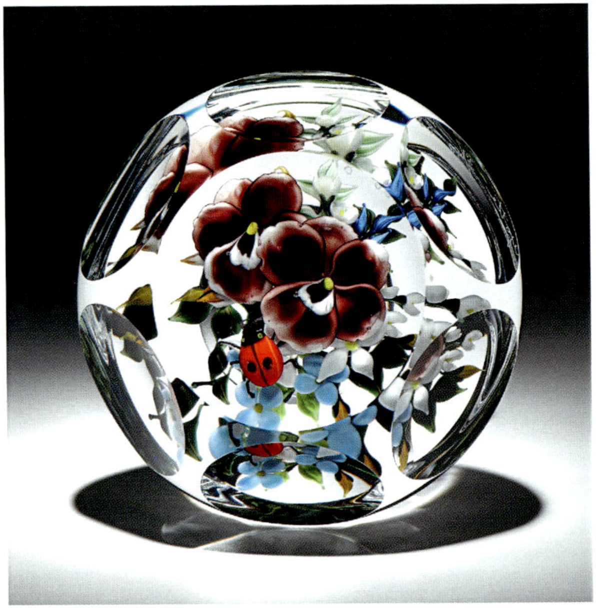

186

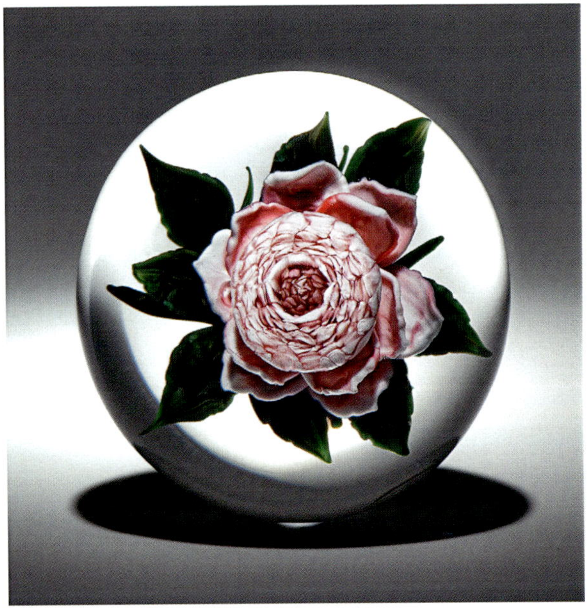

188

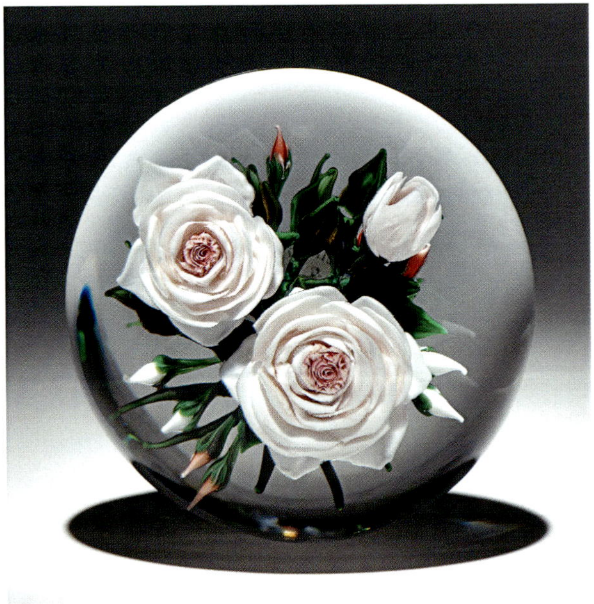

189

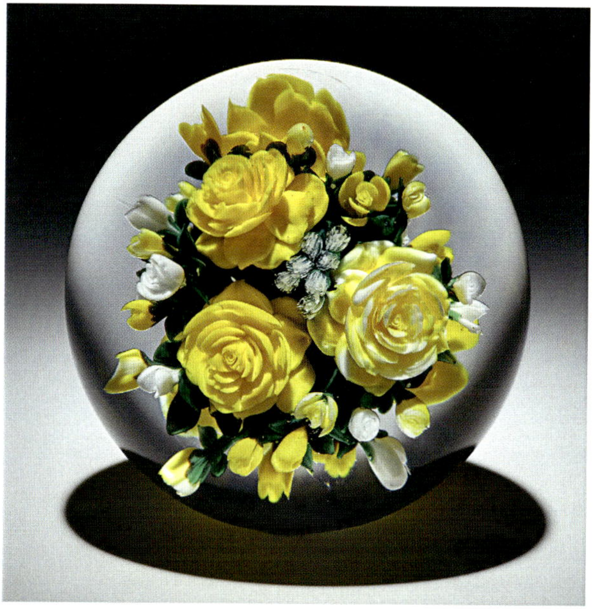

190

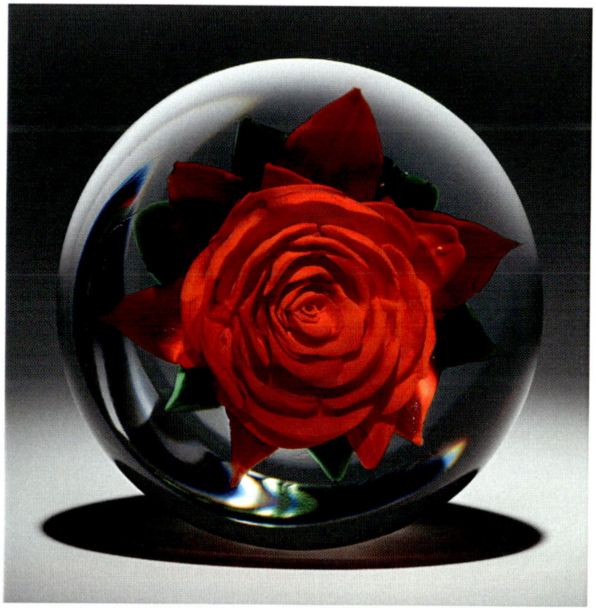

185. Rick Ayotte, American, b. 1944
Faceted Two Birds with Berries, 1987
Glass, D. 3 ⅞ inches

186. Rick Ayotte, American, b. 1944
Magnum Pink Cabbage Rose, 1989
Glass D. 3 $^{9}/_{16}$ inches

187. Rick Ayotte, American, b. 1944
Faceted Pansy Bouquet with Ladybug, 1988
Glass, D. 3 ½ inches

188. Rick Ayotte, American, b. 1944
Magnum Pink Roses, 1991
Glass, D. 3 ¾ inches

189. Rick Ayotte, American, b. 1944
Magnum Yellow Roses, 2001
Glass, D. 3 ⅞ inches

190. Rick Ayotte, American, b. 1944
Magnum Upright American Beauty Rose, 1997
Glass, D. 4 $^{1}/_{16}$ inches

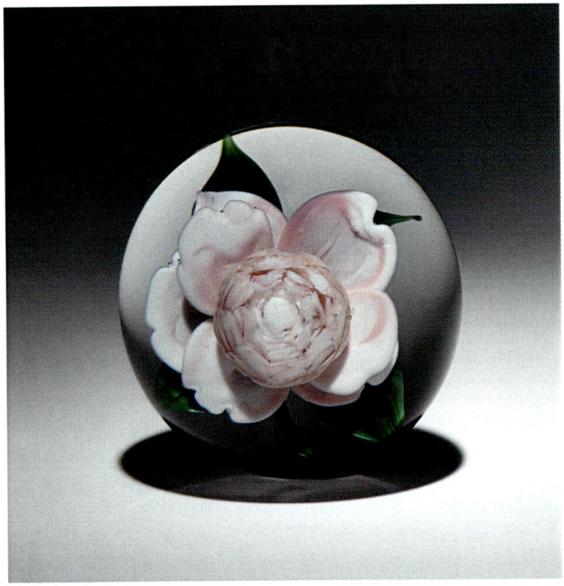

191. Rick Ayotte, American, b. 1944
Miniature Pink Cabbage Rose, 1989
Glass, D. 2 1⁄16 inches

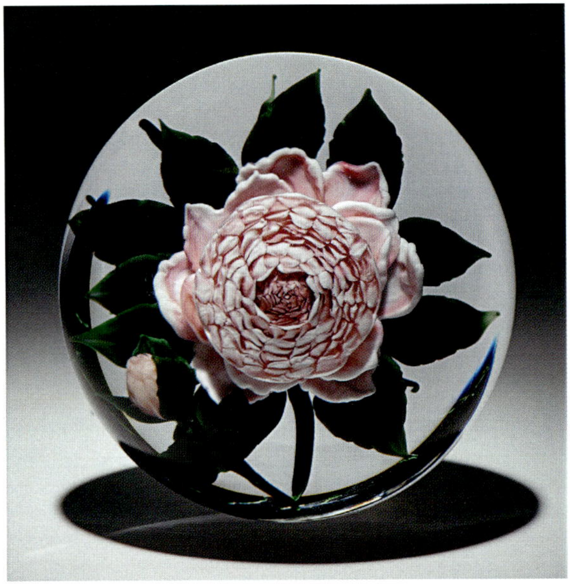

192. Rick Ayotte, American, b. 1944
Magnum Pink Cabbage Rose, 1989
Glass, D. 4 ½ inches

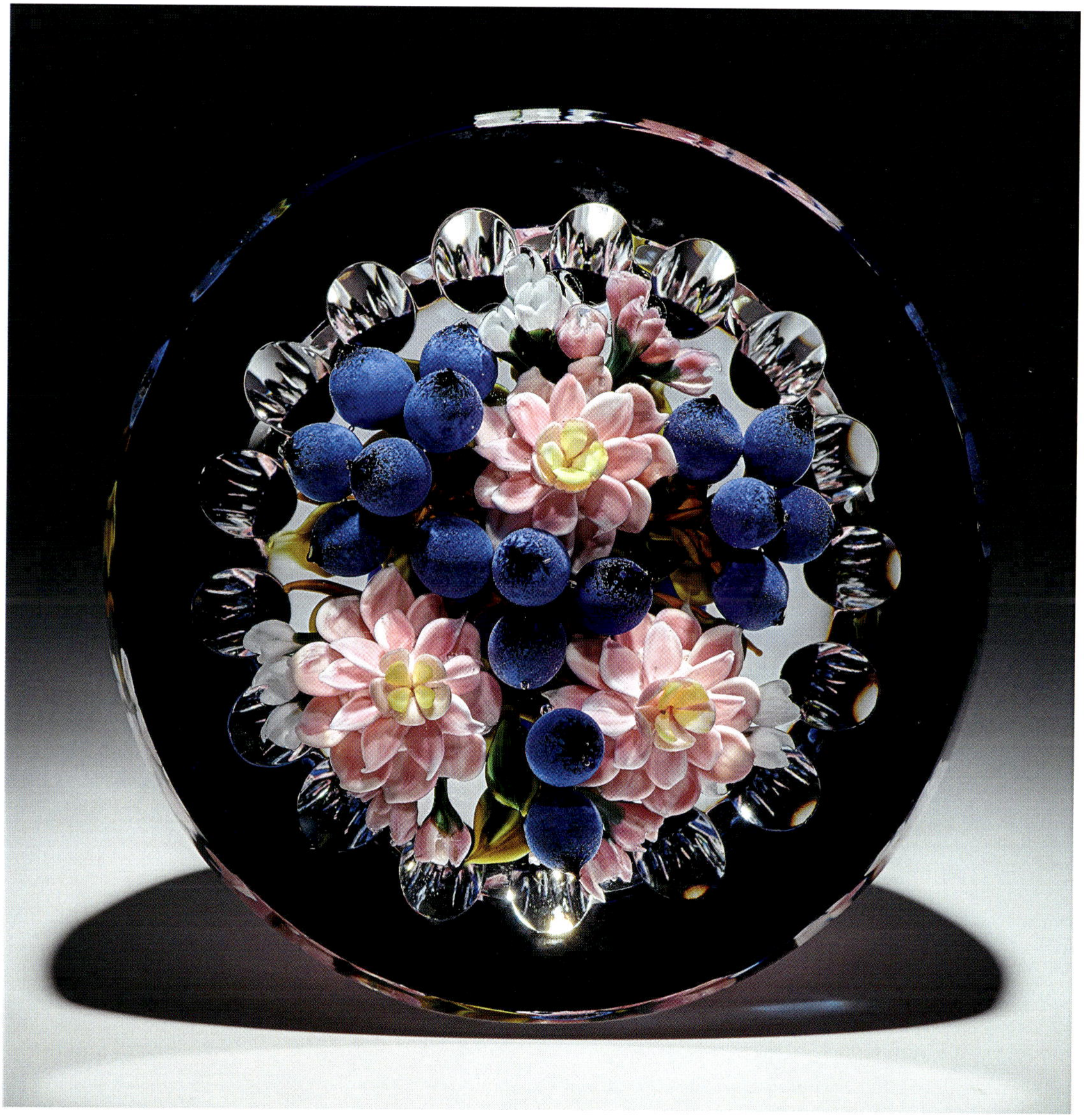

193. Rick Ayotte, American, b. 1944
Magnum Blueberries with Fancy Cuts. Glass, D. 4 ½ inches

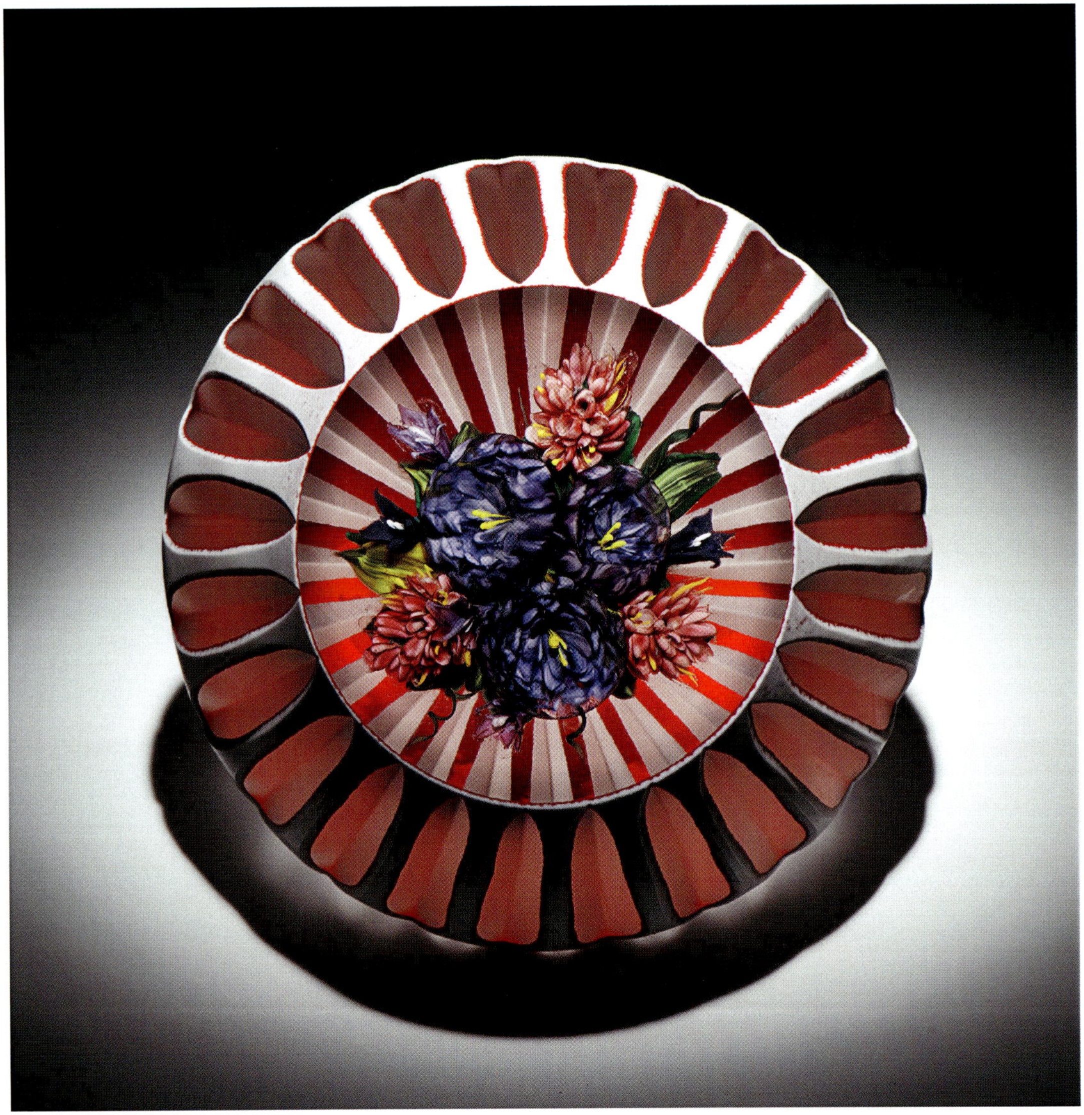

194. **Melissa Ayotte,** American, b. 1971
Faceted Cosmic Red Basket with Overlay 2018. Glass, H. 4 3⁄8, W. 4 7⁄16, L. 4 inches

Melissa Ayotte

Melissa Ayotte received her Masters at Antioch New England Graduate School in counseling and clinical psychology. Growing up with her father Rick she also apprenticed in his studio. After college this studio activity served as a creative departure from her career. Melissa started taking more and more glass and art classes. In the year 2000 she spent time assisting in Paul Stankard's studio and began working full time at Ayotte Glass Studio. Melissa pushes the limits of the historical format of a paperweight, creating pieces that reflect her sense of nature including the earthly, human, and divine. Her virtuosity in creating flowers and her expression through the use of intense colors is evident in this collection and incorporate nontraditional shapes and complex facets and overlay.

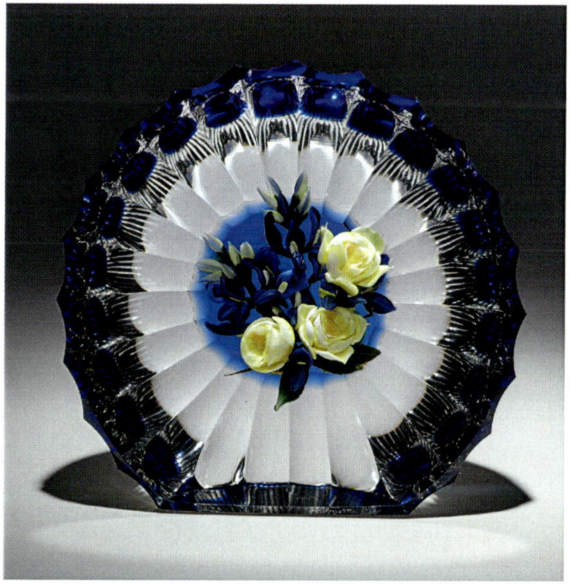

195. Melissa Ayotte, American, b. 1971
Faceted Blue Bonnet and Yellow Rose, 2007
Glass, D. 4 ¾ inches

196

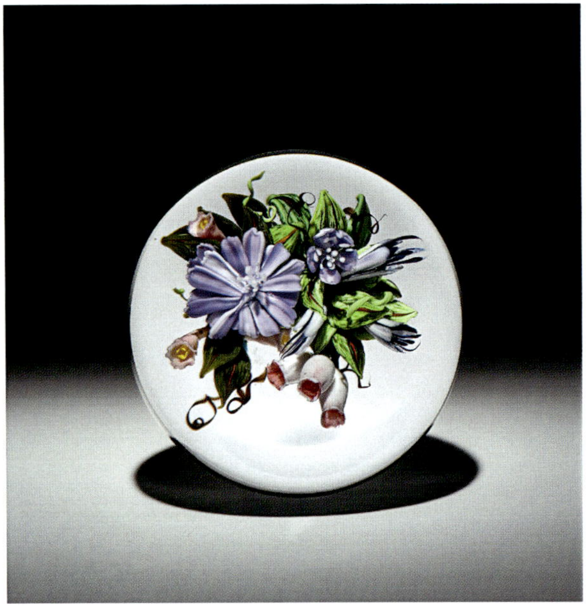

198

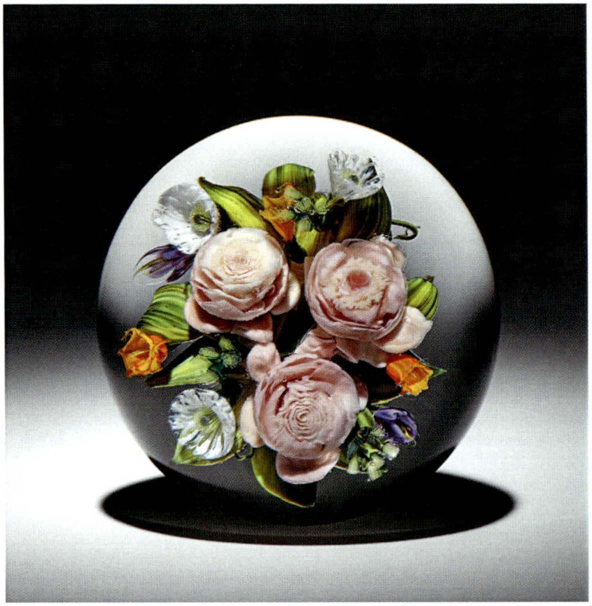

197

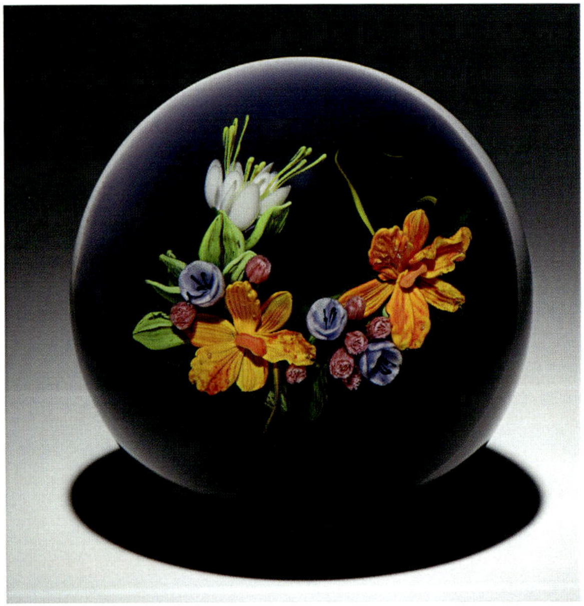

199

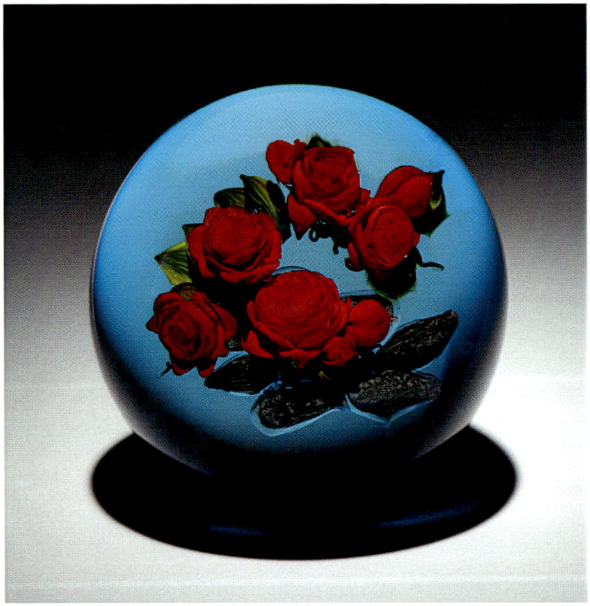

200

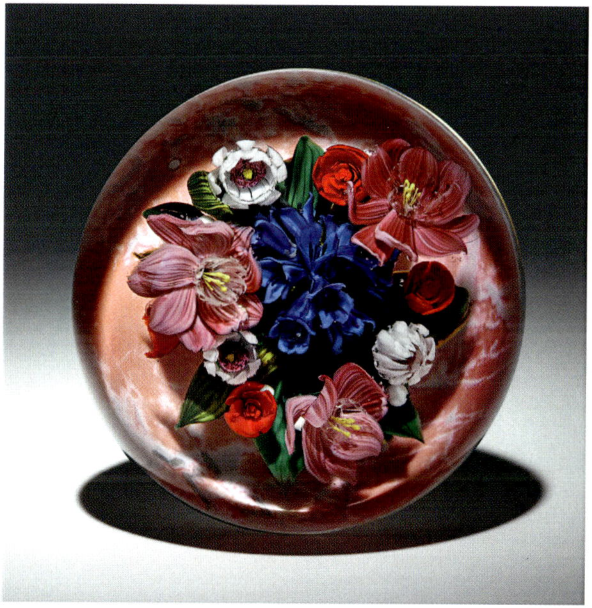

196. Melissa Ayotte, American, b. 1971
Lavender and Pink Buds Bouquet, 2004
Glass, D. 2 inches

197. Melissa Ayotte, American, b. 1971
Star Bright, 2008
Glass, D. 3 ⅞ inches

198. Melissa Ayotte, American, b. 1971
Roses and Flowers, 2018
Glass, D. 3 ¼ inches

199. Melissa Ayotte, American, b. 1971
Summer in New England, 2011
Glass, D. 3 9/16 inches

200. Melissa Ayotte, American, b. 1971
Pink Wonder, 2014
Glass, D. 3 9/16 inches

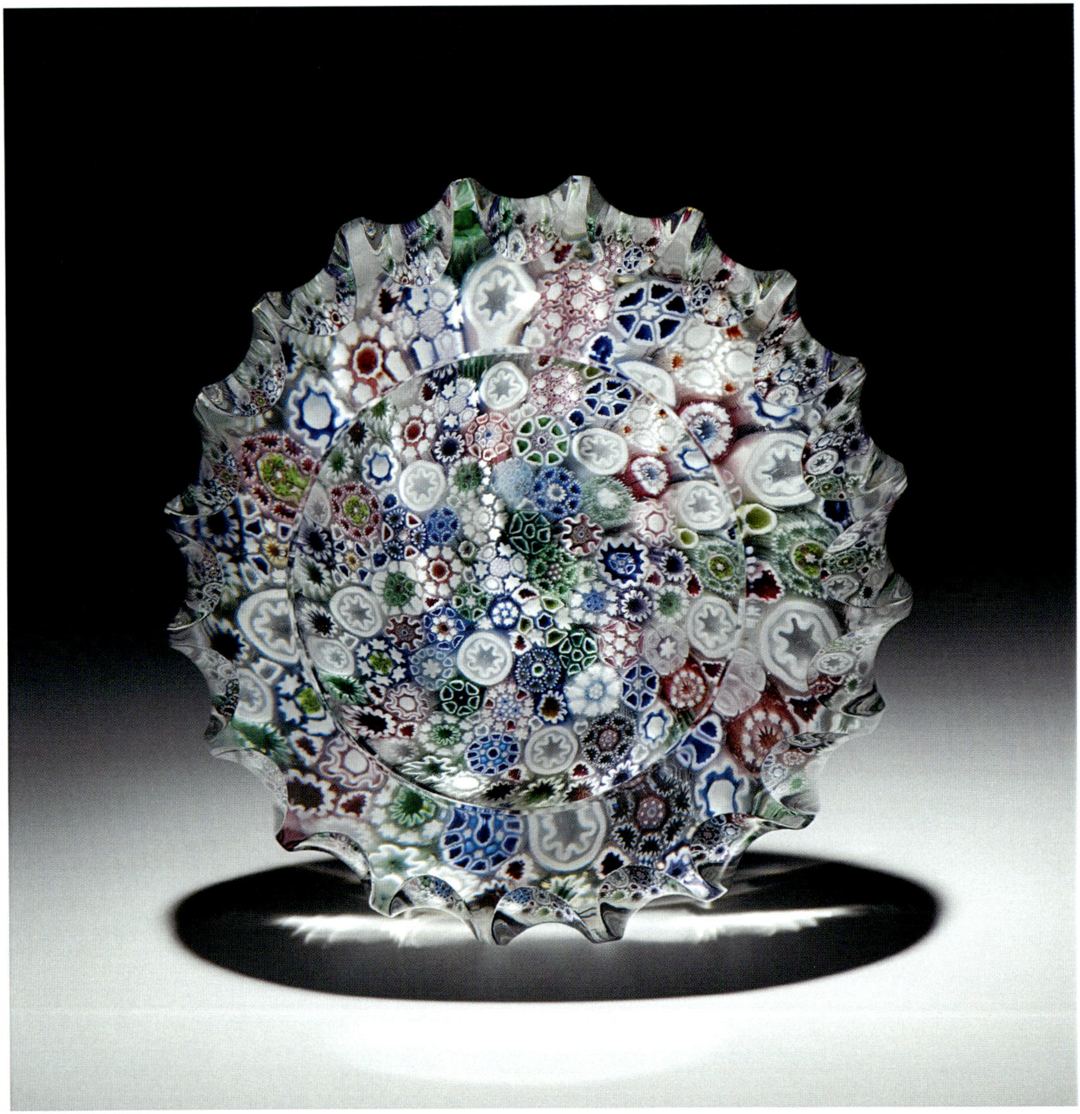

201. Jim Brown, American, b. 1949
Fluted Close Pack Millefiori, 2022. Glass, D. 3 ¼ inches

James "Jim" Brown

Jim Brown received a mechanical engineering degree from Vanderbilt University while serving in the Navy. During his career as a naval officer until 1981, he traveled throughout the Pacific. After leaving the military he continued to work as an engineer. In 1995 he became interested in collecting antique millefiori weights. In 2000 he began working with glass at the Tennessee Technological University. Since then he has concentrated on working within the style of Classic millefiori weights. He has mastered emulating the optics achieved in Bacchus weights, using large open ruffled millefiori canes in traditional arrangements.

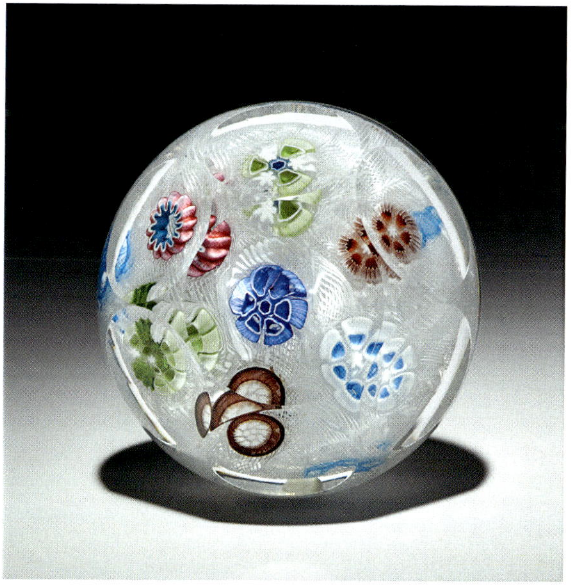

202. Jim Brown, American, b. 1949
Spaced Millefiori on Upset Muslin, 2013
Glass, D. 2 7/16 inches

203

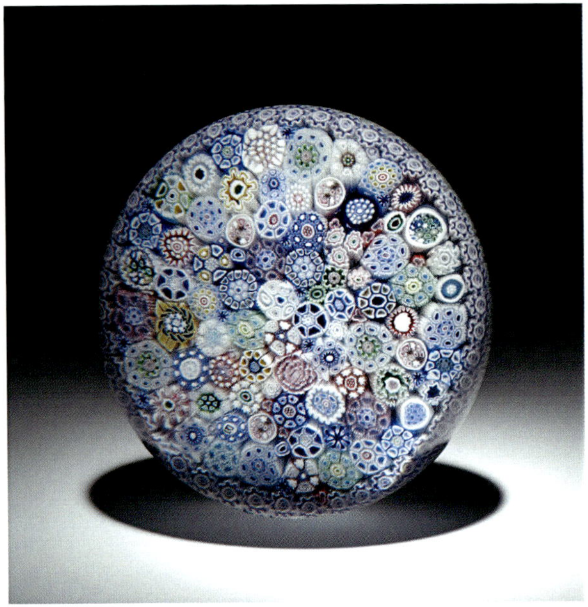

205

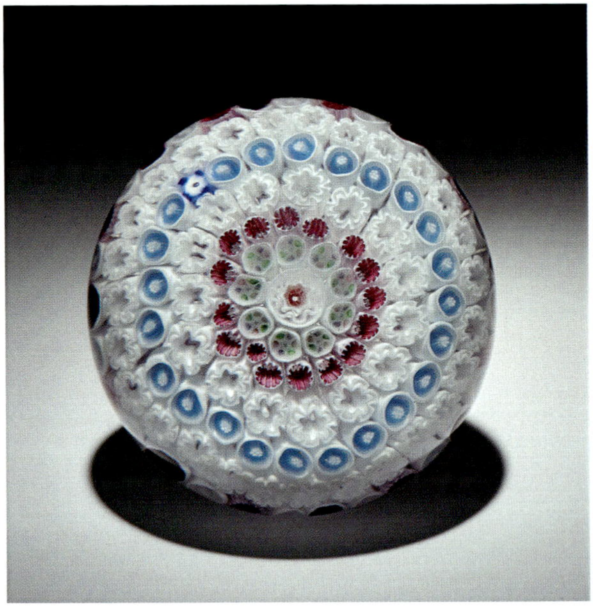

204

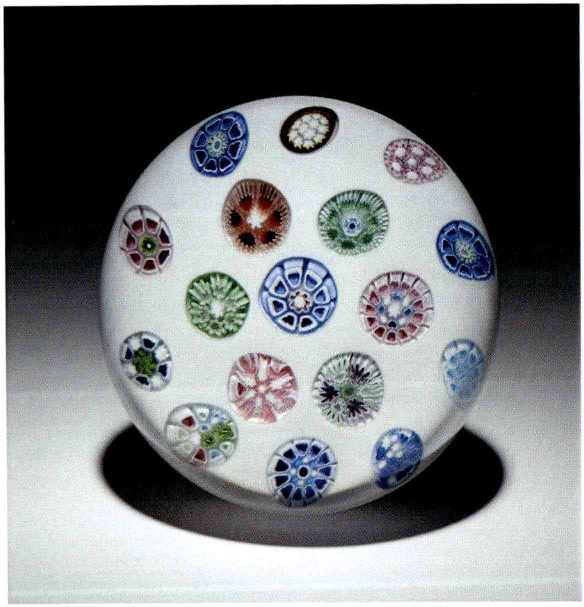

206

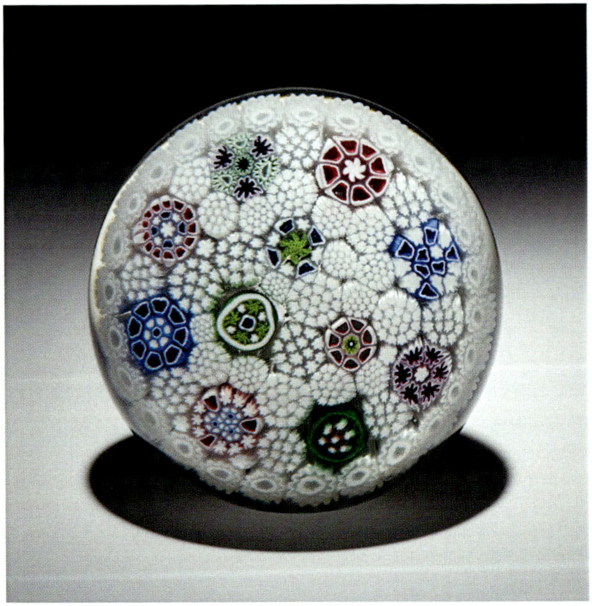

207

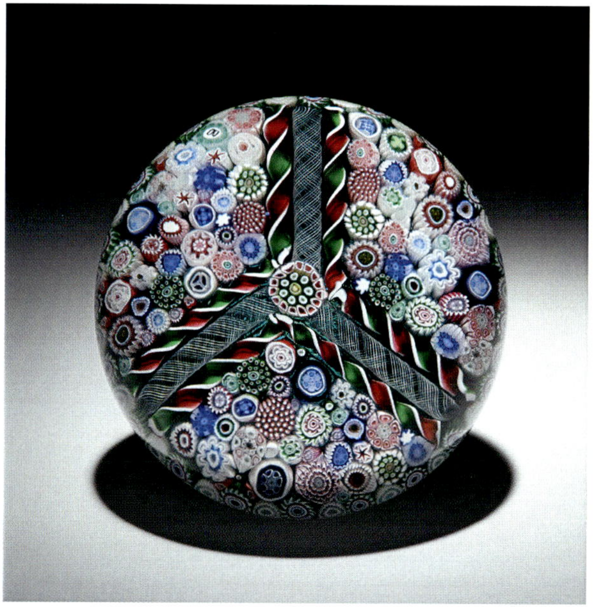

208

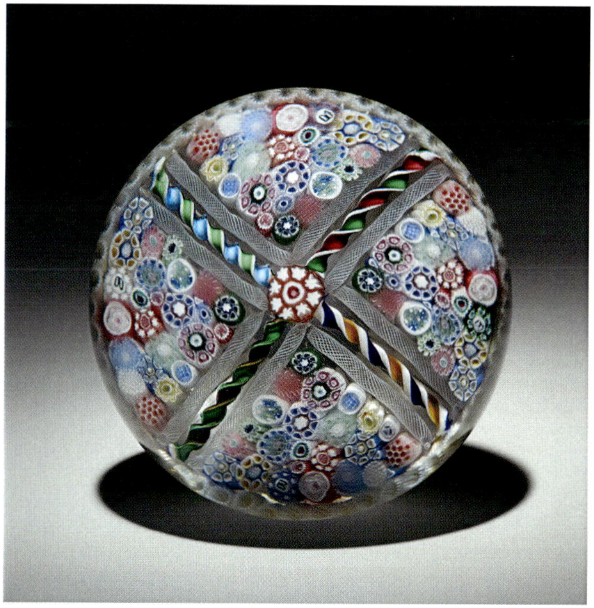

203. **Jim Brown,** American, b. 1949
Close Pack Millefiori, 2011
Glass, D. 3 ⅜ inches

204. **Jim Brown,** American, b. 1949
Spaced Concentric Millefiori on Sodden Snow, 2013
Glass, D. 3 inches

205. **Jim Brown,** American, b. 1949
Concentric Millefiori with Stave Basket, 2013
Glass, D. 2 15⁄16 inches

206. **Jim Brown,** American, b. 1949
Complex Millefiori with White Stardust Canes, 2013
Glass, D. 2 11⁄16 inches

207. **Jim Brown,** American, b. 1949
Close Pack Millefiori, 2005
Glass, D. 3 inches

208. **Jim Brown,** American, b. 1949
Panel Close Pack Millefiori, 2011
Glass, D. 3 inches

Chris Buzzini

Chris Buzzini was born and lived in Yosemite National Park until he was thirteen. He studied glass at Shasta College and California State University, leaving in 1973 to work in production glass studios in California including Orient & Flume Art Glass (founded 1972), Lundberg Studios (founded 1970) and Correia Art Glass (founded 1973). He established his own studio in 1986. Now located in Portland, Oregon, his childhood experience of living in nature informs his work in glass.

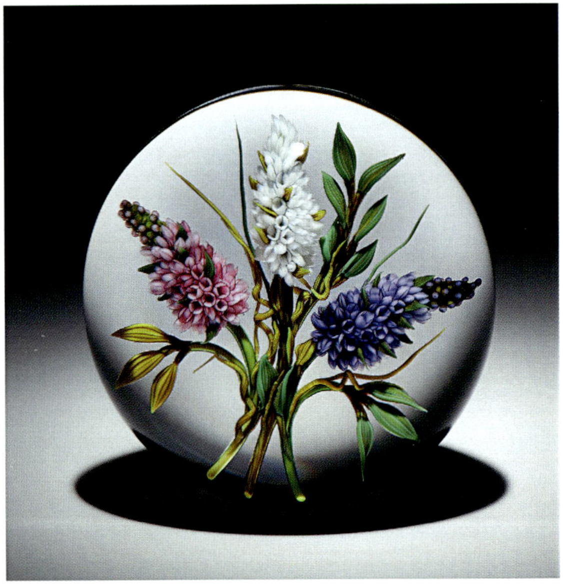

209. Chris Buzzini, American, b. 1949
Lilac Bouquet, 2010
Glass, D. 3 3/8 inches

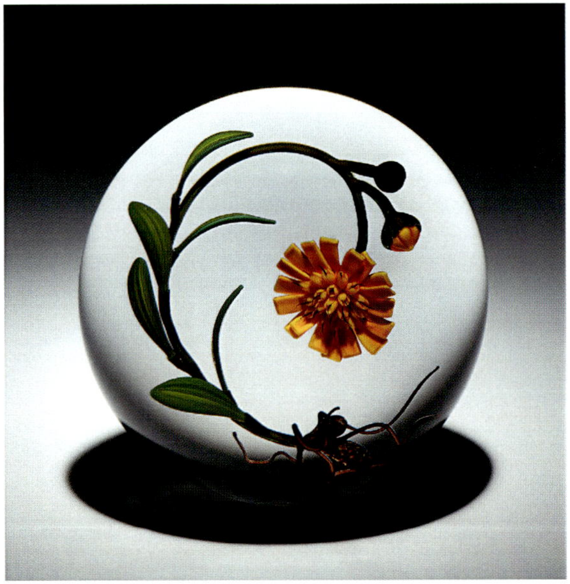

210. Chris Buzzini, American, b. 1949
Serpentine Hawkweed
Glass, D. 3 3/8 inches

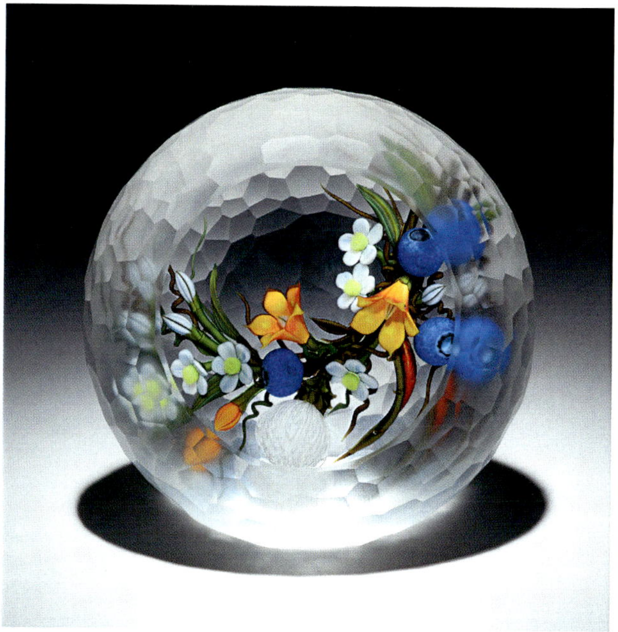

211. Chris Buzzini, American, b. 1949
Floral Gem with Battuto Finish, 2012
Glass, D. 3 ⅜ inches

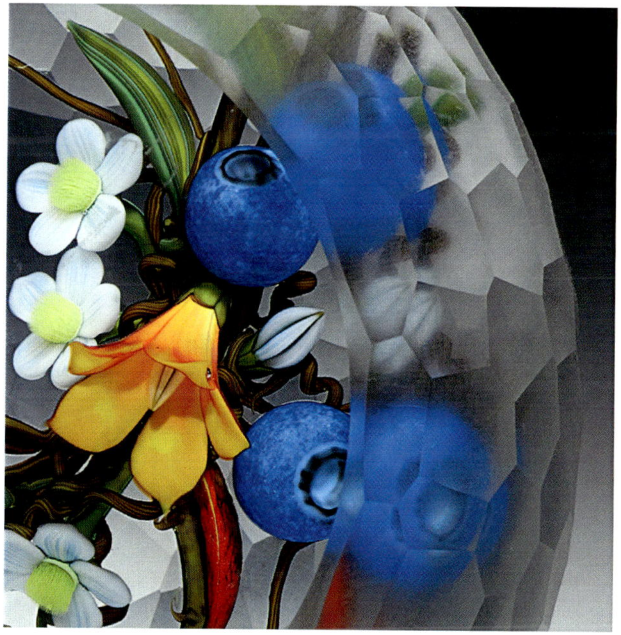

Detail of Cat. 211
This weight has a soft frosty finish that has small facets engraved over the surface of the glass called *battuto* (Italian for "beaten").

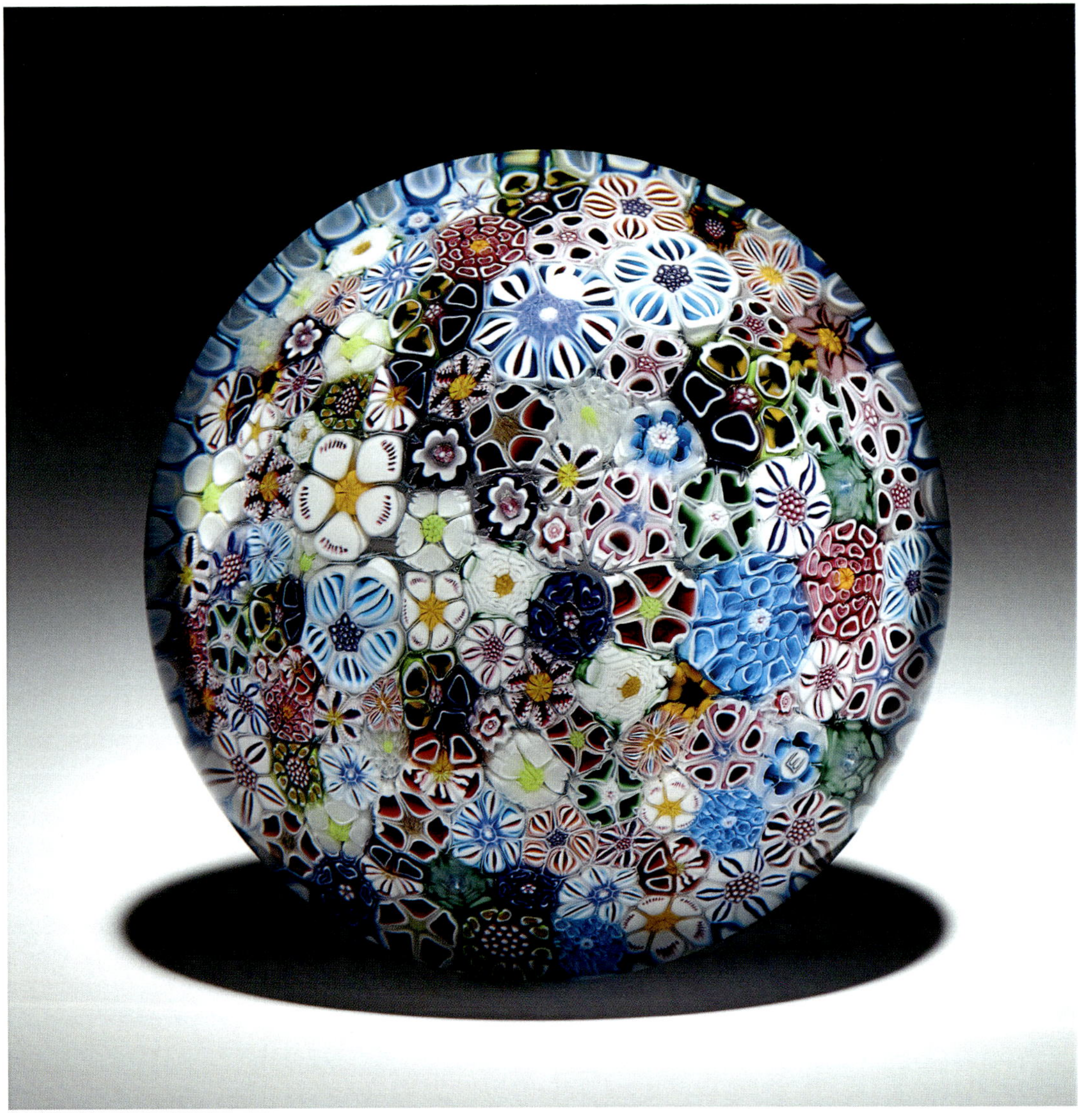

212. Drew Ebelhare, American, b. 1950
Close Pack Millefiori with Flower Canes in Stave Basket, 2000. Glass, D. 2 ¾ inches

George "Drew" Ebelhare III

Drew Ebelhare received his degree in scene design and technical theater from Florida State University. He briefly worked in stained glass before glass blowing in 1981. He recalls meeting a member of the Texas Paperweight Collectors Association in 1990, which led to his introduction to the world of fine paperweights. Ebelhare was intrigued by Saint-Louis Classic millefiori. He moved to a new studio in Colorado in 1999.

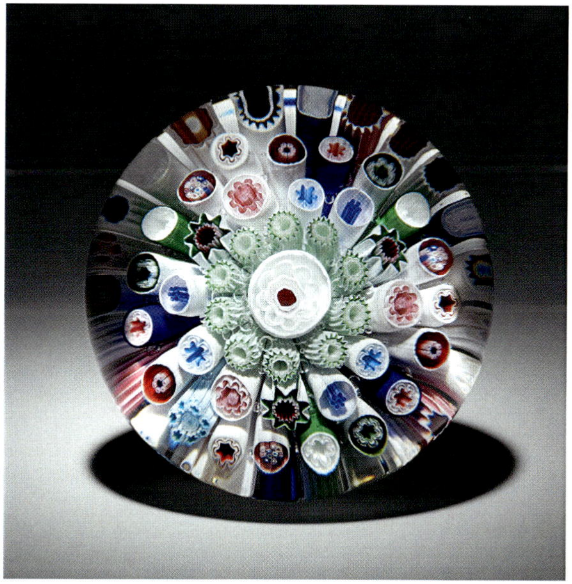

213. Drew Ebelhare, American, b. 1950
Concentric Millefiori with "Bacchus Style" Canes, 2009
Glass, D. 3 5⁄16 inches

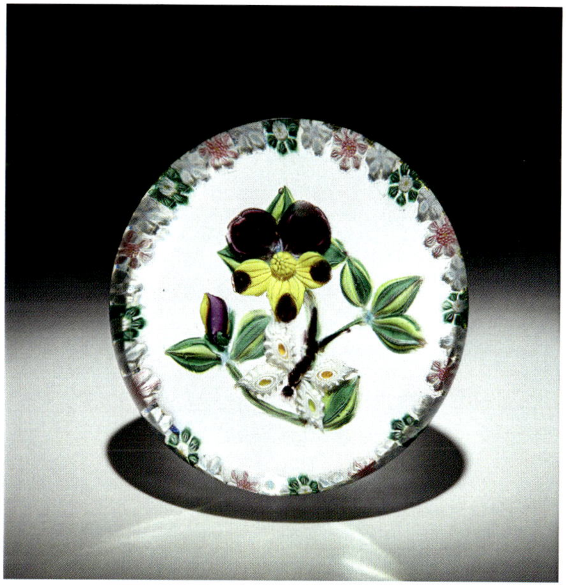

214. Drew Ebelhare, American, b. 1950
Pansy with Butterfly and Garland, 2019
Glass, D. 2 11⁄16 inches

David Graeber

David Graeber attended an area community college and vocational school in New Jersey before receiving private instruction in a variety of the arts. In 1989 he became Paul Stankard's assistant. While he continues to assist Stankard, he became an independent artist in 2009. His weights are abundant with crafted flameworked flowers and expressive bouquets. A part of his motivation to create fine glass objects is to bring the South Jersey glass tradition into the twenty-first century.

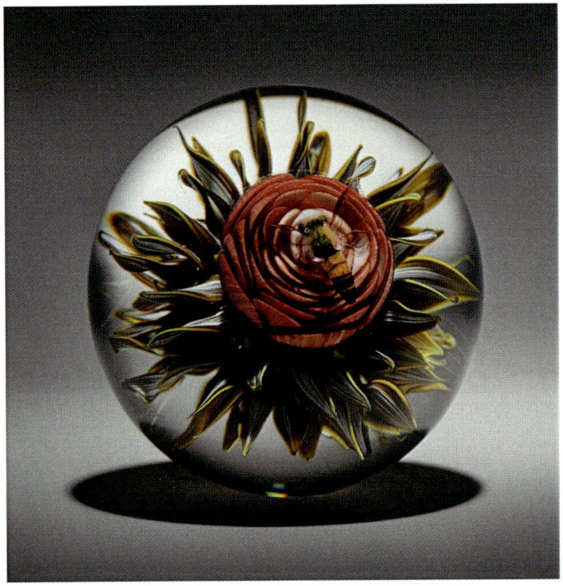

215. David Graeber, American, b. 1967
Pink Tea Rose and Honeybee Orb, 2019
Glass, D. 3 1⁄16 inches

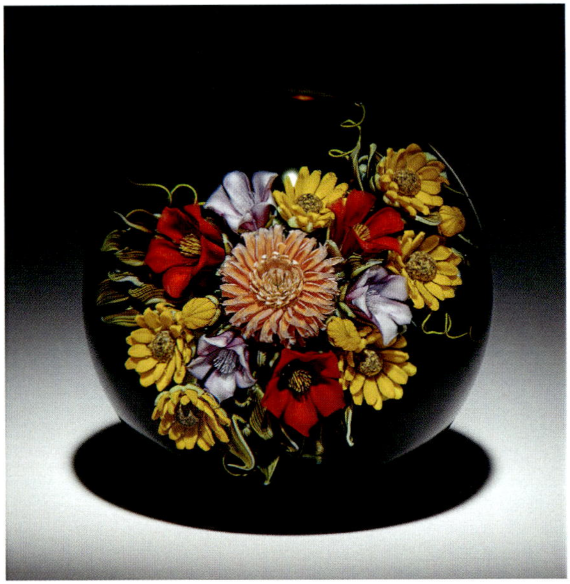

216. David Graeber, American, b. 1967
Bouquet on Dark Ground, 2011
Glass, D. 3 inches

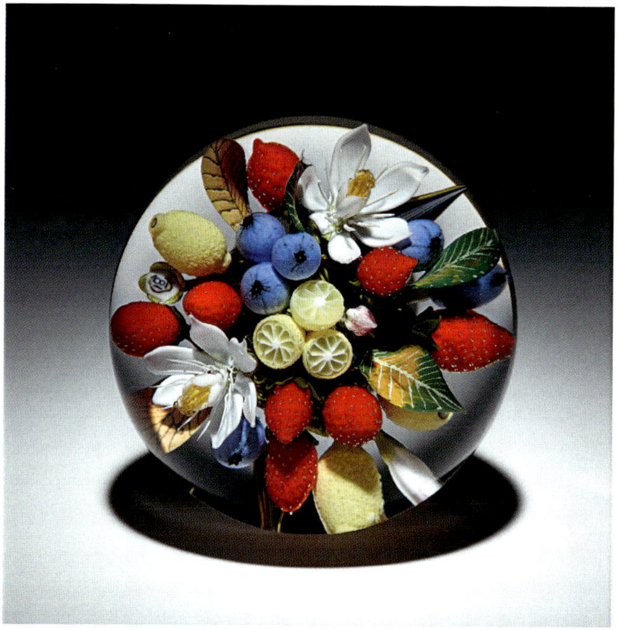

217. David Graeber, American, b. 1967
Fruit Bouquet
Glass, D. 2 ½ inches

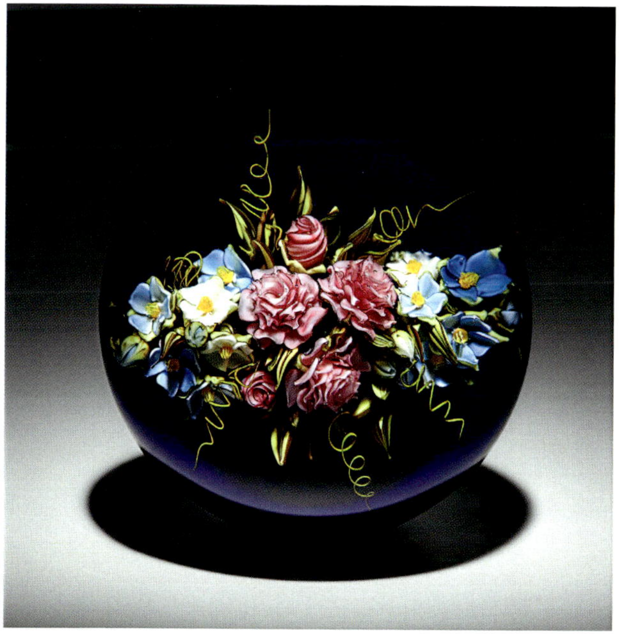

218. David Graeber, American, b. 1967
Bouquet on Cobalt Ground, 2009
Glass, D. 3 inches

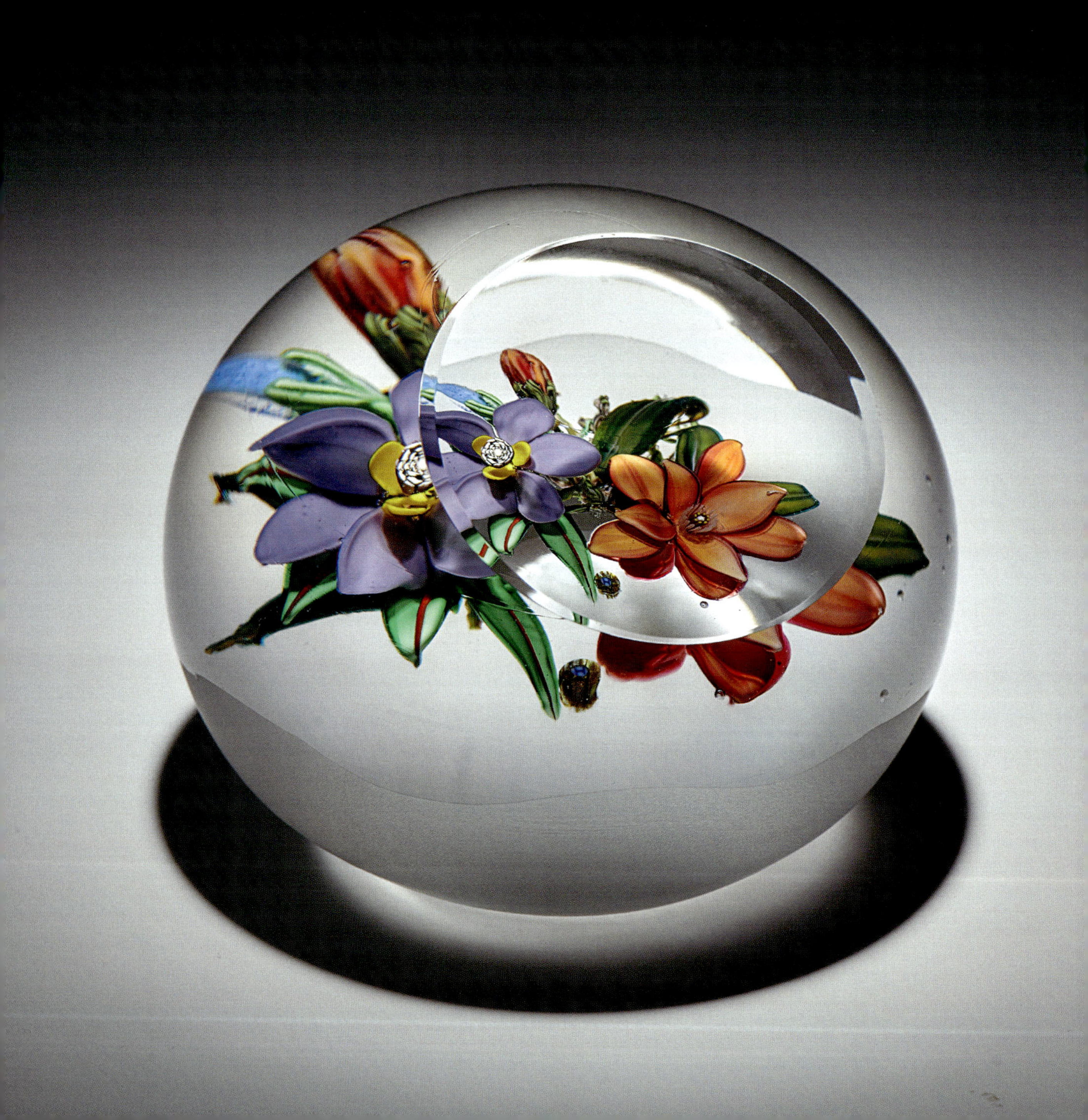

Eric Hansen

Eric Hansen grew up in California in a family of glassblowers. He worked with a torch in his family's business for eight years before joining the military. He was commissioned as a naval officer in 1984 and eventually became a pilot for a major airline. In 1994 his uncle Robert Hansen (1922–2006) taught him the art of making fine paperweights. In 1996 he started working on his own pieces. His studio is located in Argyle, Texas. **Cat. 219** is reflective of his acute sense of color and skill in rendering flowers.

219. Eric Hansen, American, b. 1961
Bouquet, 2009
Glass, D. 3 3/8 inches

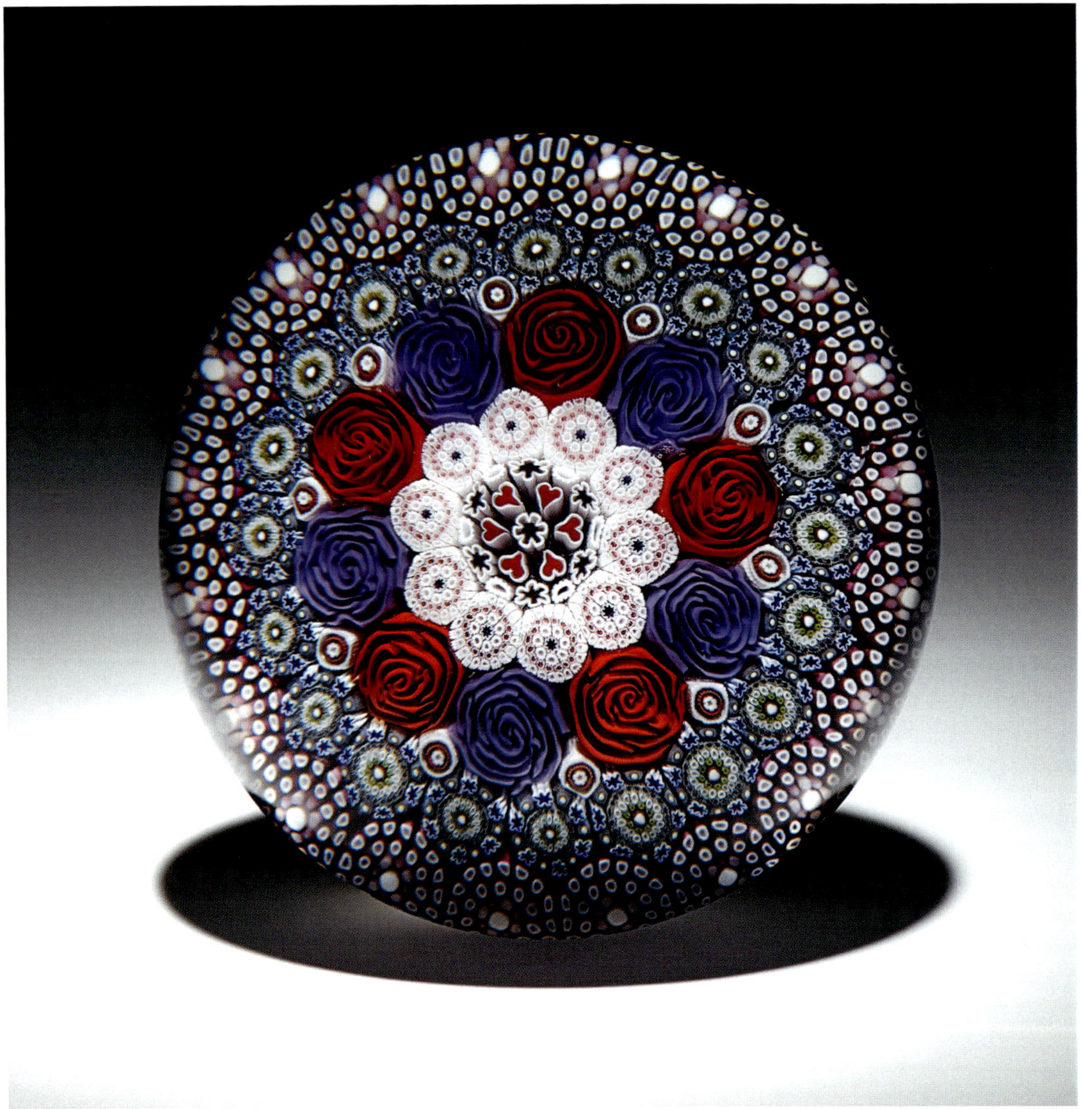

220. **Michael Hunter,** English, b. 1958
Concentric Millefiori with Roses and Hearts, 2011. Glass, D. 2 ⅝ inches

Michael Hunter

Michael Hunter began working as an apprentice for Wedgwood Glass when he was sixteen, eventually becoming a master glassblower. In 1989, Hunter moved his family to Selkirk, Scotland, to work for the Lindean Mill Glass Studio as a production master. In 1998 he and his wife Susan founded Twists Glass Studio. Hunter's weights use complex canes employing techniques mastered by makers of nineteenth-century weights. His depth of knowledge and skill in composing meticulous canes has certainly created new schemes, colors, and perspectives.

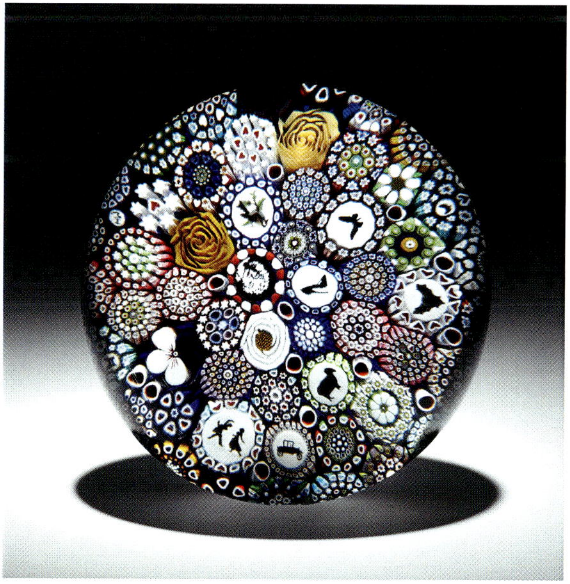

221. Michael Hunter, English, b. 1958
Close Pack Millefiori with Silhouette and Portrait Canes, 2019
Glass, D. 3 inches

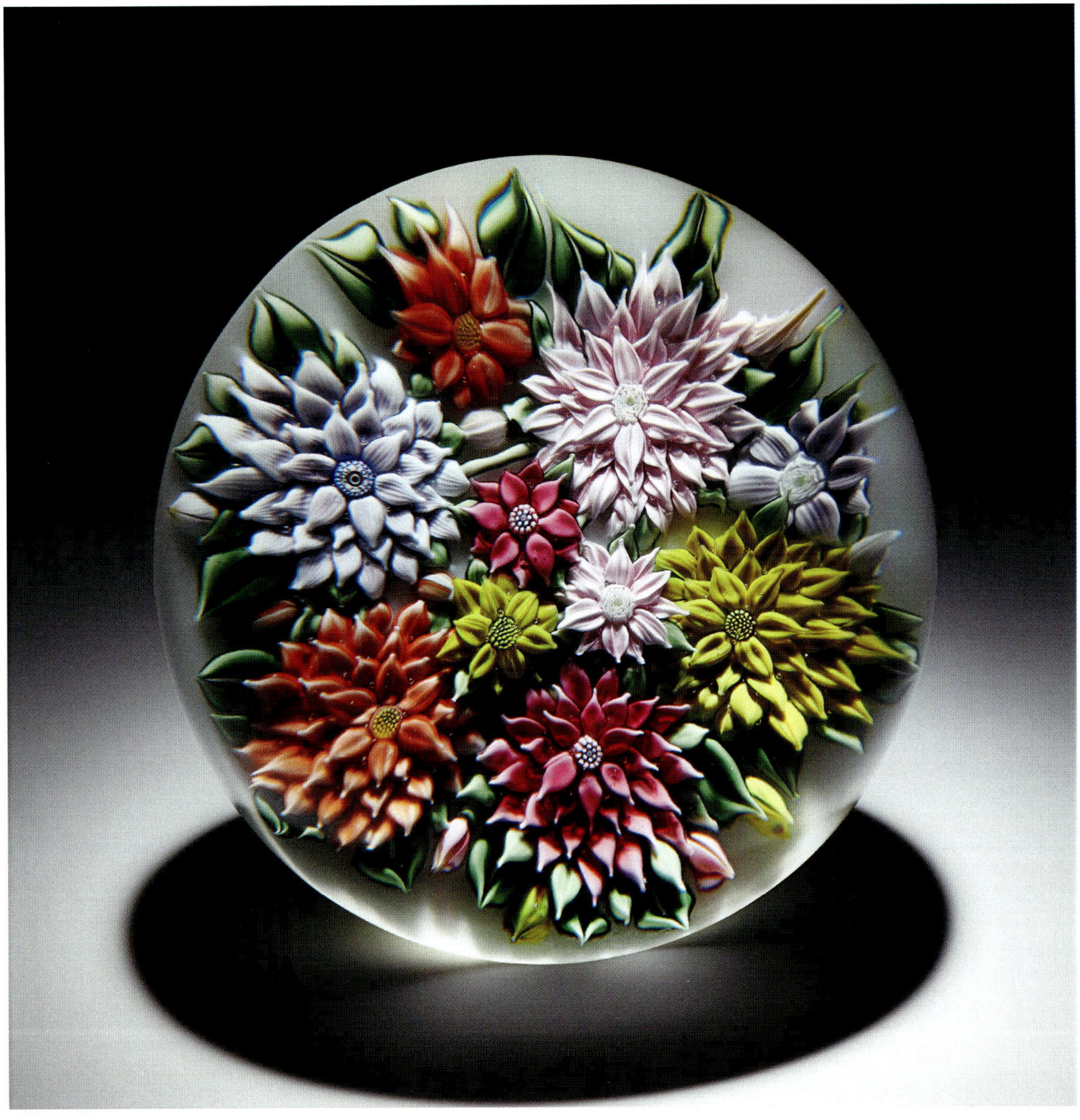

222. **Richard Loesel**, French, b. 1963
Dahlias on White Ground. Glass, D. 3 ¼ inches

Richard Loesel

Richard Loesel grew up in a family of glass workers in France. In 1980 he started working for Saint-Louis. In 1987, he was able to learn from American paperweight maker Rick Ayotte, when he taught at the Saint-Louis factory. In 2000 he continued his career working as a glassblower at the Meisenthal Glass Factory Museum. He opened his own studio in Lorraine, France, in 2017 and devoted himself to only making weights.

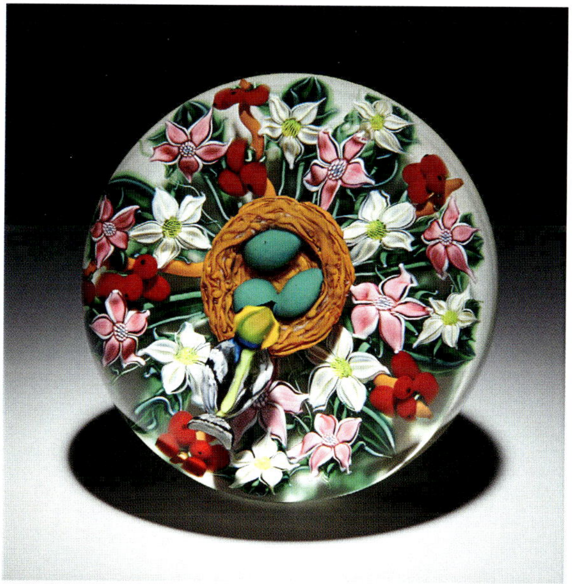

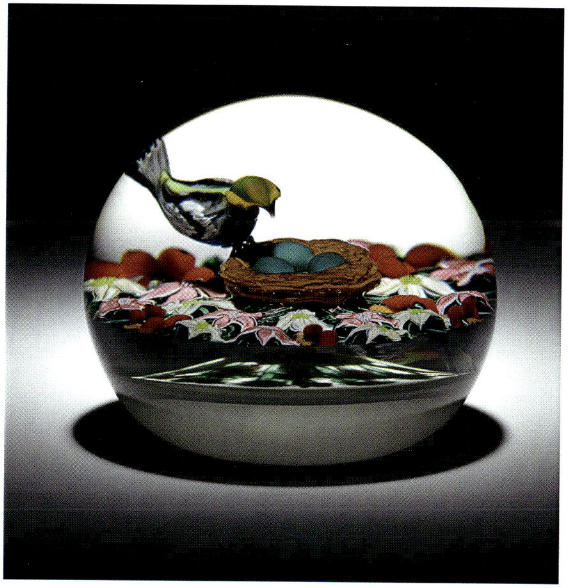

223. Richard Loesel, French, b. 1963
Bird in Nest with Flowers, 2023
Glass, D. 3 ¼ inches

This weight was part of the Paperweight Collectors Association's 70th anniversary limited edition inspired by the historic nineteenth-century Pantin weight, *Bird in the Nest.*

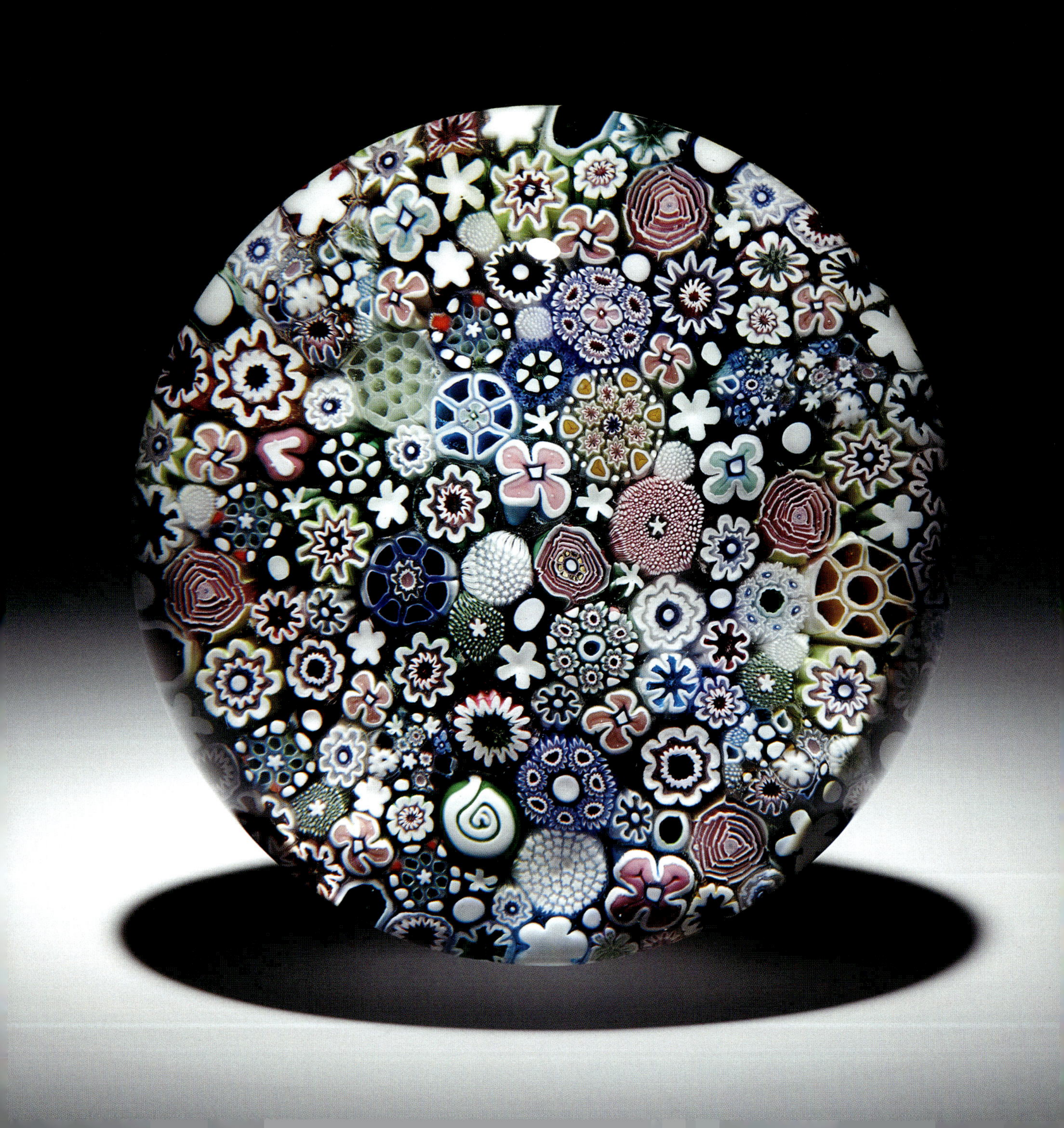

Damon MacNaught

Damon MacNaught received a MFA from the University of Illinois. In 1998, he established BareGlass studio in Silver Point, Tennessee. He also teaches neon glass design for the art department at Cumberland University. Although he has worked in hot glass for many years, he credits his interest in millefiori weights going back to 2000 when he met fellow artist Jim Brown. **Cat. 224** illustrates his crisp millefiori design.

224. Damon MacNaught, American, b. 1974
Magnum Close Pack Complex Millefiori, 2023
Glass, D. 3 9/16 inches

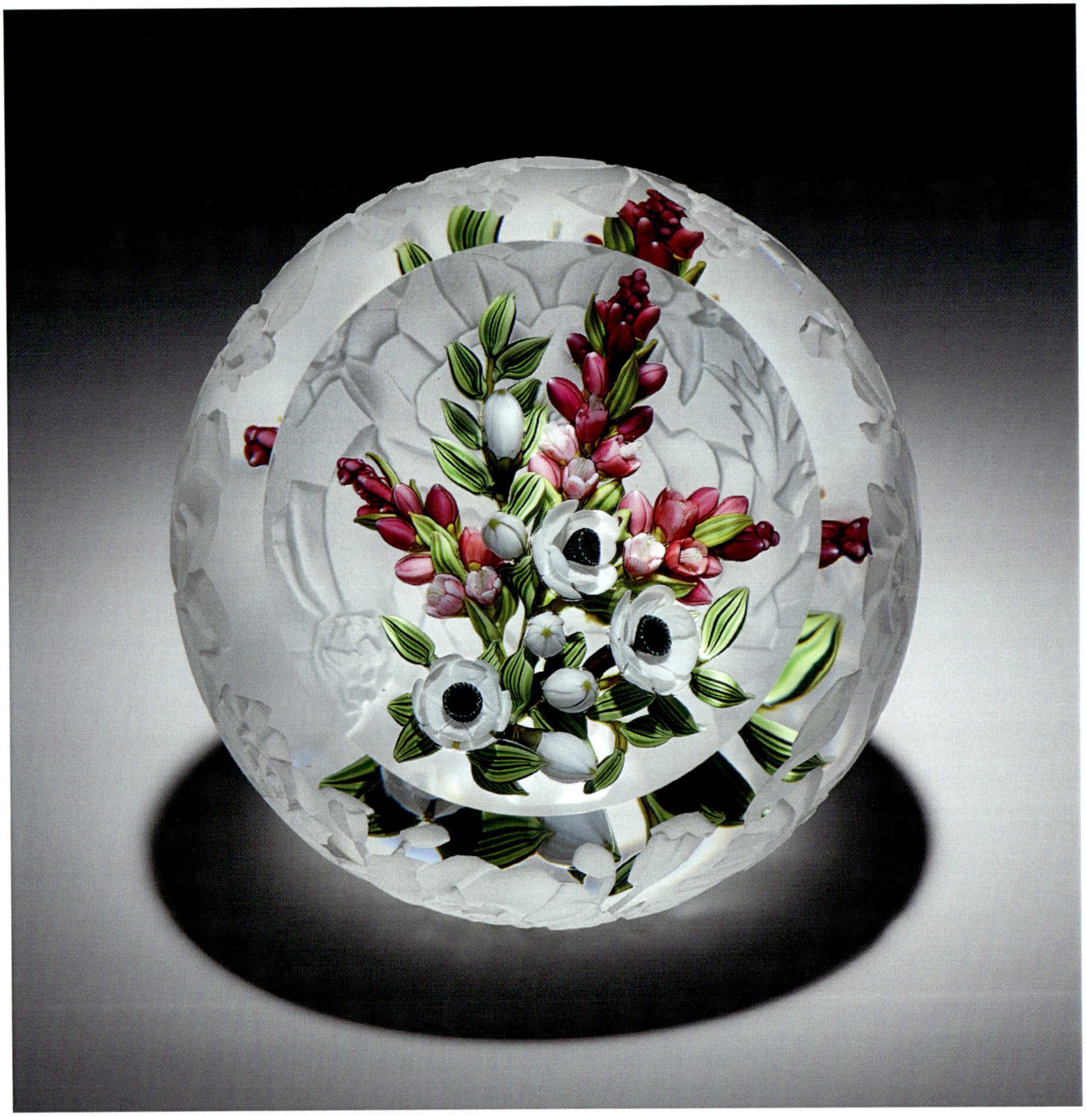

225. **Cathy Richardson,** American, b. 1949
White Poppies and Pink Meadowsweet with Etching, 2015. Glass, D. 3 ½ inches

Cathy Richardson

Cathy Richardson has a PhD from Harvard in geology and worked as a geologist until opening a stained glass studio in 1987. In 1997 she studied glass at Bowling Green University, Ohio. In 2000 she opened a studio in Winona, Minnesota. She also studied at Corning, Pilchuck, and with Chris Buzzini. Her emphasis is on personal observations detailing the phenomenon of the natural world. Her weights exhibit the interplay of light, color, and textures. She also has mastered cutting and etching, adding another layer of dimension to a piece like **cat. 225.**

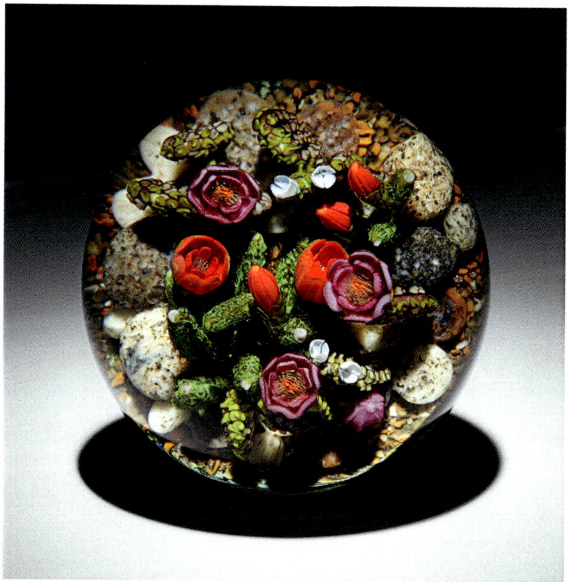

226. Cathy Richardson, American, b. 1949
Cactus, 2009. Glass, D. 3 ⅛ inches

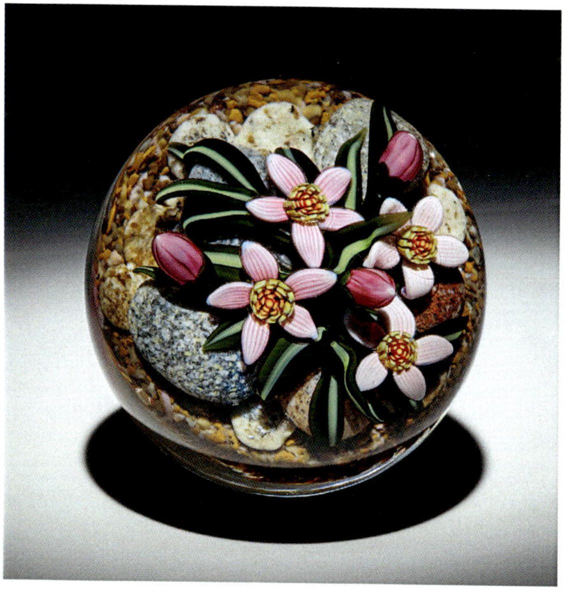

227. Cathy Richardson, American, b. 1949
Spring Beauty, 2013. Glass, D. 2 ¼ inches

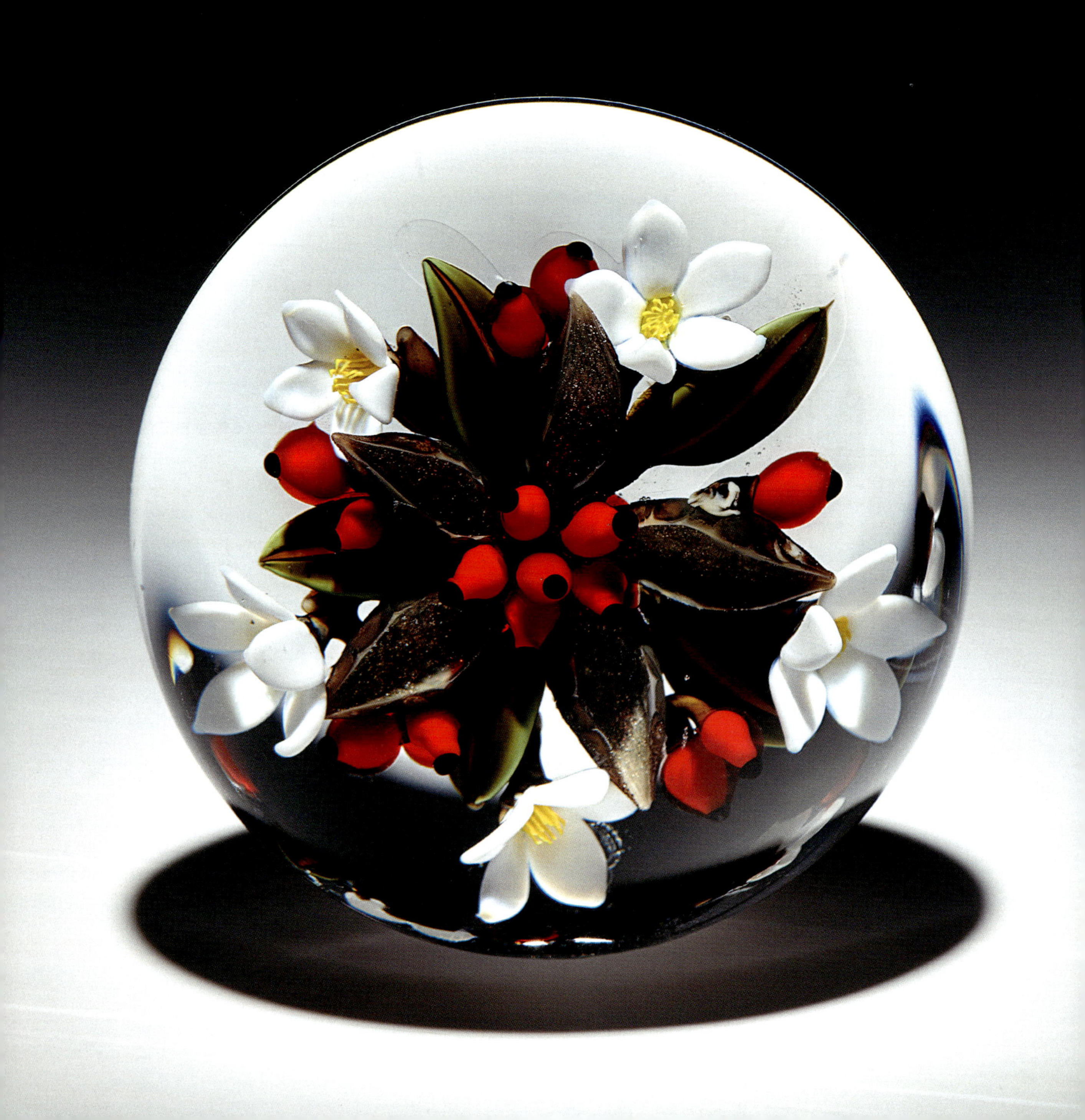

Colin Richardson

Colin Richardson received his BA from Winona State University in Minnesota. He started work in hot glass in 1994 with his mother, Cathy Richardson, and began creating his own designs in 2007. His studio is located in Burnsville, Minnesota. He finds inspiration in plant life and the ephemeral aspects of nature.

228. Colin Richardson, American, b. 1979
Kaleidoscope with Red Currants and Milkweed, 2013
Glass, D. 2 ¾ inches

Kenneth "Ken" Rosenfeld

Ken Rosenfeld received a MFA from Southern Illinois University. After graduating in 1978, he worked for Correia Glass (founded 1973). Upon leaving he set up his own studio in 1983 to focus on paperweights. During this period he worked for Radbotti (Scientific) Glass Technology (founded 1970), which introduced him to advanced equipment and techniques. From his Oregon studio he now produces skilled flameworked elements that contain intricate floral forms.

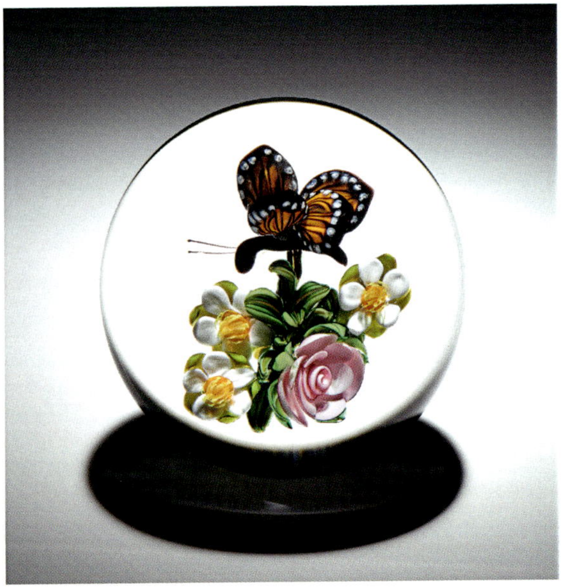

229. Ken Rosenfeld, American, b. 1950
Monarch Butterfly with Flowers, 2003
Glass, D. 2 7/16 inches

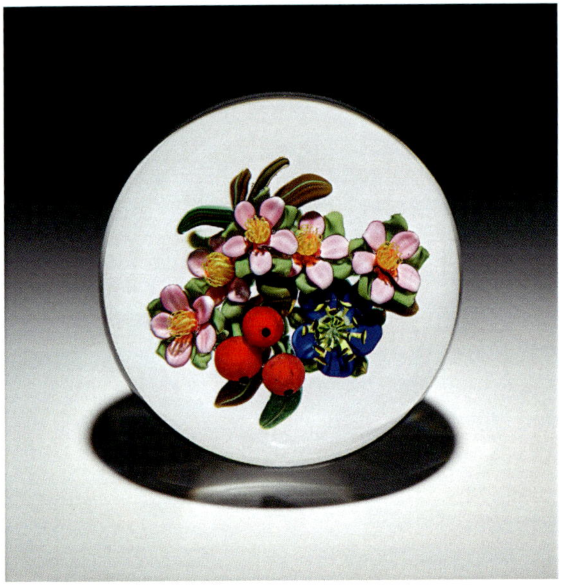

230. Ken Rosenfeld, American, b. 1950
Bouquet with Cherries, 2002
Glass, D. 2 7/16 inches

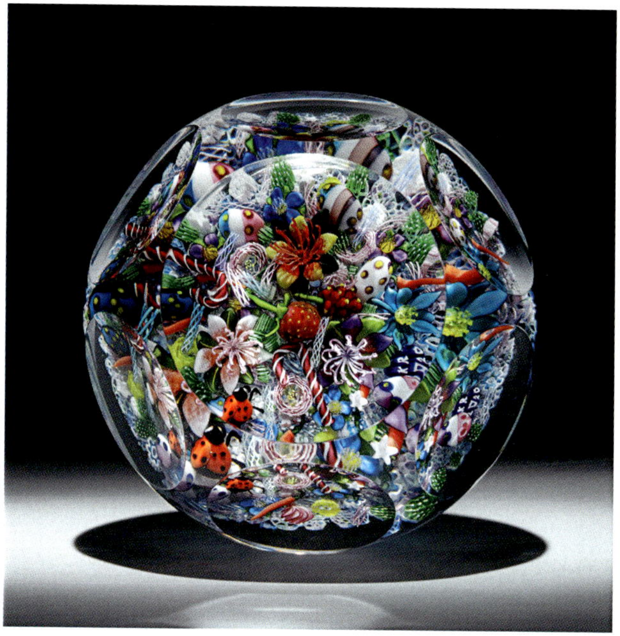

231. Ken Rosenfeld, American, b. 1950
Faceted Scrambled Canes, 2020
Glass, D. 3 ¼ inches

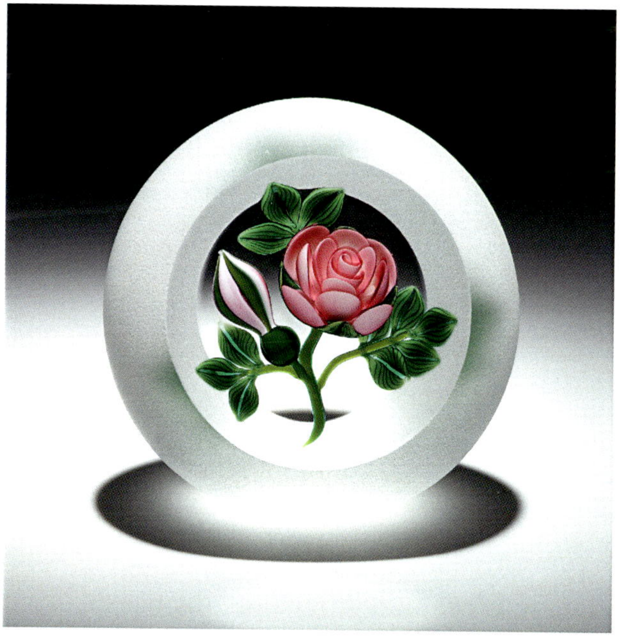

232. Ken Rosenfeld, American, b. 1950
Pink Rose and Bud
Glass, D. 2 7/16 inches

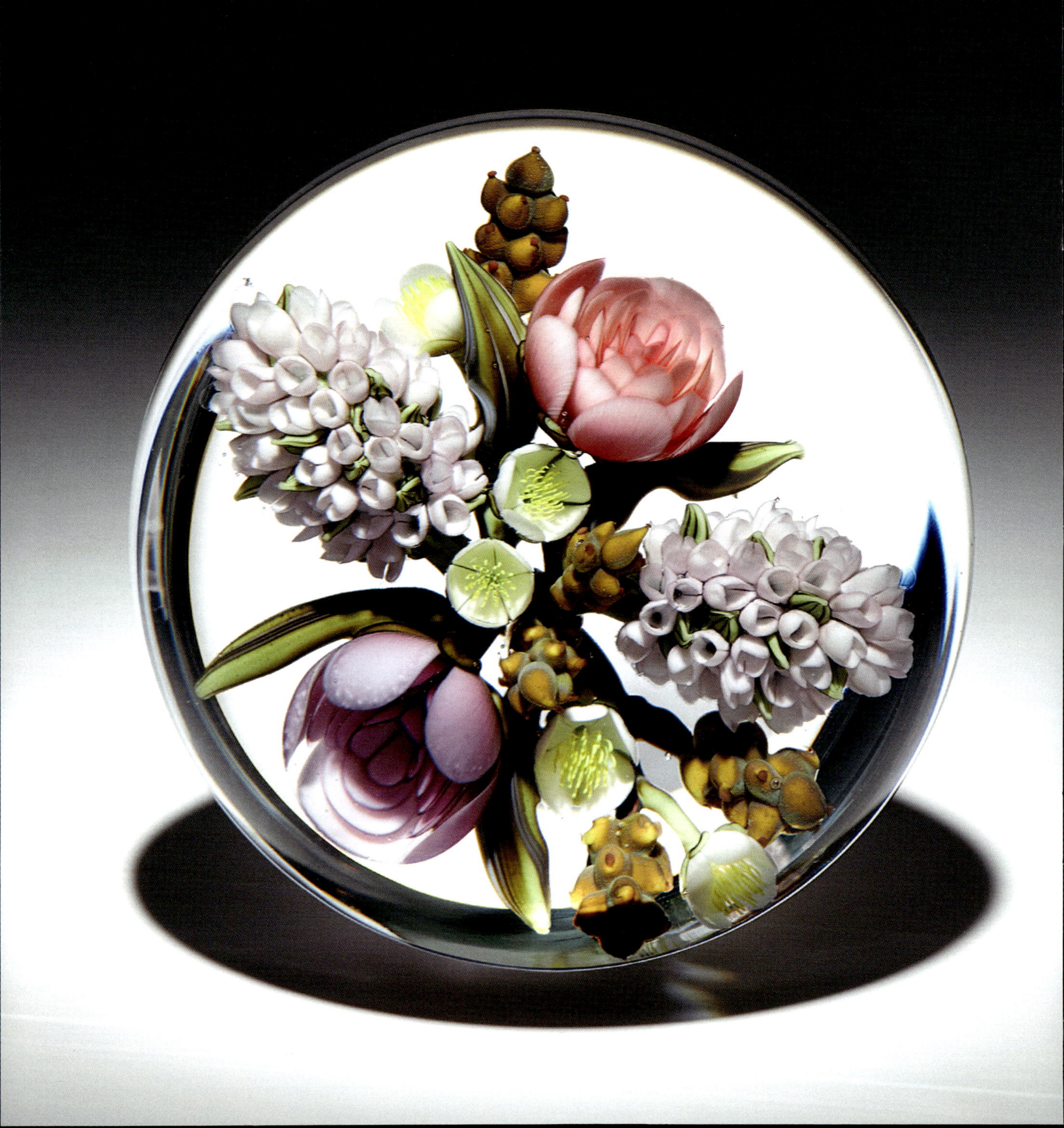

Clinton Smith

Clinton Smith was raised in northwestern Connecticut. He became interested in glass as a teenager and at ninteen he became an apprentice in the glass studio in the Webatuck Craft Village, New York. He worked in many other studios before becoming a full-time gaffer (glassworker) at Gartner Blade Glass, Ashley Falls, Massachuettes (founded 1996) where he still works part time. In 2010 he established a glass studio on his property. Smith refers to himself as a self-taught flameworker who has honed his skills to focus on paperweights. His work is directly inspired by his love of the plants and animals he sees living in Berkshire County. **Cat. 233** displays a bouquet composed of a variety of New England flowers.

233. Clinton Smith, American, b. 1979
Floral Bouquet, 2022
Glass, D. 3 ¼ inches

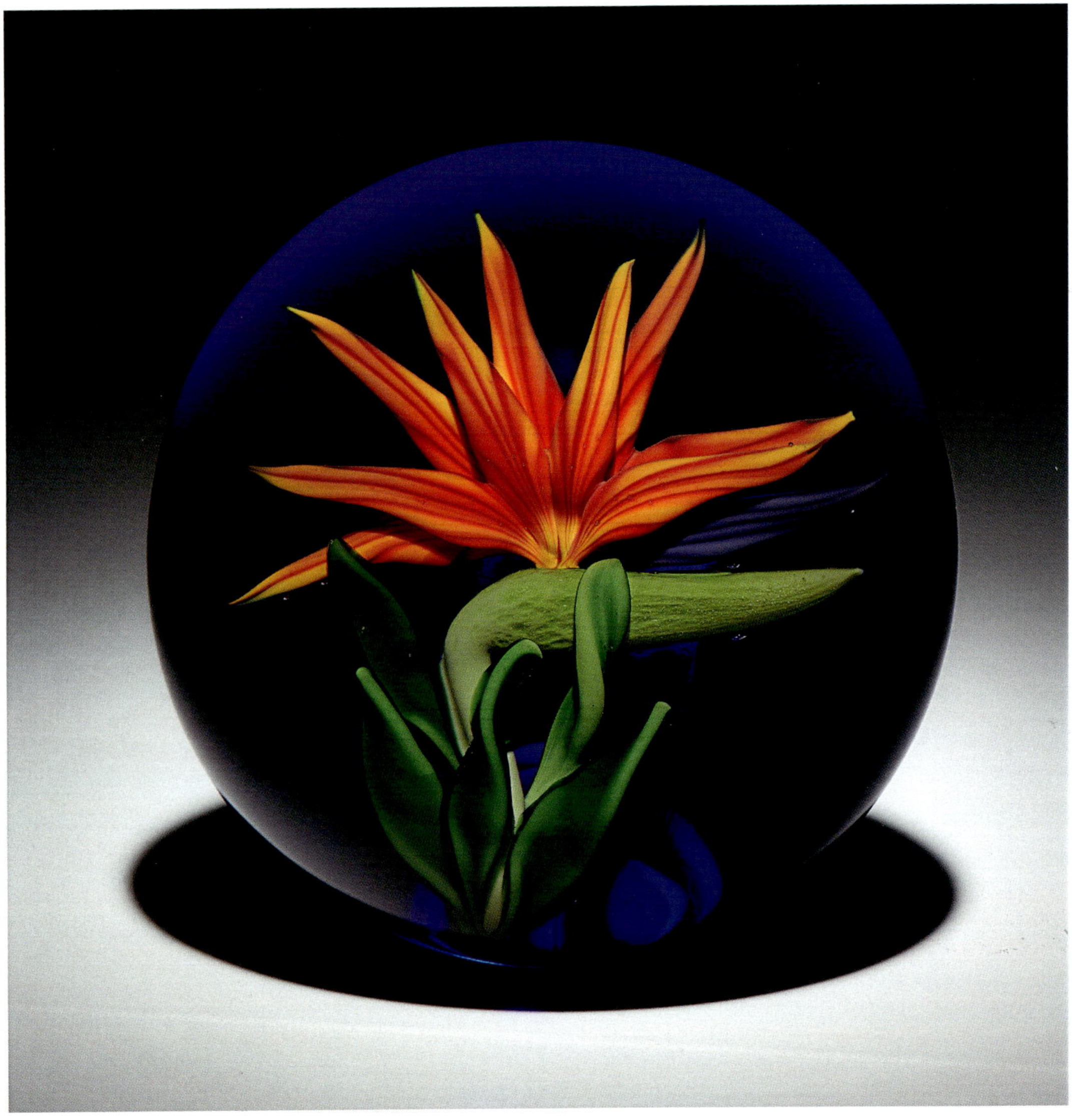

234. Gordon Smith, American, b. 1959. ***Bird of Paradise.*** Glass, D. 3 5⁄16 inches

Gordon Smith

Gordon Smith worked in southern New Jersey until moving his studio to Arizona then California. He became intrigued with torched glass work at an early age, receiving his first torch as a gift from his father when he was fourteen. After high school, he studied scientific glassblowing at Salem Community College, New Jersey. In 1980 he went to work making laboratory instruments at the Kontes Glass Company. There he was exposed to and encouraged by James and Nontas Kontes to make flameworked paperweights. He began volunteering and developing his skills at Wheaton Village glass factory (now Wheaton Arts and Cultural Center, New Jersey). In 1982, he became an independent studio artist and was recognized by Wheaton as the newest American paperweight artist. His current weights have evolved into hyper-realistic natural scenes.

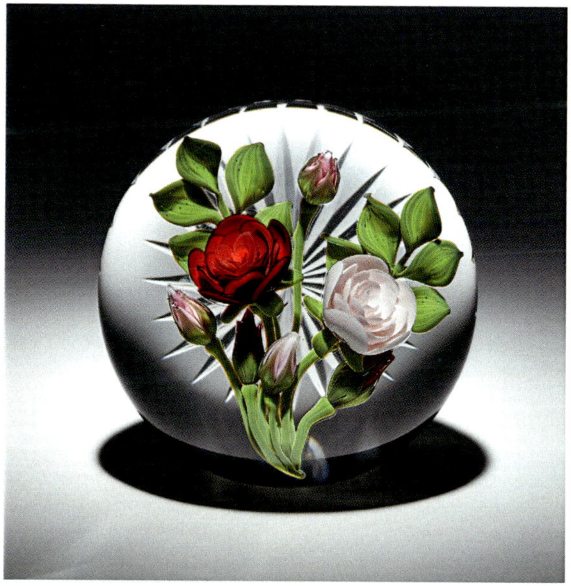

235. Gordon Smith, American, b. 1959
Bouquet of Roses, 2014
Glass, D. 3 3/16 inches

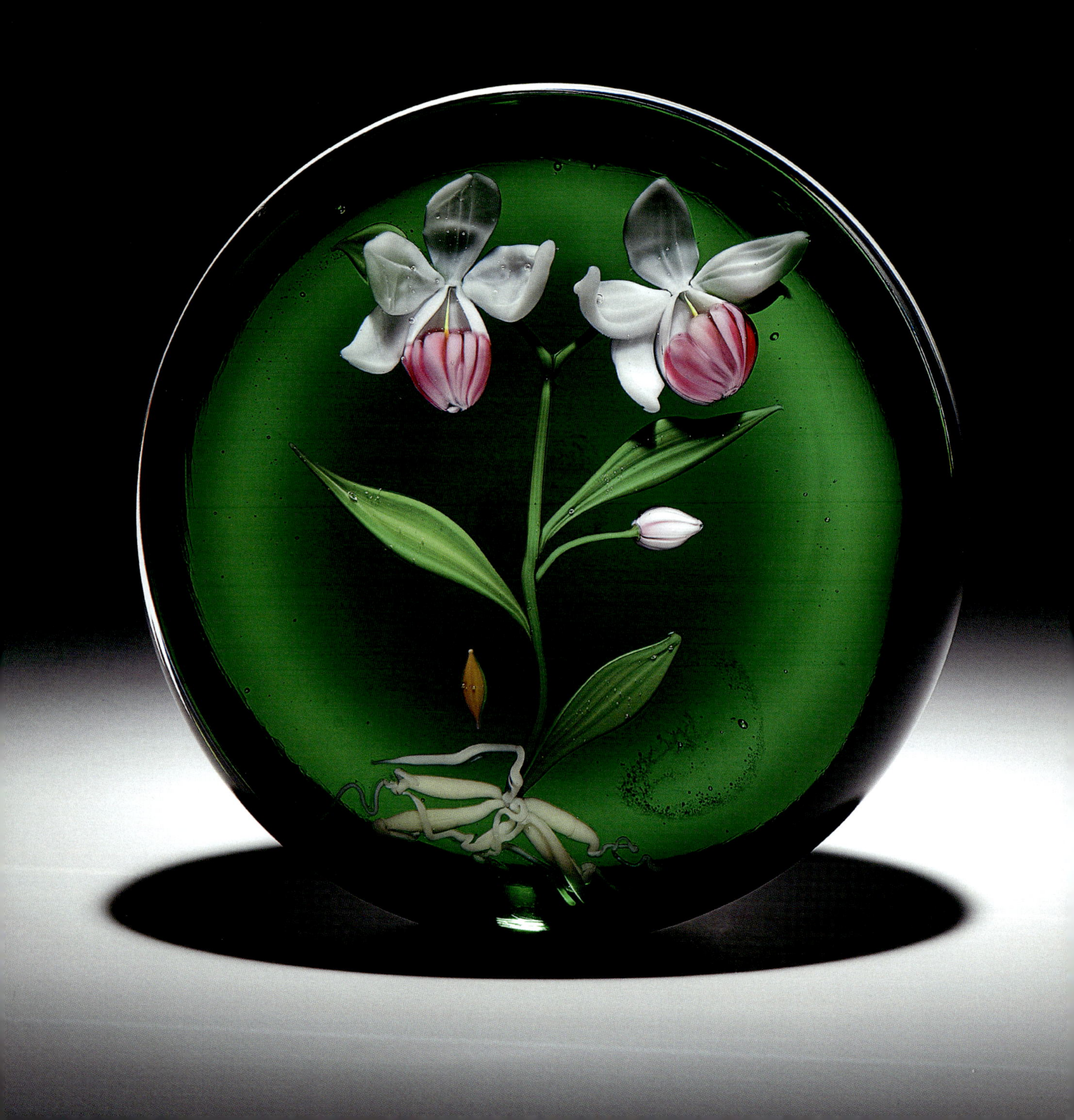

Paul Stankard

Paul Stankard completed his study at a New Jersey Technical Institute in 1963 and went on to work as a scientific glass blower at Macalaster Scientific Inc. in New Hampshire. There he met fellow glass worker Rick Ayotte. He then worked in New York and eventually moved to New Jersey, where he married and started a family. In 1969 he started making paperweights on the side to supplement his income. By 1972 he opened his own studio solely to produce paperweights. His primary focus in creating weights has been inspired by his deep love of nature, spiritualism, and the writings of poets like Walt Whitman. Technically adept, he has worked with many fellow glass artists, including David Graeber who assists him, and his five children. He has lectured, demonstrated, mentored, and encouraged students. He is known for his success in encasing complex glass flameworked sculptural elements in a variety of forms.

236. Paul Stankard, American, b. 1943
Lady Slippers
Glass, D. 3 ⅛ inches

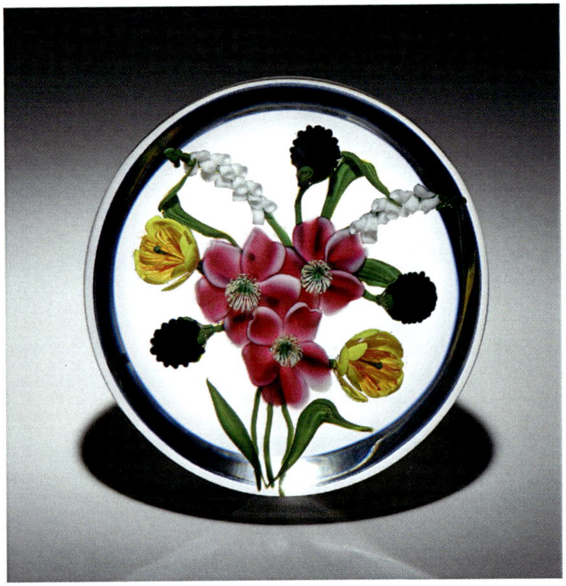

237. **Paul Stankard,** American, b. 1943
Sippewisset Bouquet
Glass, D. 3 ⅛ inches

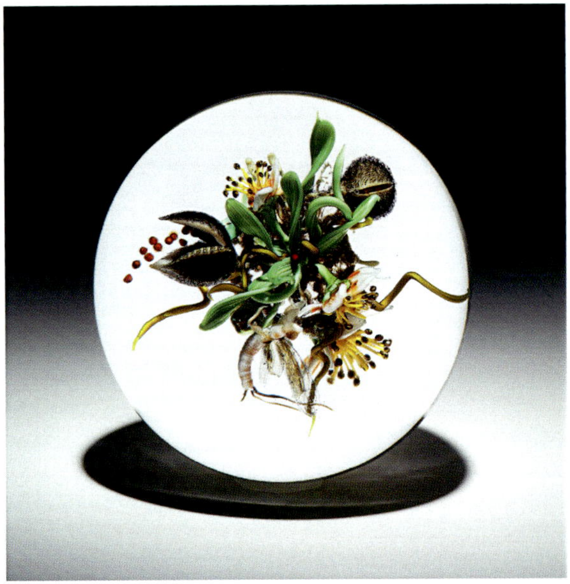

238. **Paul Stankard,** American, b. 1943
Flowers, Seeds, Mayfly, Figures, and Word Canes, 1997
Glass, D. 3 3/16 inches

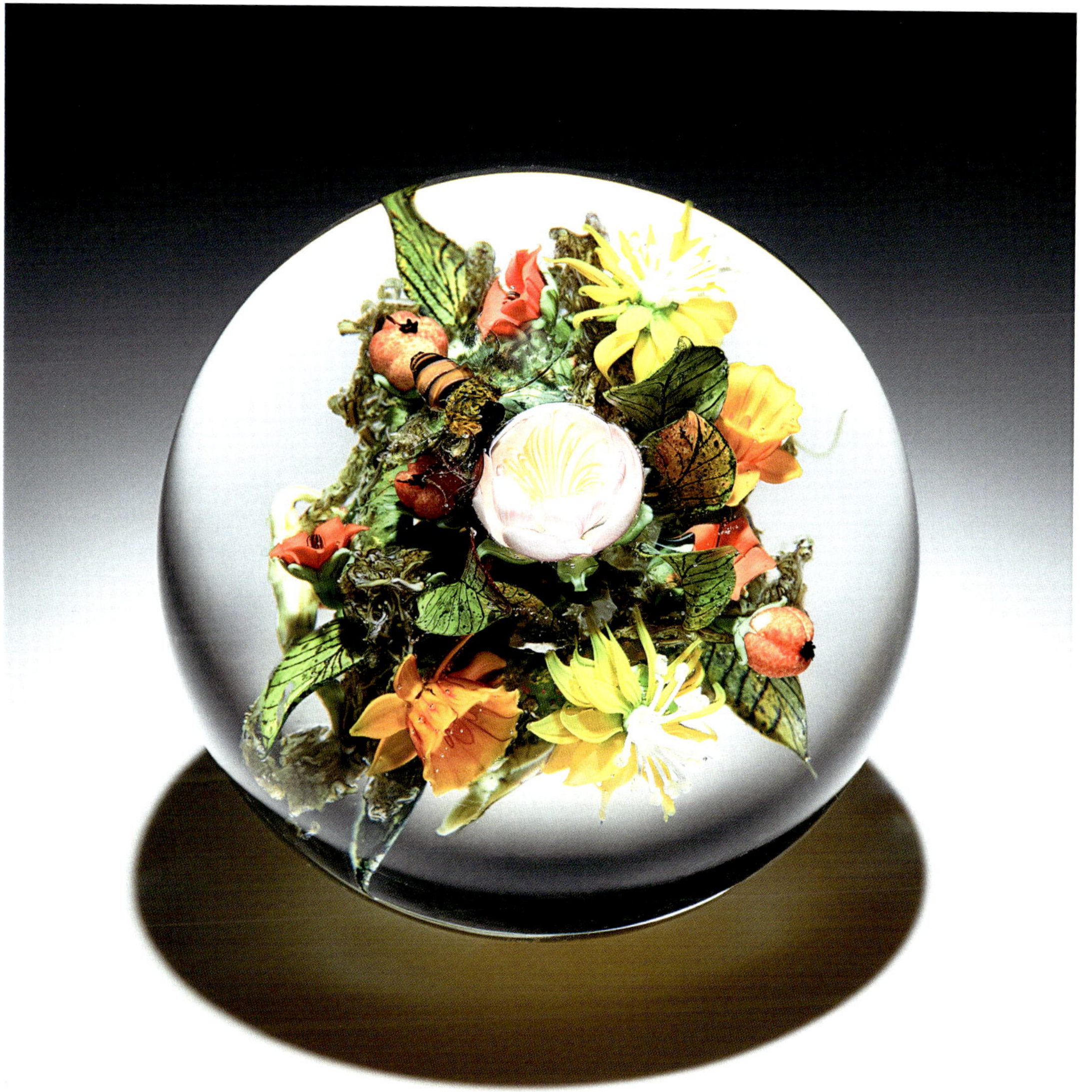

239. **Paul Stankard,** American, b. 1943
Bouquet with Bee, Mask, Ants, and Word Canes, 2002. Glass, D. 3 ¼ inches

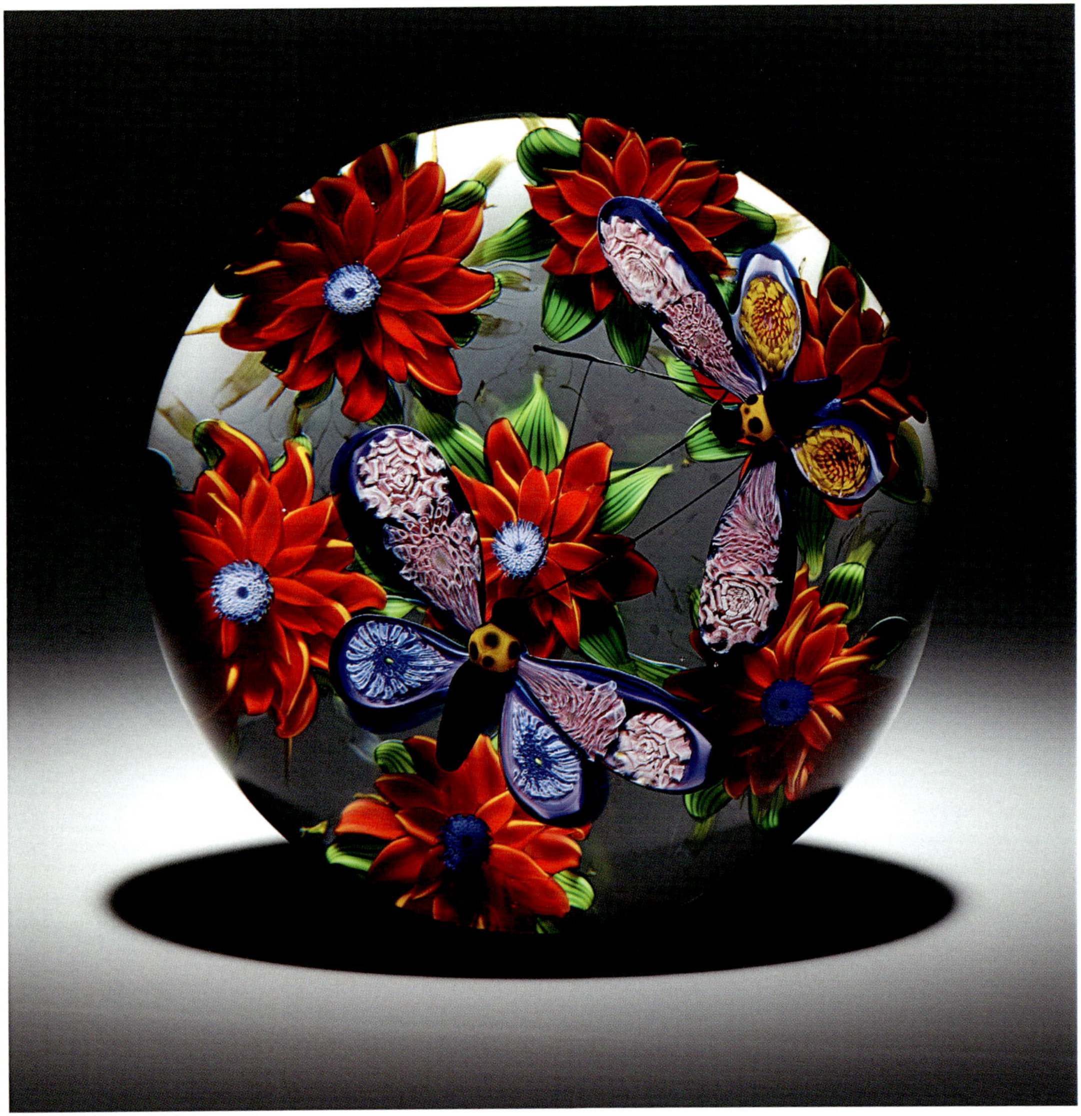

240. Debbie Tarsitano, American, b. 1955
Magnum Butterflies and Dahlias. Glass, D. 3 ⅞ inches

Debbie Tarsitano

Debbie Tarsitano was raised in a family that had a deep interest in art and antiques. She started painting as a child and eventually received a BFA from Hofstra University, New York. In 1976 Debbie and her father Adelmo "Del" Joseph Tarsitano launched Tarsitano Studio, each pursuing their own individual artworks. She also designed engravings for encased lampwork for twenty-five years with master engraver Roland "Max" Erlacher (1933–2022). Her exquisite weights have sharp details created by the use of "filament" grounds composed of hair-thin glass fibers to produce textured elements. Her studio is located in Massachusetts. **Cat. 244** was made as a collaboration with Paul Ysart.

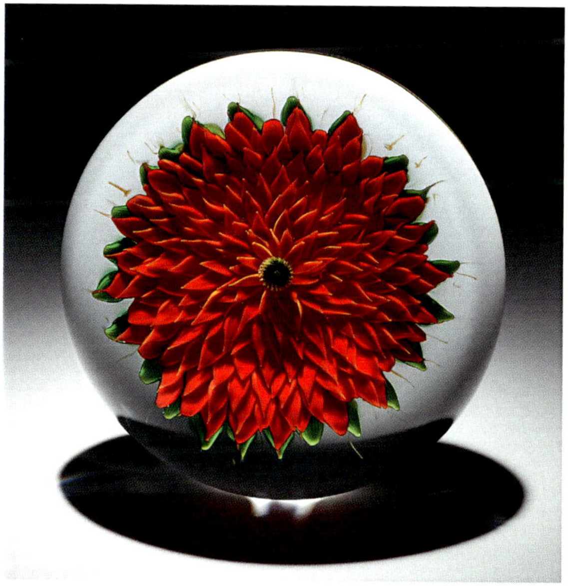

241. Debbie Tarsitano, American, b. 1955
Magnum Red Dahlia
Glass, D. 4 ⅛ inches

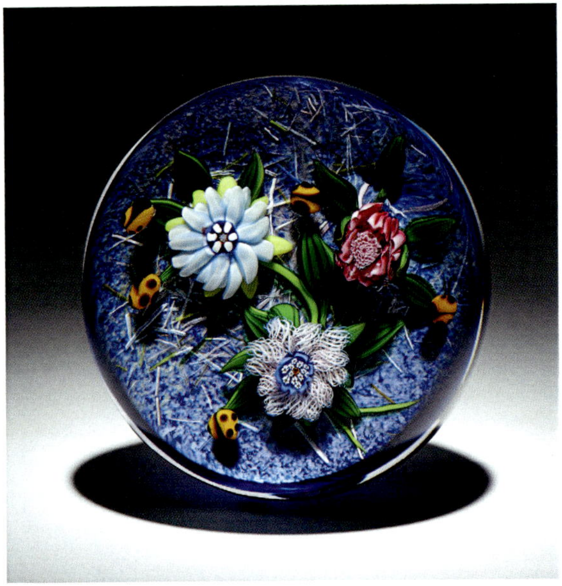

242. **Debbie Tarsitano**
American, b. 1955
Bouquet and Ladybugs
Glass, D. 3 inches

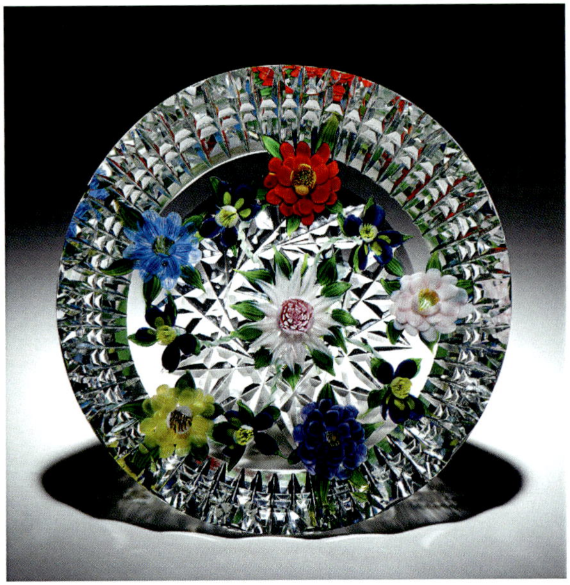

243. **Debbie Tarsitano**
American, b. 1955
Garland of Flowers Plaque with Fancy Cuts
Glass, D. 4 ¼, H. 1 ½ inches

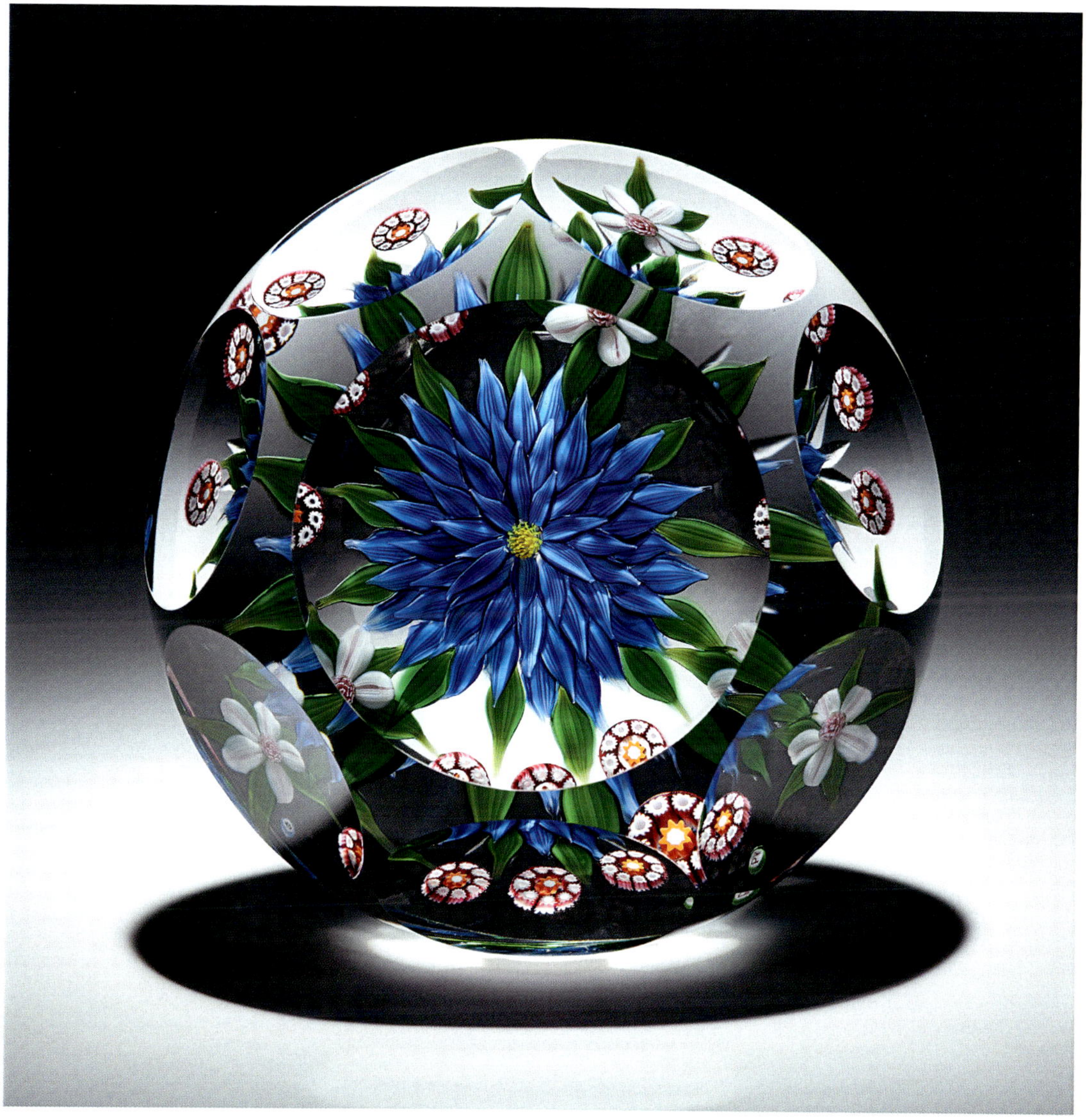

244. Debbie Tarsitano, American, b. 1955; **Paul Ysart,** Spanish, 1904–91
Faceted Dahlia. Glass, D. 3 ⅛ inches

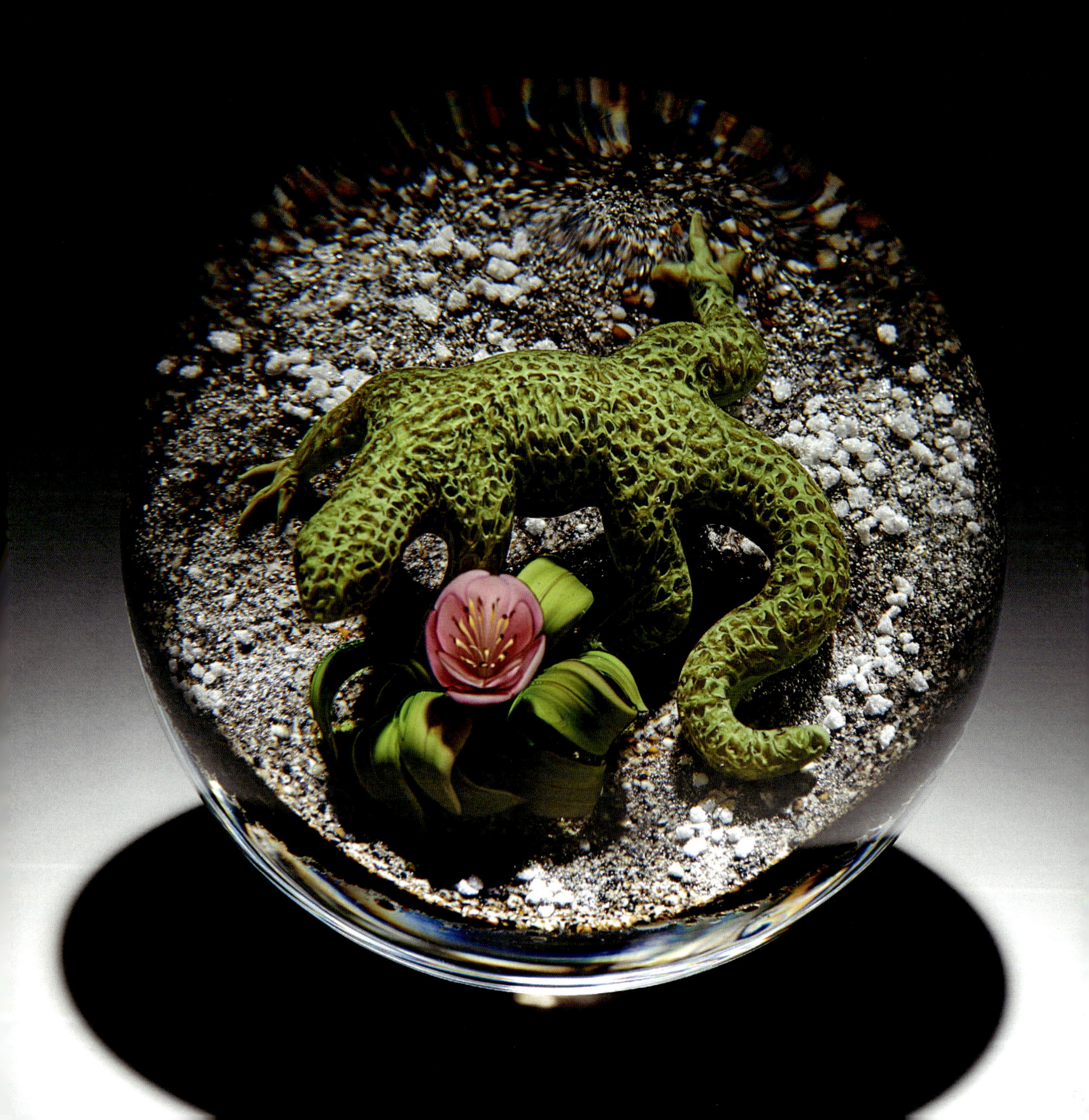

Victor Trabucco

Victor Trabucco worked for many years in construction as a steelworker. From childhood his hobby was performing magic. He became intrigued with watching a flameworker in 1974, which fostered his interest in learning about glass. He later set up a fabricating studio and in 1977, after viewing classical weights, he embarked on making them. Trabucco's expertise is rooted in his love and observations of nature and his motivation to translate its beauty into glass. One of his strengths has been his virtuosity in glass. He has mastered the ability to eliminate lines and seams within the weight to perfectly create the illusion of the motif floating within the form.

Cat. 245 is a marvelous rendering of a salamander inspired by the Pantin salamander made a hundred years earlier. Working in Clarence, New York, Trabucco Studios is a workspace shared by Victor and his twin sons David and Jon.

245. Victor Trabucco, American, b. 1949
Magnum Lizard on Desert Ground, 1993
Glass, D. 4 ⅞ inches

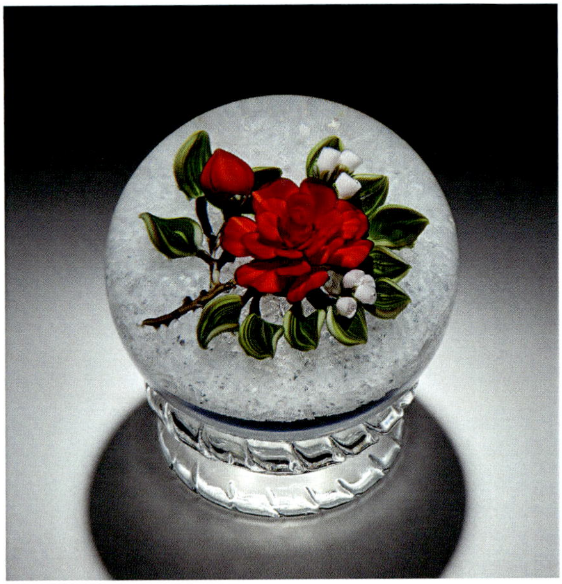

246. Victor Trabucco, American, b. 1949
Rose and Buds Piedouche, 1996
Glass, D. 3 3/8, H. 3 11/16 inches

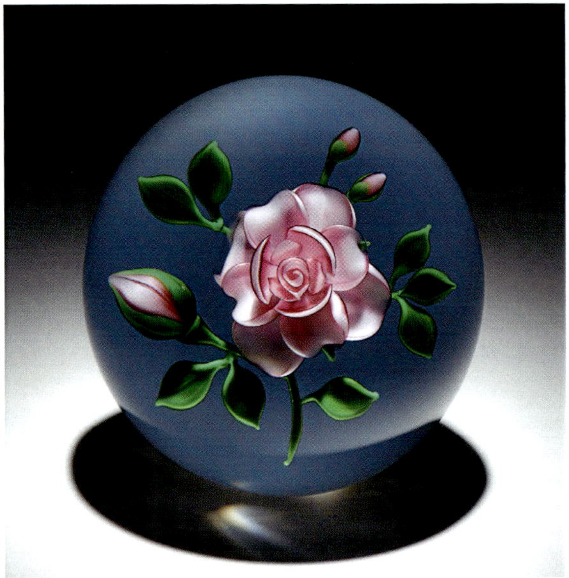

247. Victor Trabucco, American, b. 1949
Pink Rose and Buds, 1985
Glass, D. 3 1/4 inches

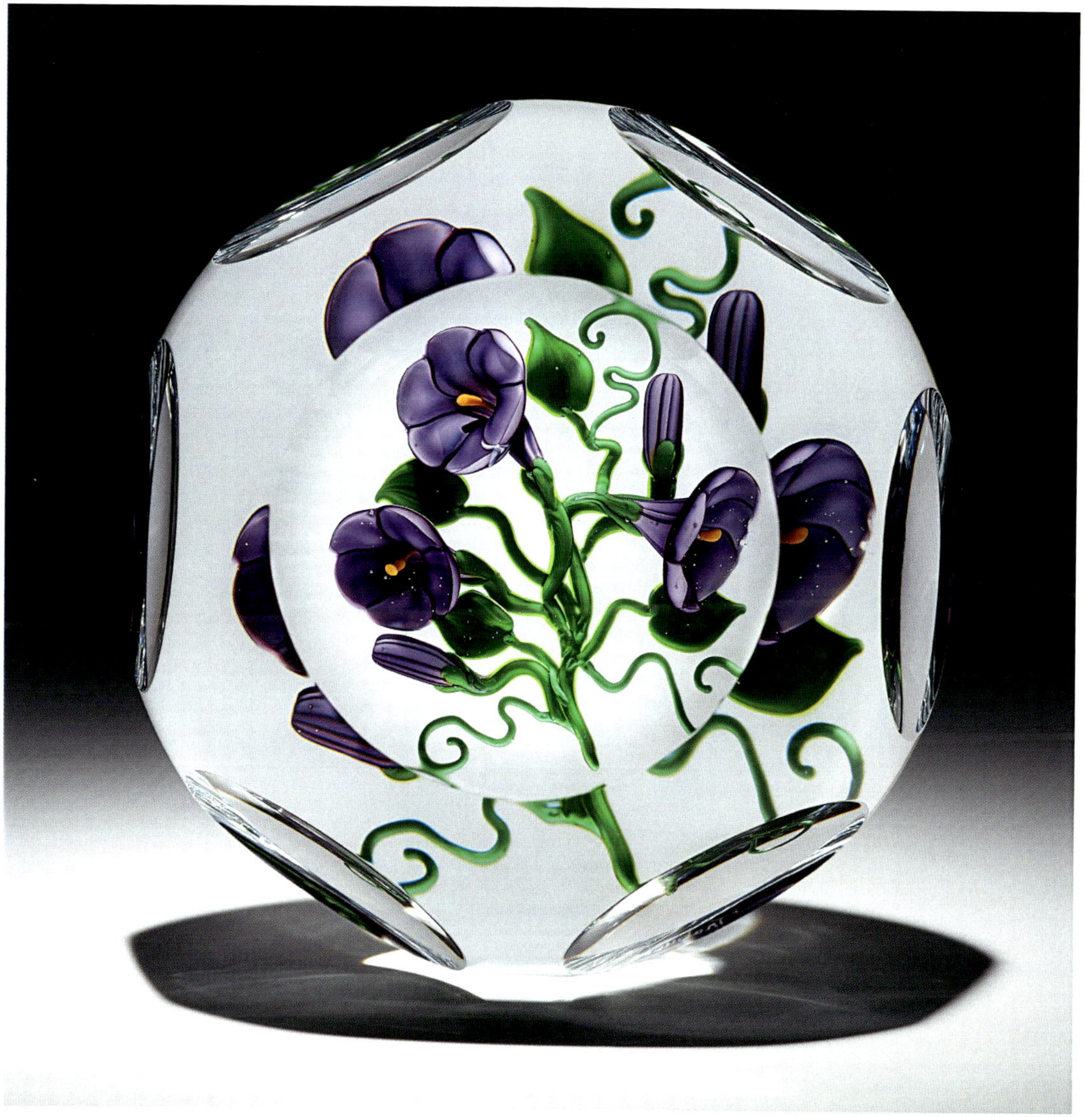

248. Victor Trabucco, American, b. 1949
Faceted Magnum Morning Glories, 1984. Glass, D. 3 ⅞ inches

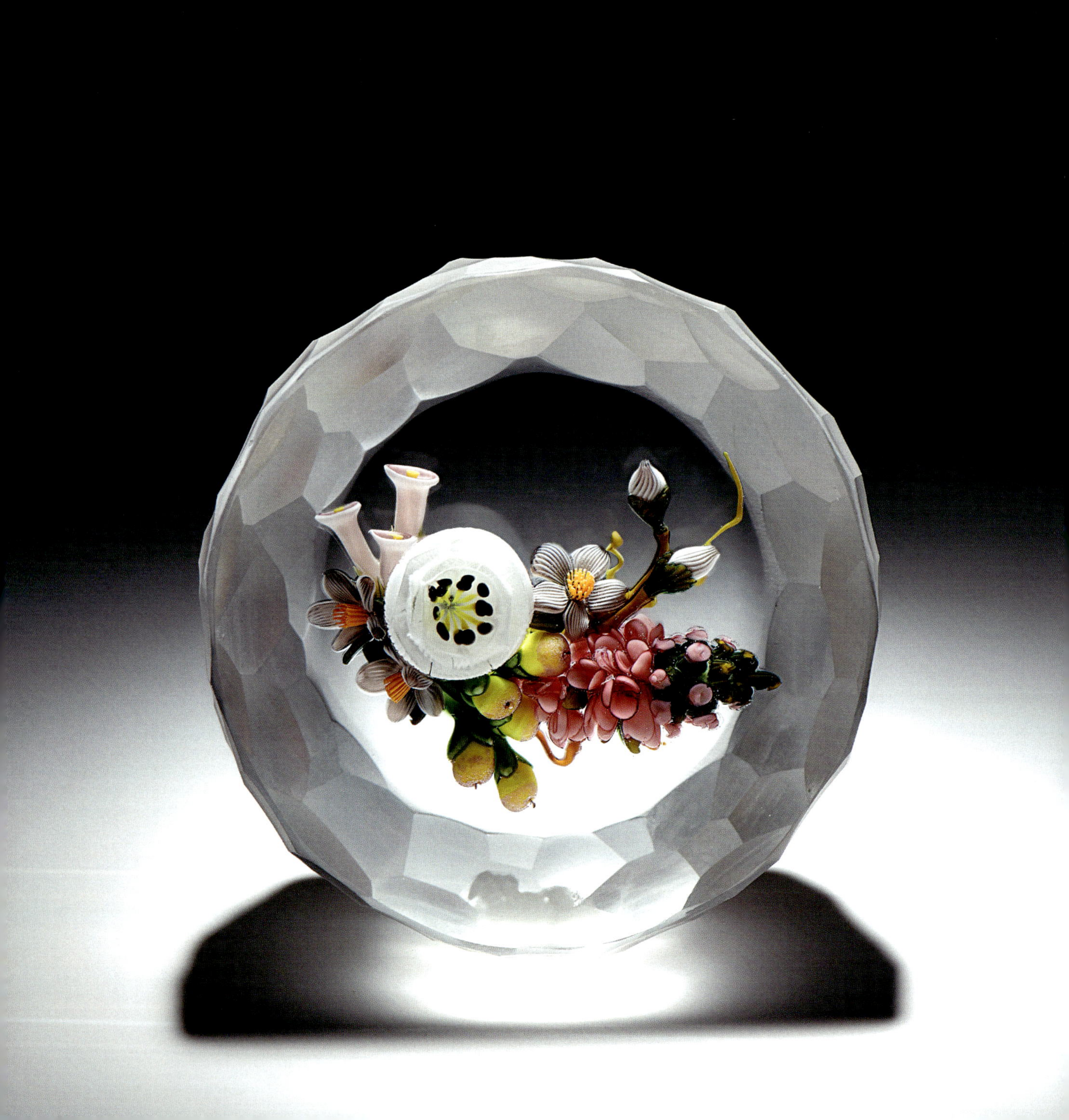

Mayauel Ward

Mayauel Ward was born and raised in Manhattan Beach, California. In 1976 he took a glassblowing class while pursuing a degree in physical therapy at El Camino College, California. That decision led to working at Correia Art Glass (founded 1973) after graduating. In 1979, he joined Abelman Art Glass (founded 1976), while there in 1988, he started his own business making flameworked weights while still working for Abelman. In 2012, Ward became an independent studio artist. Influenced by living in a sunny area and near the ocean, Ward's work presents bright, colorful, and complex floral arrangements. **Cat. 249** has a *battuto* exterior perimeter finish or engraved surface resembling hammered metal.

249. Mayauel Ward, American, b. 1956
Bouquet with Battuto
Glass, D. 2 ½ inches

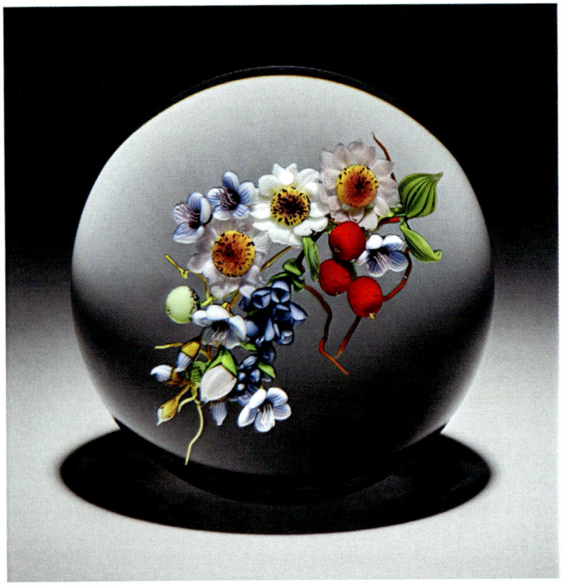

250. Mayauel Ward, American, b. 1956
Bouquet with Cherries, 2005
Glass, D. 3 $^{3}/_{16}$ inches

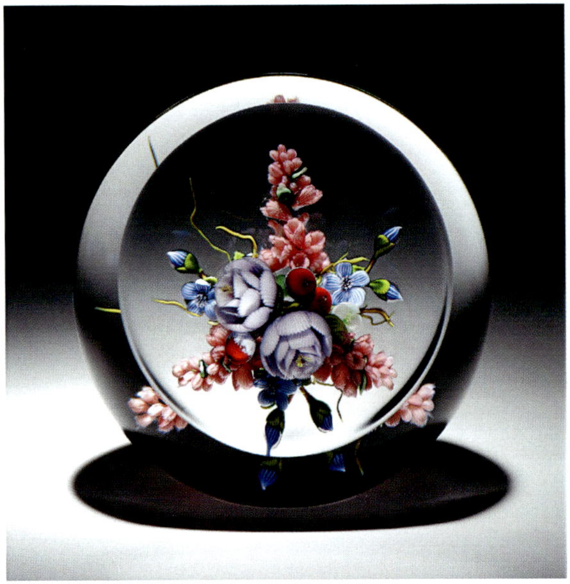

251. Mayauel Ward, American, b. 1956
Upright Bouquet, 2008
Glass, D. 3 $^{3}/_{16}$ inches

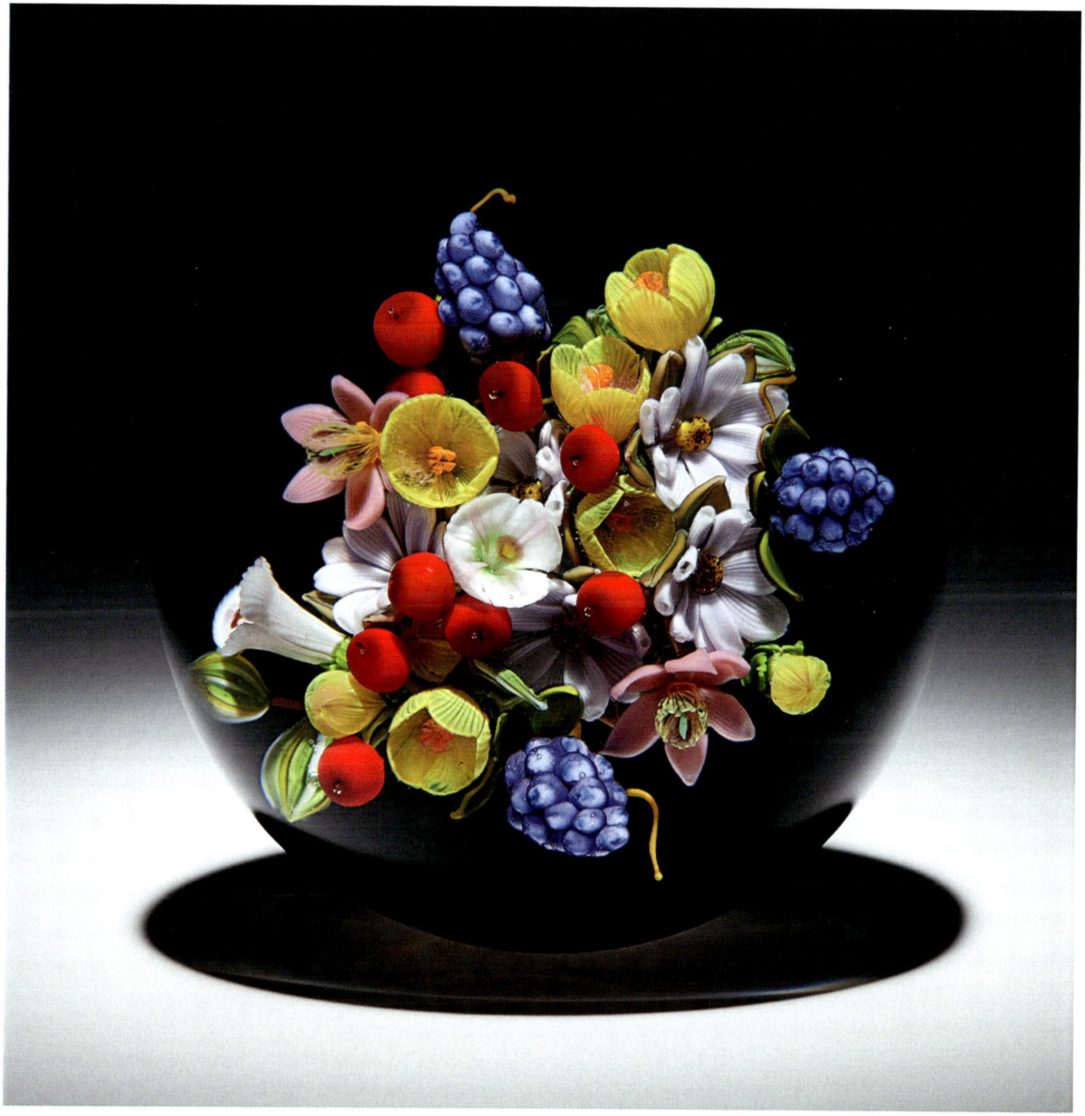

252. Mayauel Ward, American, b. 1956
Bouquet with Grapes, 2013. Glass, D. 2 ¾ inches

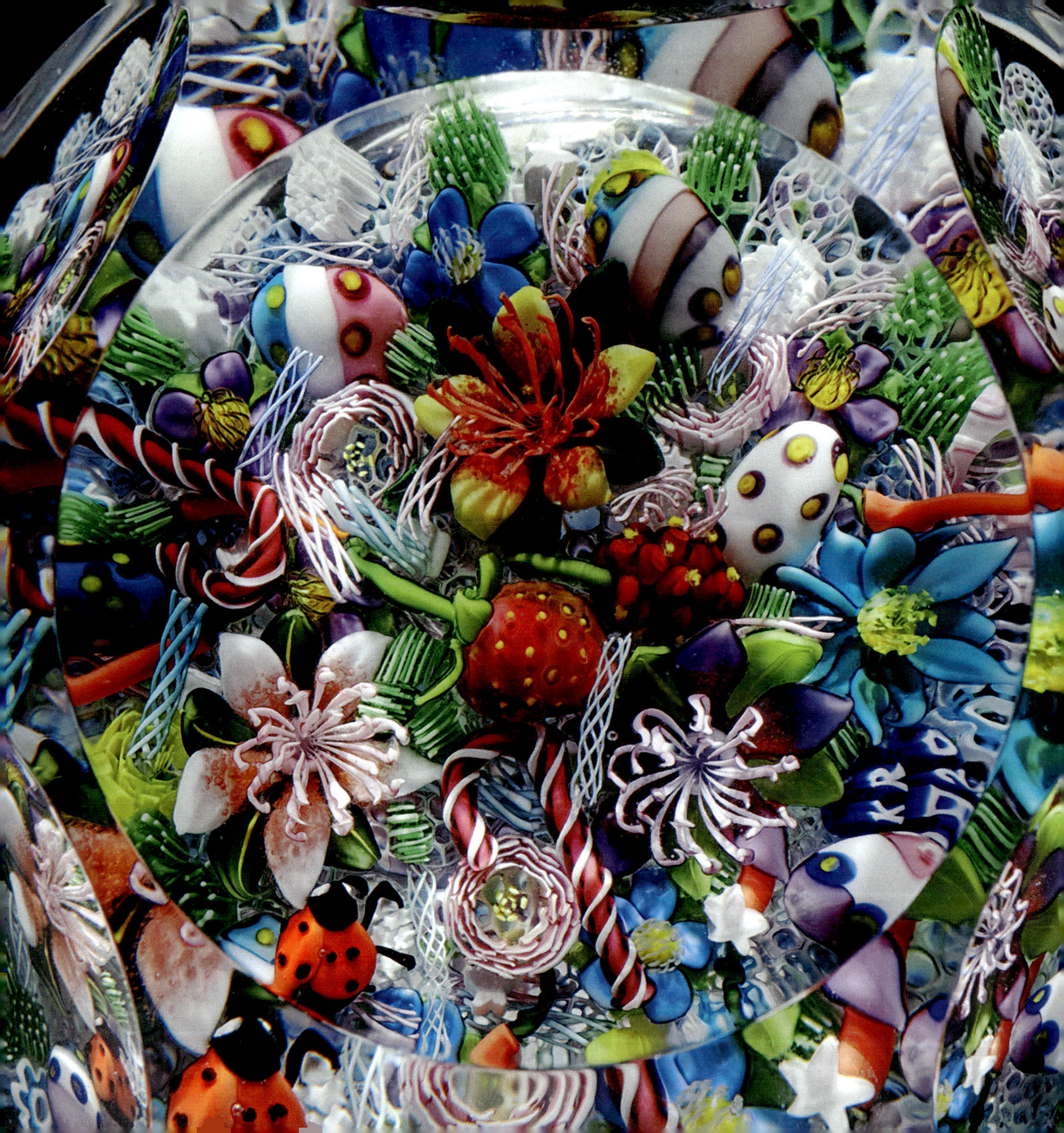

Coda

Nearly two centuries ago paperweights fit the criteria fostered by the nineteenth-century doctrine according to English artist William Morris:

Have nothing in your houses that you do not know to be useful or believe to be beautiful.

As we look at the Ellis Collection we see the magical, reflective, nature of glass that has been skillfully manipulated by artists into familiar, intimate, and accessible forms. What we also see is beauty. Viewing these small objects we are drawn into their astonishing intimate interiors. As we look, it triggers our own subjective feelings, which are drawn from our own experiences, of beauty in nature, art, literature, music, and love.

About the author: Kathryn Sharbaugh is Director of Donor Relations & Special Initiatives at the Flint Institute of Arts Museum + Art School. She received a BFA from Kansas City Art Institute and a MFA from Cranbrook Academy of Art. Sharbaugh was a faculty member of the FIA for more than 30 years before she became coordinator of several major capital and endowment campains for the FIA in 2005 and assumed the role of Director of Development in 2009. Sharbaugh's artistic portfolio has earned her numerous commissions, publications, and awards including from the National Endowment of the Arts and Michigan Council of the Arts. Her ceramic work is part of museum collections globally, notably the Smithsonian's Renwick Gallery and Cooper Hewitt Museum.

LEFT: Detail of Cat. 231

This catalogue is published in conjunction with the exhibition *A Symphony of Glass* with selections from the Eileen Ellis Collection at the Flint Institute of Arts Museum + Art School, Flint, MI, March 1, 2025—March 1, 2026.

Printed in the United States of America.
ISBN: 978-0-939896-29-5

Flint Institute of Arts Museum + Art School
1120 E. Kearsley St.
Flint, MI 48503
www.flintarts.org

Executive Director: Tracee J. Glab
Director and Curator of Collections
and Exhibitions: Sarah Kohn
Associate Curator: Rachael Hostege
Registrar: Peter Ott
Collections Manager: Heather Jackson
Curatorial Assistant: Emily Legleitner

Institutional support provided by The Charles Stewart Mott Foundation.

Publication Credits
Collection photography: Doug Schaible Photography
Design and layout: Emily Legleitner
Consulting editor: Paul Dunlop
Printing: ULitho, Ann Arbor, MI

Cover: Detail of Cat. 179 | Contents Page: Detail of Cat. 158